FIND YOUR SCREAM LIVE YOUR DREAM

Discover your inner leader

VICKI SANDLER

Copyright © 2011. All Rights Reserved.
Published by Wearthy Ideas, LLC

Cover design: Shelby Sandler
Editor: Andrea Markowitz, Ph.D.

Library of Congress has cataloged as follows:
#2011921762

ISBN #978-0-9830136-0-0

No part of this book may be reproduced, stored in or introduced into a retrieval system, or transmitted, in any form by any means (electronic, mechanical, photocopying, recording or otherwise), without the prior written permission of both the copyright owner and publisher of this book.

The scanning, uploading, and distribution of this book via the Internet or via any other means without the permission of the publisher is illegal. Please purchase only the authorized paperback or electronic edition. Do not participate in or encourage electronic piracy of copyrightable materials. Your support helps the charities who receive proceeds from the sale of this book and protects the author's rights.

Although the author and publisher have made every effort to ensure the accuracy and completeness of information contained in this book, we assume no responsibility for errors, inaccuracies, omissions, or any inconsistency herein. Any slights of people, places or organizations are unintentional.

Quantity discounts are available and special books or book excerpts can be created to fit specific needs. To order this book or obtain copyright permission, go to http://www.findyourscream.com.

ACKNOWLEDGMENTS

All of my life's experiences contributed to the creation of this work. My goal is that it will help you in your pursuit of your purpose and pure joy. It's a celebration of my personal journey. It's my life's passion and purpose—my scream—to write it. Those who have helped shape it are living their scream too. We are grateful. We are joyous. I am ever thankful to my husband, Jeff. In helping him find his heart, I found mine. Our daughter, Shelby, teaches me every day how to be objective and to see in new, loving ways. Also, I thank her for the inspired cover and book layout. Shane, our son, showed me never to be afraid and how to live as the uniquely wonderful individual you were meant to be. My faithful twelve-year-old Australian Shepherd, Samba, stayed by my side during the writing of this book. Her sage eyes displayed unwavering belief in me. Thanks to my sister and brother as we lived through the ups and downs. They have taught me much about how beliefs become reality. I am rich with my many good friends' and family's support. Thanks to my friends for relating and reviewing your stories; and for those of you who listened with undying support during all our hikes together.

Thanks to all the wonderful people I had the opportunity to lead and learn from at the electric commodity, renewables and energy efficiency company that I call GreenEnergyCo in this book. Many of their inspiring stories are told in the pages that lie ahead. I am ever grateful for the opportunities that the former chairman of our parent company, Bill, and Jack, the former CEO of the sister utility company offered me over the twenty-five years that we worked together.

My appreciation would not be complete without sending my love to those who influenced, shaped and edited this book: Laura, Joy, Sandy, Gladys, Kimberly, Michelle, Merilyn, Gene, Deb, Whitney, Jan, Linda, Evan, Diane, Becca, and Penny. Thanks to Andrea Markowitz, Ph.D., my editor who revised with love and patience so all readers could relate to the Scream to Dream

Approach to living and leading. When I became discouraged and wanted to discontinue writing this book, she lamented, "But this is your scream!"

May this work illuminate the way for you to discover your inner leader. In doing so, you will be guided to find your scream and live congruently with it for a life of your dreams.

PROMOTING A CHARITABLE CAUSE

Your purchase of this book "gives back."

A significant portion of the proceeds from "Find Your Scream, Live Your Dream" will be donated. One of the non-profits supports the development of a program to teach our youth how to find their scream to live their dream. Imagine how many young souls will lift up the world by learning about essential life skills, learning from physicians who teach them how to heal mind, body and spirit, and by discovering their inner leader at an early age. Another supports the Gladys McGarey Foundation, which promotes responsibility for one's own health and the principles of Living Medicine.

CONTENTS

9 | INTRODUCTION
WHAT DOES IT MEAN TO FIND YOUR SCREAM?

20 | ONE
HOW I FOUND MY SCREAM

38 | TWO
TRANSFORMING TODAY'S LEADERSHIP

51 | THREE
YOUR ANSWERS ARE WITHIN

93 | FOUR
EXPLORE YOUR CORE

113 | FIVE
EXPLORE YOUR ORGANIZATION'S CORE

156 | SIX
HOW DO YOU KNOW IF YOU HAVE FOUND YOUR SCREAM?

206 | SEVEN
RELEASE YOUR FEAR

254 | CLOSING
LIVE YOUR DREAM

264 | REFERENCES & RESOURCES

272 | MY SOUL SONG

INTRODUCTION

WHAT DOES IT MEAN TO FIND YOUR SCREAM?

Take heart to the beauty of who you are and never let it go.
— Laura Alden Kamm, author and medical intuitive

There's a special scream deep inside every one of us. It's the scream of our life's joys and gifts, and once it's out, there's no stopping our potential as individuals and leaders. A scream doesn't have to be loud—you just need to hear with a new ear—one that listens within.

The metaphor of a scream goes beyond just representing your likes and wants. It reaches into your innermost internal voice. It's your scream of pure joy that comes from the creative forces deep within you, from your heart-energy, your core! You can make life choices driven by a need for survival, which is fear based, or from the force of creation, which is love based. Identifying the difference between these two choices is transformational. While you have intuitively known and heard that creative voice within you, like most of us, in disbelief, you have ignored it.

Answer these questions for yourself:

- Are you living and loving your life's work?
- Are you expressing the essence of who you are in what you choose to do?
- Or are you climbing the corporate ladder, so to speak, only to risk discovering it's leaning against the wrong wall?

The right wall awaits.

To find your scream, it may be as simple as reconnecting with what you loved to play as a child—when time stood still. What shoes did you dream of filling? Are the shoes you are walking in now too big? Does that create a fear that you will never fill them? Or are your shoes too small—stifling you and creating pain in your life?

When you walk in your "best-fit" shoes, you become aligned with who you truly are—with your talents, values, innate passions and drive—your actions will be congruent and supportive of your scream. This congruence causes an internal shift from dependency on outside forces to acting in alignment with your own integrity. The shift creates a space where the greater good and your own well-being can dance in synchronicity. Finding your scream and taking actions consistent with it at work and play set you on the path of your dreams. Instead of your life consisting of a list of things you have to do and being full of drudgery, your life unfolds as a natural expression of your scream.

When you find your scream:

- You express your natural creative gifts, your genuine self in your life and work.
- You work smarter, not harder: you accomplish more in less time and with fewer resources.
- You have an abundance of energy and exuberance.
- Your work brings you bliss.
- You are fulfilled as a person and a leader.
- You help others find their scream.
- You are at the top of your game and couldn't dream of living any other way.

The concepts in *Find Your Scream, Live Your Dream: Discover Your Inner Leader* (a.k.a. the Scream to Dream Approach) transform your life and work. This approach shows you how to live and lead from the inside out. It's about discovering the wisdom of your inner leader. It's a uniquely integrated, multi-dimensional, multi-cultural approach. It blends the best of analytical data-driven information with the power of intuitive knowledge. It's the accumulation and culmination of thirty years of personal growth and leadership experience that resulted in ever-increasing happiness and productivity for my employees and for me.

WHAT DOES FINDING YOUR SCREAM LOOK LIKE?

Just as every one of the almost six billion people in the world has a unique signature, fingerprint, iris and DNA, your scream is individual to you. If you are a musician your scream might look like Diana Ross finding her distinctive voice singing, "Ain't No Mountain High Enough!" Or if you are an athlete, it might look like Shaun White holding the American flag after clinching a gold medal in snowboarding on his first run. On his next run, he threw his riskiest big trick, the double McTwist, that he had worked on for four years. Or like Kim Yu-Na from Korea, seizing the gold medal in the 2010 Olympics figure skating event. Or like Kurt Warner, former Arizona Cardinals quarterback, throwing a touchdown pass.

If you are a political or spiritual leader it might look like Martin Luther King receiving the Nobel Peace Prize for his relentless efforts to create equality among blacks and whites. Or like Sandra Day O'Connor sitting as the first woman on the United States Supreme Court. Or like the current Buddhist spiritual leader, the Dalai Lama (Tenzin Gyatso), who also received the Nobel Peace Prize.

If you are a business leader, living your scream could look like Bill Gates creating the computer software giant Microsoft from humble beginnings in his home. Or like Jeffrey Swartz, CEO of Timberland outdoor apparel, leading the company as a community whose values match those of his own family. Or like the first African-American billionaire, multiple-Emmy Award winning talk show host, Oprah Winfrey.

Sure, I have named relatively famous people who have found their scream because many of you are familiar with them. I cannot attest to whether they fully live their scream because I don't know if they are also balanced in mind, body and spirit. But you probably know "ordinary" people whose actions and achievements honor who they are, people who are healthy all around. They, too, live and lead fulfilled lives that are in concert with their authentic inner self, what I call their "scream."

LEADING WITH YOUR SCREAM

Looking back, I realized that most of the leaders with whom I've worked had not found their own scream, so they rarely were able to help others find theirs. Leaders who have found their scream create an inspired work environment and illuminate the way for others to find their scream. As a result, they cannot help but achieve optimal productivity for their organization. It's a natural consequence. Everything comes from the inside out to create their dream and everyone's success. It's truly something to celebrate!

The importance of finding your scream may seem alien to you, especially if you are analytically inclined. At first, it surprised me, too. I have been described as the poster child for the analytical, intellectual type, an "arm-chair engineer." I was a Phi Beta Kappa economist and an attorney who was indoctrinated by engineers and immersed in a highly technical electricity transmission and pricing arena. Yet I was fortunate enough to listen to my intuition, which guided me to lead instead of to advise. Leading people and helping an organization succeed became pure joy for me.

My awakening came when I was the legal counsel for the largest utility in Arizona, after I had argued a $23 million energy contract case before now Supreme Court Justice Scalia. Despite my ability to do this type of work successfully, I found my scream by leaving it. I mustered enough courage to take a leap of faith. I became a self-taught leader who, during the turbulent period of electricity deregulation, grew a startup competitive commodity and green energy business from zero to more than 100 employees, from negative $10 million to $220 million in revenues per year for ten years and to $80 million in assets.

Sure, there are leaders whose resumes dwarf mine and who lead far bigger companies, but my ultimate scream is to share with you how to achieve your scream. This book maps the process through which I grew to articulate the Scream to Dream Approach.

I am grateful to have had the opportunity to incubate these principles at the company I'll call GreenEnergyCo. While I draw upon the real company and real customer and employee examples to provide insights for you, my purpose is not to have you repeat what we did. It's for you to find success in your unique way. I have utilized other names for all but the experts with whom we worked to maintain privacy. I was privileged to see the Scream to Dream Approach work among our varied employees, who included electrical engineers, people who served on nuclear submarines, financial engineers who were quantitative whizzes, commissioned salesmen who loved golf, IT-types, corporate middle managers, MBAs and data entry and administrative support people. What I learned is that by becoming more aware of who I was and then enabling others in our workforce to do the same, we could accomplish much more with much less resources, time, resistance, struggle and money.

I invite you on this journey with me to find your scream and live your dream. You and your company, organization or solely-owned business will be the winners because the principles in this book apply to you as a person, as a leader and as an instrumental contributor to guiding your own firm. In this age of instant information, it can be an overwhelming task to find the best personal and business solutions. Finding sincere mentors and insightful coaches can be challenging. While they can offer valuable ideas and solutions, you'll learn from reading this book that you have had the answers all along.

Moreover, in today's turbulent economy, it's more important than ever to be creative and resilient in the skills and ideas that you offer, since it's very probable you will change jobs a few times.

This book will show you how to find your answers, just as my employees and I found ours. And yes, if you are wondering, I initially pursued the money in the job without considering whether I was internally aligned. But because I eventually found my scream and made effective choices, the money flowed and it's no longer a concern.

When I first started working as an attorney I had no guidance—I wasn't awake and didn't see that I was out of alignment. My goal is to shorten the learning curve for you and show you how to live and lead in a different way that will work optimally for you.

HOW DO YOU BEGIN?

Ask your inner leader. On August 14, 1996, I made an entry into the journal I kept by my bedside. I was forty years old and did not feel fulfilled, although by societal measures, I was certainly successful. Nonetheless, I began to reassess my life goals. I decided to do a simple rating of eight aspects of my life on a scale of one to ten. Ten represented the highest score for how fulfilled I felt in each area. "How do I rate?" I asked myself. Here are my recorded responses:

Play: 5   Romance: 7
Personal growth: 7   Spirituality: 3
Career: 7   Friendships: 5
Wealth: 7   Health: 8

I then asked myself, "What do I want?"—All 10s! "How will I know when I have them?"—There would be noticeably more time for me, and I would be more relaxed, more patient, and more supportive with others. I would have more time for friends, my children and husband. I would be physically healthy and emotionally less stressed. I would love my work, instead of looking at it as something to pay the bills. My family and I would be financially sound. And I would be living amongst green trees, not in the scorching hot desert where I spent most of my life and work.

Now you try it. (Or you can wait until the end of chapter 1 where this exercise is set forth for your completion.) Ask yourself how you rank each of these eight areas in your own life on a scale from one to ten. Also, next to each area and ranking, estimate the average amount of time you spend per day on that aspect of your life. If you are a "weekend warrior" when it comes to exercise, for example, just average the time you spend on your health over the week. Don't overthink it! There's no right or wrong answer. Keep your list handy because you will revisit it.

WHAT DOES FINDING YOUR SCREAM FEEL LIKE?

Finding your scream feels like a score of all 10s in each of the above eight rated areas of your life, plus much more!

Finding your scream feels like you are in perfect alignment with what you value. You are in the flow from which success grows. I don't mean that success comes without effort—just without the pain, frustration, stress and struggle of going against the flow. It feels like time stands still. You find you have stopped pushing the boulder up a hill, only to have it roll back onto you and crush your spirit. Instead of beating your head against the wall to get ahead, it feels like you are ascending your ladder of success to reach the stars!

When you find your scream you move beyond self-improvement. You feel as if you have transformed—the caterpillar morphs into a butterfly; the yellow-and-black hot-rod Camaro in the film *Transformers* turns into Bumblebee the Autobot with a bottomless well of luck, determination and bravery.

When you find your scream your life flows in and around obstacles like a river weaving through a canyon. It finds the path of least resistance. You will be less frustrated as you manage your way through the perceived chaos of life. You'll face problems with a clear mind and you'll be able to stay true to your course. What you clearly want will come to you without exhausting your energy to make it happen. You will fit what you do. You will be inherently happy. You will be at peace with yourself, content, grateful and appreciative. You will observe. You will treat your body well and eat mindfully. You will speak thoughtfully. You will have endless energy. If leading is what you are meant to do, you will lead effectively and meaningfully.

I know how it feels to literally let go of the rigid lessons of the past—vocally, intellectually and emotionally. The water in the river flows over you, and all of your anger, strain and toxic emotions—those beliefs that have drained you of your optimal energy—wash away. I experienced this feeling with the indigenous people in the waters of the Kusane River in Karkloof, South Africa. The power of our intuitive wisdom was so dramatically brought home to me that I can now share it with you.

You will know when you have found your scream because

you will feel balanced in mind, body and spirit. You will feel fulfilled in all areas of your life. Sounds like a dream? It can be your reality.

And how do I know this? I now live it. Most every day.

WHY THE SCREAM TO DREAM APPROACH WILL UNIQUELY BENEFIT YOU

The Scream to Dream Approach is a multifaceted, multi-cultural approach to discovering your inner leader. It weaves concepts from different disciplines and traditions into an integrative and whole-person system. It also dares to plunge into more imaginative, mysterious depths. It connects many seemingly unrelated topics. But keep in mind, one of our greatest cognitive thinkers, Albert Einstein, actually attributed his genius to connecting things you wouldn't necessarily think of as fitting together by using his creativity and imagination.

This approach takes you back to the basics—as basic as listening to what indigenous people, that is, the native descendants of the ancient, original people, have to say. You may find that the integration of the perspectives grows on you. Or you may not relate to everything or feel immediately comfortable with some of the concepts. That's just fine, because the overall goal is to enhance your self-awareness—to get you closer to, and hopefully, to fully find your scream. Just use whatever prompts you in this book and elsewhere to dig deeper into yourself to discover your inner leader.

The Scream to Dream method also goes straight to the heart of the issue—you. You will discover you and your leadership from the "inside out." You will validate or deny whether leading others is even your best fit. It's critical to know either way for your optimal success, joy and fulfillment.

As I already mentioned, to understand is to transform. You don't have to be a psychologist to understand yourself. You will be shown intuitive ways to find your answers within. You will learn how to listen to your clues. This information is already available to you but in a language you may not have understood previously. You will also be provided with data-driven references, tools and assessments rich with insights. Illumination from the combination of both analytical and intuitive sources creates the clearest, most well-lit path "home"—to the place where you belong, where you are totally accepted and valued for who you are at your core.

You will explore your "whole person." This includes your natural talents, what you truly value, your passion and drives. You will learn how your mind and body do and don't work together for the results you want. For example, your body's ailments can tell you where you are not in alignment. Disease and distress are intriguing outward signs of your discontent.

I provide exercises that anchor each of the three principles of the Scream to Dream Approach and include both personal and workplace examples of what have and haven't worked. You can learn from them and apply them in a way that bests fits you as a person, leader and as a company or organization.

One of my most poignant personal examples is how I catapulted from an unhappy attorney "mis-fit" to a successful CEO "best-fit" by becoming self-aware, releasing the fear to change and inspiring my employees to do the same. Learn how to find your "best-fit" and become an inspirational "you" and leader, too, if leading others is your best-fit.

The promise for you, as a leader, and as a reader, is that you will:

- Become balanced in mind, body and spirit, and as a result, be more fulfilled and productive as a person and as a professional.

- Gain a sustainable competitive advantage for your company—inexpensively.

- Increase productivity by aligning your desires and strengths and those of your employees with your work and with that of your company's mission and goals.

- Optimize the use of your intuition as a person and leader.

- Create an environment in which you and your employees want to engage in meaningful work.
- Recruit and retain qualified, inspired best-fit employees.
- Reduce health care costs by creating a healthy environment and by using a whole-person approach.

Realize that transforming your life may require some fundamental behavior changes. You will be different, not just act differently. This book will get you started on that path. You will need to be committed to your desired change and to dig deeper into the supplemental resources that accompany this book to achieve sustained change. I provide resources to assist you, but ultimately, I want to inspire you to make your own changes and follow through with them.

This book will enhance your understanding—not about your expertise, you already know that—but about yourself. When you understand yourself, you can attain a permanent shift to a better place that brings success and fulfillment. Typically, the biggest rock blocking the road is you: when the rock is removed, you are free to flow and go!

THE THREE PRINCIPLES TO FIND YOUR SCREAM

To help you find your scream, I've distilled my experiences into three principles that worked for my employees, my family, my friends and me. I trust the principles will work for you, too. I have applied them in both personal and corporate settings. If they seem unconventional, trust me when I tell you that even ardent engineers became sincere believers in their effectiveness. My successors continue to use the principles.

The three principles to find your scream and live your dream are:

1. **Find Your Answers Within.** Access all available information from your own personal answer room. Learn to live and lead in an inspired, intuitive way. Find the answers in your heart—in other words, your gut, your intuition.

Work smarter, not harder, by doing more of what you love and do well.
2. **Explore Your Core.** Explore your core through key tools that provide insights into what you value. Rediscover your natural gifts. With this information, you can identify your best-fit, actualize it, and your energy will be optimized. Identify when your gut and goals align! And then you can begin to help others do the same.
3. **Release Your Fear.** Learn to release your fear so you can move toward alignment, to congruency. Find the antidote to fear and frustration by recognizing when your ego, perception, beliefs, biases and judgments prevent you from changing and being optimally productive and fulfilled. Learn how to change so you can realign with your scream and live your dream.

ONE

HOW I FOUND MY SCREAM

I can see clearly now the rain is gone. I can see all obstacles in my way. Gone are the dark clouds that had me blind. It's gonna be a bright, bright, sunshinin' day.
— JIMMY CLIFF, "I CAN SEE CLEARLY NOW," WE ALL ARE ONE: THE BEST OF JIMMY CLIFF, 2002

When I began mapping my process of self-discovery and transformation, I reflected on my youth:

It's a warm, sunshiny day in October of 1963, and I am seven years old. I'm on my knees playing marbles outside our small home in Central Phoenix, Arizona, with five neighborhood kids.

"Kip," I squeal, "I'm going to win your black and yellow bumble bee boulder when I hit it outside the circle!" I've got the biggest killer marble, a steelie, lined up. BAM! "Kip, to get it back, you will have to trade me two cats-eye marbles."

Within that moment time stood still. It was pure joy. I was winning, trading and playing outdoors with my friends.

Thirty-three years later on another October day, I'm leaning against the elevator wall at 2 a.m. with an electric utility company director beside me at our corporate headquarters in Phoenix. As the in-house energy attorney, I'm working on data requests for the umpteenth rate increase case. I've run out of the half-gallon-sized bottle of TUMS® that I've been living on for too many years.

Bleary-eyed, I look at the director and announce, "I'm not doing this EVER AGAIN! I will not be the utility lawyer who handles tedious rate cases anymore!" My entire body is shaking and vibrating with frustration and anger. I'm tired of standing on the sidelines as an advisor, and not directing and making the business deals which I am confident I can do as well as any of the other leaders.

I finally had the conscious realization that I was living incongruently. I was out of alignment. I wasn't living out of my heart's joy.

Within a week I presented a proposal to our vice president: I asked to lead the parent company's new electric commodity group that management was forming to take advantage of upcoming electric competition. As the company's attorney and expert in this area, I essentially had been making many business decisions, so why not lead the new business? Leading was very familiar to me—I had been president of my senior high school class and many college clubs and civic groups in the past.

The vice president's first reaction was, "And throw your law degree away?"

I had to overcome the perceived obstacle that I was a woman in a white-male engineer-dominated workforce, a former behavioral economist and an attorney—three strikes against me, at least if you have heard the stereotypical jokes about how un-bottom line, un-business-like economists and lawyers are perceived to be.

Persistence is a strength of mine, however.

I had been the vice president's attorney for fifteen years. He was well aware of my capabilities, strengths and weaknesses. I had a track record of success that had built his confidence in me. Ultimately, the vice president gave me the chance. And later it became very clear that my law degree wasn't a waste; it was all part of the "plan"—my path. All the money that came in and out of our doors required contracts—and I knew all about contracts!

The new group started with one member—me. I wrote the proposals, made the sales calls and contracted for the delivery of the competitive electricity services. I used to joke that I had a bloody nose because the learning curve was so steep.

In less than one year, the new electric competition group

was expanded to ten employees. In January of 1998, we became the core of a new, separate startup subsidiary energy company, "GreenEnergyCo." The company focused on sales of competitively-priced electricity, green energy and energy efficiency services to business customers. When our group merged into the new company, I was made vice president. The head of the utility company's marketing and customer service departments was initially made president.

Within two weeks of moving into our new location and starting up GreenEnergyCo the president left. She followed her dream to become the CEO of a Southwestern utility company. Our board of directors started a nationwide search for a new president and I was on the interview team—awkward but necessary. I threw my name in the hat. I also wrote a memo to our parent company's executive who was heading up the interview team that enumerated why I would and would not be the best candidate for president. Essentially, it was a strength versus weaknesses list. Because I was generally aware of what I didn't like to do and wasn't good at, I was very forthright. Moreover, if the executives didn't support or believe in me, I didn't want the frustration of fighting against the current.

I knew the risks and rewards of making money through commodity electricity sales. Electric power is the most volatile-priced commodity in the world. If, say, our gross profit was $2.00 per MWh (megawatt-hour, the units in which bulk electricity is sold), we could lose our gross margin and more in a mere five seconds. The price could change by over 30% in the real time market in less than a minute from say, $60 to $90 per MWh! That is why we hedged and covered our sales to the greatest extent possible by ensuring we had locked in the price of power at wholesale before we guaranteed the downstream retail price.

While I liked sales and knew how to make the money, I did not like "accounting for it." By that I mean tracking all the detailed and SEC accounting rules. Thus, I advised the executive, I would need to "back-fill" this area with a top-notch financial leader. Without that complement I would not be the right choice for president. After interviews with three men who wanted a higher salary, more resources and greater board commitment than I had received to date, I was chosen and made president.

Over a ten-year period I experienced the joy of leading truly committed people—people who wanted to be at work. It was the experience of a lifetime. Looking back at what I am most proud of, it is not all the money we made during our glory years, or the legacy of green projects that we built for our customers, but how many of the employees found their scream!

So, how did I happen to know at that moment on an elevator in October of 1996 that I was living out of alignment with my life's joy? In retrospect, I realize that a series of clues led to my epiphany. I was only two years into practicing law when I left the original law firm that I'd joined after clerking for an Arizona Supreme Court judge. I was disenchanted with the real world of law, discovering that at many times, I could not attain practical results for my business customers through the legal process. You could succeed in a judgment against the offender, but there would be no assets from which to collect it! It was a world of tireless conflict.

I missed economics. So I sought and was hired for the job of rate analyst for Arizona's largest utility company. This job combined economic analysis and legal practice in that we compiled cases to present before regulatory bodies. I kept my legal license active even though I was working behind the scenes. I was getting married and knew I would want time for a family. The hours were far more reasonable, but the work environment was not.

Less than a year later, in 1983, I was fed up with being told by my curmudgeon of a boss that I was displacing a man by working in my job. He advised that I would gain recognition and a badge of courage if I worked most weekends. After repeated, blatant, sexist statements, I sought "greener pastures." I was qualified to join the utility's in-house legal department and at my request, transferred there in less than a year. This compromise afforded our family a good income while I worked fewer hours than in a law firm. But off and on for the next almost fifteen years as senior attorney in the legal department, I longed for more, having settled for less. Looking for answers to why I was discontented, I attended most of the work-life-career-balance sessions that the company offered.

At one such event, the "giveaway" (like a party favor) was a deck of 52 cards—*Calling Cards*, by Inventure Group, which help people discover their calling. Their purpose is to help you find fulfillment in the workplace by answering the question, "What work would I most enjoy?"

From the 52 cards you select the five cards that best fit your natural preferences. Then you select which one of the five answers this question best: "What would you most enjoy contributing to others?" I selected the card for "empowering others through enthusiastically leading by example, explanation, and demanding and rewarding excellence." The work environment that correlates with this type of work is "enterprising." I also chose the sub-category "pioneering."

My choices made sense to me. As I reflect on my youth, boy, was I enterprising and not afraid to take risks as a "pioneer." Not only did I have an enviable marble collection, which I had largely competed for and won, but I was the one-girl, human version of eBay. I created all kinds of paintings, paper-mâché flowers and items that my friends and family bought. I would trade and re-sell these and other items very profitably! All of these activities were pure joy. They were like a game, and all the while, I made a lot of money doing them.

Along the path from childhood to adulthood, I deafened to the voice of my inner leader. I let my head lead instead of my heart. I was guided by fear, not love, and the many desires of others. I didn't pay attention to the multitudinous clues available to me as I became misaligned. My body talked back! It hurt or became ill. I covered its cry with constant busyness and over-activity. While this experience is common to many of us, what I also desire to become common from reading this book is your rediscovery of what you have lost.

I rediscovered my heart's joy when I listened to my intuitive wisdom. I courageously released my fear of leaving the known practice of law. I took the leap of faith to once again become enterprising by starting up the new energy group. I lived and led the people of GreenEnergyCo in an inspired, intuitive and empowering way. And I am still living my dream today by inspiring, writing and speaking.

ACTIVATING MY INTENT

On August 14, 2001, I scribbled in a new journal that while our GreenEnergyCo business was spectacular, I would not fully realize my calling until I wrote a book. I knew we were onto something big, so I wrote about my personal and professional journey. At the time, I did not know that this was the book that I would write and that I would not complete the book until over nine years later. I labeled this journal "Finding My Calling and More, 2001—The years of doing what is important to me and those that matter!"

What I realize now is that I set in motion a very specific intent. I intuitively decided it was best to live with passion and follow my heart, which I had already accomplished once by leaving the practice of law to help start GreenEnergyCo. I was going to continue to do what I was naturally gifted at and interested in. I did not know the timing of when all the desired changes would come, and I started small. I balanced my home and career life better by occasionally leaving work early. I signed up for a ceramics class. Although I had been an economics major in college, my minor was in fine arts. I longed for a creative release.

Recall the eight areas of my life that I rated in my previous journal in 1996. Well, after leaving corporate America more than thirteen years later on October 28, 2009, I ranked them again. Here's where my intent to achieve all 10s in my life led me:

Play: 10   Romance: ascending
Personal growth: 10 Spirituality: 9+ (most improved)
Career: infinite   Friendships: 9+
Wealth: plenty   Health: 9++

Wow, the Scream to Dream Approach was really working! I learned that to manifest my intent, I must have a deeply-held belief over time. It requires both quality and quantity of thought. Now that my aspirations and inspirations are aligned, my potential is truly being realized.

ENERGIZE!

I have a saying that no matter what you face in life, if you are inspired in your heart, you naturally inspire others around you. Energy flows where your intention goes.

Why not take the easiest path for your energy to flow to create the life of your dreams?

The connectivity between my professional background in energy and my beliefs about how energy influences your personal life offers a compelling metaphor. As you may be aware, everything is made up of energy, even rocks and you. (As Albert Einstein explained with his famous formula, $E=mc^2$, energy and mass are two different forms of the same thing.) When you are living who you are, your energy readily flows, like the way Ohm's law works. It states that electrical energy flows most readily over the transmission lines that have the path of least resistance. Power lines can only carry the produced energy to the consumer if the lines are not congested. The flow of energy through transmission lines is analogous to the way energy flows through your body. The point this metaphor makes is that your thoughts and feelings direct energy, and to attain what you want in your life, you must direct your thoughts and feelings in a manner that's completely consistent with what you want. When energy is not flowing within you, you can become congested physically, emotionally and spiritually. What you intend to happen does not happen.

If you are out of balance or congested, or resisting who you are (which makes it impossible to be in alignment), your energy will not readily flow. Think of a kinked water hose, for example. Finding your scream is about being in your full personal power or potential and commanding your full energy. As the leader in GreenEnergyCo I found my scream and was energized by enabling every person to find his or her scream.

I observed that when you find and live your scream you have all the energy you need. You get things done by working smarter, not harder.

Imagine that you work like the compact fluorescent lamp (CFL) 60-watt bulb instead of the old Edison incandescent light bulb. They both accomplish the same thing because they emit the same amount of light in your homes, schools and businesses. But the CFL performs the work using 25 percent of the energy used by the incandescent bulb. Imagine what you could achieve with that extra 75 percent of energy!

Not only does the CFL bulb use less energy, it lasts up to ten times longer and helps our environment. When you do what you are naturally good at, you will use less energy because life will not be the struggle it once was. You will love what you do and it will energize you. In any event, don't you want to create an environment where you and your employees work healthier, smarter and not harder, like that CFL?

When you live and work in alignment with your scream, you will use your energy efficiently. It's the same with power plants or transmission lines—whenever we don't use them to their fullest capacity they are less efficient, less productive and more costly to operate. We have incurred the cost of installing a certain sized wire—its capacity—but aren't running all the energy through the line that it's designed to carry. Conversely, if we try to flow more energy through a wire than it can hold, it becomes congested and can burn up. The less strain on an electrical outlet, the more juice flows.

The same principal holds true for you and your employees. When you are in alignment, when you find your scream, you reduce your strain. When you help your employees find their scream you reduce their resistance and strain. Less strain on you, less strain on every individual, allows greater output utilizing the same human capacity.

So to command your full potential, you must energize — transmit your unblocked energy into optimal action. This happens when you find your scream and live it.

I knew without a doubt that I had found my scream when the leadership principles I believed in—and incubated—helped create best-fits out of mis-fits. We accomplished far more with less people due to the alignment of our employees.

FROM MIS-FIT TO BEST-FIT

Why don't people want to go to work? Do they dread it because they are mismatched with their work? Imagine the productivity of a company of best-fits in contrast to a company of mis-fits.

GreenEnergyCo is an example of what happens when many employees find their scream in a company. It demonstrates what can be accomplished when the people are aligned with their natural strengths and when their roles and goals are aligned with those of the company or organization. In the beginning, it seemed like GreenEnergyCo's startup was akin to the original 1964 holiday movie special, *Rudolph the Red-Nosed Reindeer and The Island of the Misfit Toys*.

You may have watched one of the film's many versions on TV. The island is a sanctuary for defective and unwanted toys such as Charlie-in-the-box (misnamed, but otherwise a normal Jack-in-the box), a cowboy who rides an ostrich and a train with square wheels on its caboose. Rudolph the Red-Nosed Reindeer feels outcast after the other reindeers in the North Pole ridicule him about his glowing nose. He runs into the forest where the Abominable Snow Monster chases him. Rudolph flees to the Island of Misfit Toys.

But when there's too much fog on Christmas Eve for Santa to make his deliveries in his sleigh, Rudolph saves the day. Rudolph lights the way with his brilliant red nose! Santa stops by the island and picks up all the mis-fit toys to match them with children who very much want and love them. One of Rudolph's friends, an elf named Hermey who wants to be a dentist instead of Santa's helper, was also a misfit. Now Hermey gets to open a dental office in the North Pole. All the mis-fits become best-fits.

I've related this tale because, like Rudolph and Hermey, the story of GreenEnergyCo is, in large part, the story of how helping people find their scream turns mis-fit employees into best-fits. Prior to becoming the President of GreenEnergyCo, as the senior energy attorney, I had worked with many senior-level leaders and individuals in the electric utility company's different departments. I recognized innate talent in some of the people who were treated like outcasts or discounted in the conservative, regulated culture because they were different from "the mold." I intuitively knew that these "mis-fits" (or in some cases "dissed-fits") could become "best-fits" in a different, more entrepreneurial environment.

Several of GreenEnergyCo's most successful leaders blossomed after they transferred into an empowering environment where they were allowed to create their own future. For some individuals, however, our business would have been too unknown, ambiguous and unsettling for their nature. I also understood firsthand from my previous work experiences how it felt to be a mis-fit in environments that don't match your strengths and style, which is what prompted me to ask to run the competitive affiliate.

I knew the culture that I wanted to foster at GreenEnergyCo was very different from the one I had just left in the regulated utility—and that it had to be. Many of the skill sets had to be different, too. In a highly-regulated industry, the regulators judge your performance in hindsight. They dictate the level of your economic opportunity by establishing what level of return you may earn on your invested capital. Caution and compliance are critical because you could be slapped on the wrist after the fact for erroneously anticipating market price movements. Since no one can ever correctly guess such movement, there's no upside in taking any risk. Fear is the motivator.

But in a startup, smart risk taking is essential. It's about the money, honey. You have to pay the bills to grow. So I looked for talented people who might have been perceived as the square pegs in the round holes of my former workplace—ones who would fit perfectly in our competitive enterprise.

During the first week of employment at GreenEnergyCo we offered all of the employees the opportunity to take the

DISCProfile™ and Motivators™ assessments because these tools help people discover their best-fits. Everyone willingly agreed. We divulged their results only to each individual employee, although many ultimately discussed them with one another.

The DISC tool identifies employees' natural strengths and values. I found it to be quite helpful to my employees, leaders, family and me. I had observed over the years that many people don't know themselves well. So I invested in all of my employees to help them understand who they were, how others perceived them and what they valued. Until people become aware of what they naturally do well, they don't always get placed into the best job for their talents. And when they are unaware, they don't take action to create their best-fit, obviously, because they don't know what it is.

We observed that some of our people were results-oriented, bottom-line types; some were relationship-oriented customer service or sales people; some were natural problem solvers who liked process; and others wanted to carefully conserve or preserve assets; and so on. These descriptions merely typify what we could see on the outside, but we didn't necessarily know what inspired them on the inside.

Once our employees understood their strengths and values, the company leaders could work with them to determine their best-fit. This didn't mean we could immediately change the position they were hired to perform. However, we worked toward finding them the best jobs or key projects to optimize their strengths. We encouraged cross-training and switching positions, where practical.

As background, we had three business lines—a three legged stool—so that our income streams were diversified. We had a profitable, but more volatile commodity electricity services and renewable energy sales business line; an asset based district cooling plant and distribution pipe system business that returned income more like an annuity; and an energy efficiency and performance contracting business where we were paid as construction progressed and we functioned as the general contractor. We carried the risk of energy savings for years on some of these jobs.

Having a common way of viewing ourselves helped new employees and leaders integrate with other team members. It supported a sense of community. One of our consultants, Joy Schwertley, Ph.D., who participated in the beginning stages of the "find your scream" principles that GreenEnergyCo employed, observed:

> "Vicki's people were all naturally interested in learning about themselves through, among other things, the DISCProfile™ and Motivators™ assessment (DISC). She demonstrated that management cared about each person as a whole person. When a person sees value, it can lead to buy-in, so there wasn't much resistance to the process. If the highest leader does not buy into the use of the DISC, for example, it won't work. Odds are, however, that if the leader had a magic wand that could change the most important thing to the leader immediately, the DISC would help in achieving that. Key is that the leader take it to heart and make any needed changes in himself or herself first."

Here are a few examples of how GreenEnergyCo became home for mis-fits turned best-fits. (I've included many more stories throughout this book.) Charles, the eventual leader of one of our three business lines, was "realigned" twice before ultimately finding his scream. Charles was a professional engineer who had been the head of energy sales. During a reorganization I reassigned him to develop a technical area and work with our joint venture partner, instead of pure sales, which wasn't his best match. While I could see the potential, Charles took a little longer to accept this opportunity for change. Ultimately, we terminated the joint venture, and with a new team that he hired, a successful new business was created. We were all thankful that he became a best-fit!

One of our leaders, Roberto, actually left his former workplace and a significant bonus behind because he saw the opportunity to make a difference in a startup. He joined us because I gave him the independence and operating room to satisfy his interests and values. He had many interests beyond being a commodities trader, at which he was currently succeeding handsomely. He had the mental agility to understand how the world of regulation intersected with marketplace rules and pricing. As a result, he and his team found profits for our company and savings for our customers.

The company's philosophy of looking at each person as an individual also included customizing employees' incentive plans, work hours and work environments to match their values. For example, we eventually worked it out so Roberto could commute one week a month from Minnesota to Phoenix. As I describe in Chapter 3 he continued to successfully lead our top-performing team.

SCREAMING WITH A DECADE OF SUCCESS

By creating an environment for mis-fits to become best-fits who are aligned with their natural strengths and values, we gained not only loyal, satisfied employees, but also loyal, satisfied customers. We accomplished this with only one-third of the employees that our competitors had on staff. Our success was due entirely to unleashed and optimized human potential and energy. Our people wanted to create a dream green energy company and believed that business and sales integrity was a long-term strategy.

We have all witnessed the public's loss of trust in brokerage firms after investors were misled by financial derivatives market executives. Also, adjustable rate mortgages were sold to unsophisticated homebuyers, contributing to the foreclosure crisis. There are parallels in electric commodity markets. Prices can race up in seconds if, for example, the weather gets hot suddenly and creates a peak demand. We would not advise a lower risk type customer to float with market prices in this environment, even if initially the floating price was much cheaper than a fixed price for electricity. If we lost a bid because our price didn't appear as cheap as our competitor's price, so be it.

Yes, we lost many requests for proposals (RFPs), especially to Enron. For good reason. In 1997, we had a "good loss." We responded to one of the first-in-the-nation RFPs for the largest competitive electricity sale to the combined University of California and California State University systems, which encompassed 33 campuses with approximately 200 MW of energy (the equivalent of more than 200,000 mid-sized homes in the Southwest).

My newly hired pricing leader and I anxiously sat outside the Long Beach administrative conference room awaiting the bid interview. Out strutted Enron's team of eight—which included four women in short skirts and stilettos—carrying briefcases. We were next in line for questioning by a panel of fifteen different university facility and procurement managers. It was clear to us that their expectations were unachievable. This was a bid to lose. Enron won the five-year contract.

Four years later, Enron was sued for failure to perform. GreenEnergyCo responded to the University system's new bid request, along with many competitors that were much larger and better capitalized. We won the bid because we were aligned with our customers' values. They were educators, and we took the time to explain how the market worked and provided them with decision-making tools, not just prices. We taught them about the volatile electric commodity market and worked with them on pricing that matched their budget cycle. This enabled them to take control of their procurement of energy. We continued to win their bid each of the next five years. It was a challenging, progressive and mutually beneficial relationship.

As I mentioned earlier, GreenEnergyCo steadily grew from our negative earnings as a startup to $220 million in revenue each year. We built $80 million in assets, hired more than 100 employees, and utilized the expertise of many shared services groups from our parent company, such as accounting, legal, credit and risk management. GreenEnergyCo provided commodity electricity and energy services in four states. We traded, scheduled and supplied electricity competitively. We bought energy for delivery to schools, hospitals, industrial and retail corporations, buildings and city facilities under a variety of states' diverse rules.

Because we were small, we had to rely on the strength of every person. Much like a trek to Mount Everest, each of us carried provisions for the others, without which none of us could have survived. If someone was not a best-fit for the particular role, typically everyone knew it, and he or she (with support and encouragement) would self-select to take on a different task. We quickly learned at what we excelled and what we didn't.

We became the general contractor who kept oversight of the projects because our reputation was behind every one of them. We decided to outsource trades to subcontractors. Using this model, for example, we won more than $100 million of energy efficiency and performance contracting work for Arizona State University (ASU). We were the general contractor who oversaw the installation of the first solar facilities on one of ASU's parking garages. We designed and constructed the approximately $25 million Sun Devil combined heat and power (CHP) facility. This may not sound very sexy but it's one of the most cost-effective ways to be energy efficient if you have a large campus.

While there are many qualified construction and engineering companies that might have performed the work, we carefully selected a high-level account manager who supported the campus leadership. His account management skills were critical to our joint success. There are many competing agendas in any organization, and harmonizing them for the best overall energy program was a skill-set that we harnessed, apart from the technical work.

Empowered people's genius never ceases to amaze me when an environment for ingenuity is created. I witnessed that genius when the City of Flagstaff, Arizona hired us. Nestled in the tall pines of Northern Arizona, Flagstaff is an outdoor, environmentalist community. Many people there want to be as green as possible. To show residents that the city was "greening-up," we started their comprehensive energy program with a very visible 15 kW solar array installed on the roof and exterior facade of the south side of Flagstaff City Hall. When you drive by it on Route 66 going through the heart of the town, the black solar panels are unmistakable. The real "guts" of the program, as far as saving energy, however, was a project the public cannot see. It involved capturing methane gas into a digester from the city's Wildcat

Hill Wastewater treatment plant. Flagstaff uses this otherwise wasted by-product to power a turbine that creates electricity for the plant. It replaces electricity that the city would otherwise have to purchase.

Because we were wholly owned by a generally risk-adverse parent holding company, we were cautious in how we pioneered these green projects. We did not invest in unproven technologies. For instance, we did not build a $50 million bio-digester that held promise. The concept was a completely sustainable farm. The cows and chickens would create the fuel for the turbine and the chickens would eat some of the fly ash left over from the combustion process. (I learned more about the importance of consistency of these fuels than I care to remember.)

Other innovative projects were completed, however. A real testament to our people's creative problem solving was the energy savings accomplished at the then Bank One Ballpark, now Chase Field. Chase Field is a covered baseball arena in downtown Phoenix, where the Arizona Diamondbacks play. GreenEnergyCo's out-of-the box idea was to use the ballpark's already-existing large chillers that provided air conditioning to the enormous facility (it holds more than 48,000 baseball fans) to create ice at night, and melt it during the day for cooling. At night, the cost of electricity is often over three times less than daytime prices. By selling the excess chilled water to other businesses, we could pay the Ball Park for the use of their chillers.

We expanded the system by adding another chiller plant that made a giant Popsicle™ in the basement of the Phoenix Convention Center, in a tank the size of five Olympic swimming pools. A five-mile radius of piping delivers the 34-degree Fahrenheit water to buildings where, in essence, they blow the almost ice-cold air into the buildings with fans. This system allows the building owners to avoid the capital investment and maintenance of large chillers, at a competitive price.

Still, between 2007 and 2008, GreenEnergyCo ceased commodity operations, about ten years after the company began. It was not because we weren't successful, but because our business was no longer compatible with the parent holding company's focus on its primary utility business. We no longer fit the parent company's business model. We became a mis-fit. We had a different risk profile and more volatile earnings.

Shareholders wouldn't reward the parent company for owning a subsidiary company that delivered value through growth, not dividends. Shortly after the closing of GreenEnergyCo's commodity business line, the parent company also sold its district cooling business. Fortunately, the energy services business has continued its work of helping organizations be more energy efficient, since this business complements and continues to fit the parent holding company's strategy.

At first, the end of such a great experience felt like death for those of us who moved on. However, we eventually realized the many blessings that resulted from being set free. Our deals had become increasingly difficult to execute, due to the parent's tightening risk rules and approval procedures. After we left and found new positions, we once again became valued for our scream in our new jobs. I know that most of the people who left GreenEnergyCo are excelling in their new opportunities. Even those who were reassigned and assimilated into the sister utility company's environment have adapted more readily, due to the perspectives and experiences they gained at GreenEnergyCo.

Interestingly, because they were on the forefront of many industry issues in our entrepreneurial company and had so much responsibility, many of these people now lead teams and key projects. Some GreenEnergyCo team members have voluntarily set up annual reunions, where many of us came together recently to celebrate the good old days. I know for sure that when we worked together we had the time of our lives (so far)! And so can you.

EXERCISE

Rate the following eight aspects of your life on a scale of one to ten. Ten represents the highest score for how fulfilled you feel in each area. Don't overthink it. Next to each ranking, estimate how much time you spend each day in this area. If, for example, your play time totals two hours of exercising on Saturday and Sunday and no play the rest of the week, average your play to about 35 minutes per day.

Area	Ranking	Time per day
Play:		
Personal growth:		
Career:		
Wealth:		
Romance:		
Spirituality:		
Friendships:		
Health:		

TWO

TRANSFORMING TODAY'S LEADERSHIP

How do we inspire ourselves to greatness when nothing less will do? How do we inspire everyone around us?

— Morgan Freeman as Nelson Mandela in Invictus

WHY WE NEED TO CHANGE HOW WE LEAD

We are in the midst of the breakdown of our old ways on many levels. Fast and vast disruptive changes are occurring in our world. In the last ten years of my life, I have seen more earthquakes and volcanic eruptions, tsunamis, drought, tornados, economic crises, health care crises, and ongoing war than I remember in prior decades.

As I said earlier, the old models of leadership don't work in this chaotic environment; so let's not waste time merely improving them. Corporate greed should be dead, and command-and-control leadership should be dead, at least, for any entity that intends to thrive in our ever-changing world. Leaders who are interested only in lining their own pockets are being exposed and should no longer be tolerated.

On top of that, our educational practices need to develop independent, creative thinkers. To date, the major approaches to organizational learning and change have been based on the same underlying model: learning from the experiences of the past, according to Dr. C. Otto Scharmer, Senior Lecturer at MIT and creator of the Presencing Institute. Leaders increasingly face challenges that the old tools don't address. They need a new core capability: the ability to let go of the past and lead by tuning in to the possibilities of the future. That capacity, Dr. Scharmer calls, "presencing." Presencing, explains Scharmer in his book,

Theory U: Leading from the Future As It Emerges, is a blend of the words presence and sensing, and means to sense and actualize your highest future possibility.

The Scream to Dream Approach that I offer has similarities to presencing and is a "way of being"—a *Tao* in Asian philosophy, a *path* in English translation, or an *experience*. It begins with you becoming the best individual and leader you can be by living and leading consistently with your scream. You follow the three principles of: 1) increasing your self-awareness through finding your answers within; 2) exploring your core and listening to your body; and 3) releasing your fear of change if you are not living in alignment with who you are. You become balanced as a whole person, in mind, body and spirit. There is a persuasive body of research demonstrating that a leader's level of self-awareness is the number one criterion determining effectiveness.

Once you find your scream, you can then enable others to find theirs within your company or organization. Ultimately, the organization or company cannot help but be the best it can be. I see this as a new and emerging way of leading—one that is based on connectivity, collaboration, co-creation and community—one that awakens the spirit and focuses on each person as a *whole person* who is connected with everyone and everything else on this planet.

For instance, we are all connected through the World Wide Web. Did you know that the third most populated "environment" after China and India is Facebook, with a growing half-billion visitors? Why? Every human wants to belong. By first understanding ourselves better, we can find where we fit. Each one of us is searching for answers to the most fundamental questions about who we are and what we want. And each of us has our answers—within! You and I are creating our world together. You and I—all of us have a need to grow and evolve. We want to contribute, collaborate and be part of a community. A company, in essence, is a tribe—a community—and everyone wants to belong where they are a best-fit.

To collaborate as a leader is to co-create; this is power *with*, not power *over*. It's not command and control leadership. Leaders and teams who build collaborative, community environments will be more creative and productive, as I illustrated with the example of the small team at GreenEnergyCo winning over Enron.

With the advent of globalization and the shrinking of our world, we have an unprecedented opportunity to expand our knowledge, and a responsibility to use it wisely. Therefore, you as a leader have the power and responsibility to find your scream and to help the people with whom you work find theirs. The future of our world requires that we find our individual screams. Each of us can, and innately wants, to make a difference. To do so in a leadership capacity, we must transform how we lead, if we lead out of fear. All thoughts, ideas, decisions, choices and actions are based either in fear or love. We must lead out of love, not fear.

LEADING WITHOUT FEAR

Identifying and acknowledging fear is a critical principle in the Scream to Dream Approach and in leading in a new way. Fear is a huge dark cloud that obscures who you are and what you want. Your fear manifests false limitations. When you learn to recognize your fear, you will identify when your ego is ruling your decisions. Your ego guides you based on your fears of what you "should" do, not what your heart chooses to do. Your heightened self-awareness will allow you to catch your ego in action and replace it with beliefs of the limitless opportunities that you have to be all you can be. (I explain this concept more thoroughly in Chapter 7.)

Leading without fear, leading when you are aligned, increases productivity. How? Because you help your employees find their screams so they are no longer living in limitation and swimming upstream. For example, when I encouraged a contract analyst to apply for the pricing leader position, she accomplished the work of two former employees. Her strength was clearly with numbers, and when she became aligned with her scream, both the employee and the company were the winners. She was effective in contracts, but not optimal. That is the difference. Her innate ability to build pricing models eliminated risk for us while allowing us to price more competitively.

Our mission rallied our heads and hearts. At GreenEnergyCo, we existed to make a difference in the health of our customer's business and our world by offering customized commodity and green energy solutions that fit our customers' needs. This was our organization's scream, in effect. Much like the alignment required to be balanced in mind, body and spirit as an individual, alignment of the organization's mission and values is critical for success.

The work environment that we created accommodated individual work-style preferences. We allowed telecommuting and we didn't *fear* that people would not get their work done if they weren't being watched. This was in contrast to my experience in other work places.

We led without the fear of being open. We created a place where it was safe to be yourself, where people could have fun and even act goofy during staff meetings.

We created an alternative to the type of environment in which people viewed withholding information as a way to climb the ladder. We encouraged people to "open up," to collaborate and share their ideas and information. It was important for you to understand not only to whom you handed off your work, but also how others utilized it, and ultimately how it affected the company and the customer. It's critical to foster a safe, open environment because it's the most efficient way to empower everyone to make informed decisions, especially when they're located in different states. It's very inefficient and costly to have to pry information from the "owner."

To create a culture of openness, I led by example. I had previously discovered through self-awareness and information from the DISC and other assessment tools, that my self-confidence and results focus could be intimidating. I wanted to encourage discussion for the richest debate and idea generation in order to co-create our future. In order to get the most out of our people, I realized that I had to put on my brakes during discussions and not always cut to the chase.

To create community we added a break room out of an area that was under utilized.

Another example of our open work environment was at our quarterly all-hands meeting where we had the leaders responsible for our top corporate goals present their results in fun, creative ways. They would have us guess at the scores through a Jeopardy format, a skit or competitive question and answer game. These meetings routinely included a playful yet informative health awareness session. We had a nutritionist from the YMCA guide a guessing game about food labels, for example. We issued pedometers and had a miles-walked-during-the-quarter contest. The purpose was to raise awareness about the importance of simple activity and stress the need for balance in health and work performance. The message to employees was that we cared about their business and personal success.

We did all of these things inexpensively and realized a demonstrable cost/benefit gain.

We also gave back to our community in several ways. For example, the entire company volunteered for a day at the Salvation Army. We utilized our construction trucks to hang a basketball hoop. We fixed potholes. Those who had an artistic scream painted cartoon characters on the nursery walls.

We held all kinds of company team building events, such as outdoor, Outward Bound exercises to increase trust in one another. The three business lines played a big-betting, "slightly" competitive softball game and we hunted each other down during a friendly laser tag game. (As I painfully recollect, I was shot hundreds of times!). We went to a Diamondbacks baseball game and played the dollar hand-off (you passed your dollar each time your batter failed to bring in a run, and when a run was scored, the person holding the dollars at the end of the inning got to keep them). And there were plenty of good-humored pranks, but I am saving those for later. The goal was to foster a sense of community where you support one another so everyone can succeed.

Our leadership approach was intentionally different from others I experienced. For instance, some of my prior leaders subscribed to a "show-me" style: you show me I should put my faith in you and trust you to deliver. Then you might get a key project. Prove you can get results (I have no qualm with that). But each time after demonstrated success, you start proving yourself all over again. In other words, even after you repeatedly demonstrated competence and reliable completion of a project or task, your vice-president, director or manager would still hover, micromanage and even assign the same project to multiple groups.

Assigning the same project to more than one person or group is incredibly inefficient. I've seen it occur when managers lacked confidence in a person's ability or inclination to perform. Assign the task to two people and see if one of them succeeds. This practice creates confusion about who's really responsible. Even more important, it communicates that you don't trust your employees. True leadership requires that you stand up for, believe in and support your employees.

My preferred leadership approach is to start by selecting the most capable person for the job. Clearly delineate what is expected. Describe the reward and consequences for performance. Ensure that the responsibility, expertise and needed resources are within that person's province to accomplish the job. Then I say, "I trust you as being capable. If you let me down, we will both have difficulty dealing with the disappointment, because I gave you the benefit of the doubt." This type of leadership is quite simple. It's based on trust, honesty, and staying out of the other person's defined sandbox, that is, their business.

However, you cannot be naïve as a leader. You have to place boundaries and checkpoints in case employees don't meet expectations—sometimes just due to miscommunication. You must also give continuous feedback to ensure the leader or employee is on track. Empower within defined parameters. Delineate leaders' and employees' sandboxes.

To put it another way, you must establish the guardrails and let the accountable employees drive the cars between them. The guardrails need to be set at the appropriate width. You don't want people driving off the cliff or on the wrong side of the road. There needs to be an appropriate balance between prescribing how the goal is to be achieved without unfettered freedom. I describe how to achieve this in Chapter 5.

Of course, GreenEnergyCo had growing pains, so we assigned a neutral facilitator to intervene before miscommunications became unproductive. A massage chair positioned in a quiet room awaited our tense employees. Our human resources leader encouraged stressed employees not to speak out of anger and to "cool off" in "the chair."

Generally, people self-selected out if they were ultimately not a best-fit after efforts to reposition them to match their scream. However, there were occasions that required intervention when the individual's value system did not match those of the company. It's better for all involved that he or she be released to find the place where he or she can excel.

The incredible results that GreenEnergyCo's leaders achieved by leading in a new way are corroborated by other successful companies' philosophies. Even in today's tough job market, employers such as tech powerhouse SAS, Edward Jones, and Timberland are looking at their employees as whole people. These best-rated companies in Fortune magazine's 2010 top 100 companies offer unusual perks to go out and play, creative recession busters, and much more. There's increasing recognition among top-rated companies that the personal and professional sides of people are merged. You don't leave your personal self at home! These companies are investing in a balance of building the mind, body and spirit of their most valuable resource, their employees.

Outside magazine (May, 2010) listed the 50 Best Places to Work, based on a company's policies, practices and benefits, and employees' satisfaction. The practices they included are those that enhance employees' enjoyment of active endeavors—their environmental and social involvement. They know that benefits like onsite gyms and fitness classes, reimbursements for ski passes and sports racing fees and support for community service during work hours make their employees happier, healthier and more productive. And the business case for investing in employee health in a recession is more important than ever.

Doing the "right thing" by not only investing in employees' health but also in the health of our environment reaps financial returns as well. Companies on Fortune's annual list of the 100 Best Companies to Work For in America have consistently returned 14 percent per year, compared to 6 percent per year for the overall market, according to Alex Edmans, a professor at The Wharton School, University of Pennsylvania, where he analyzed these 100 companies' returns over the period from 1998 to 2005.

A 2009 study conducted by A.T. Kearney came to similar conclusions. During the three-month period of September through November 2008, the performance differential tracked across the 99 firms on both the Dow Jones Sustainability Index and the Goldman Sachs SUSTAIN focus list of green companies was 10 percent and over six months it was 15 percent. "This performance differential translates to an average of $650 million in market capitalization per company," the report said.

GreenEnergyCo worked with business customers from all sectors to customize their sustainability plans. The key to success in every instance was CEO endorsement—as is the case with success in any new organizational initiative, including implementing the Scream to Dream Approach.

You can also succeed as a leader and a company without viewing the world as one in which you have to ruthlessly compete for scarce resources. When we changed our perception to one in which you can cooperate and succeed with greater ease, we saw that there's abundance. There are plenty of customers for all excellent companies. So no, you don't have to follow the old leadership model that promotes pain, struggle and fear. When you create a work environment of connectivity, collaboration, co-creation and community, you will have success with far less effort. You can find and follow your scream to create a new leadership vision that transforms your organization for the better—better for you, your employees, your bottom line and our world.

WHAT WOULD YOU LOVE TO CREATE?

Now is the best time to seek new opportunities, in this economy, in these times. Maybe you have less to lose right now. Maybe your fear of change and of doing something different has lessened, too. Did you know that Chevron, Disney and many other strong businesses emerged during a recession?

In my community, Ahwatukee, Arizona, I recently visited a new healthy eatery, the Pomegranate Café. It was started by three generations of women who used their own seed money. They saw the opportunity for a great deal on a lease, had low startup costs and successfully followed their passions of healthy cooking. Over the last year, the Pomegranate Cafe has grown consistently and steadily. Success is attributed to having great food that appeals to anyone, not just vegetarians. Patrons also gain health awareness as a positive side effect. "Our success comes from the fact that we are family-owned and offer something unique to the area. It's heartfelt, and customers appreciate that," said the owner, Cassie Tolman, in an interview with the *Ahwatukee News* on October 20, 2010.

My daughter, Shelby, joined Boon, Inc. in June, 2010 as a graphic designer. This company exemplifies a young entrepreneurial leader's creativity in realizing her vision. Rebecca Finell founded Boon, Inc. in 2004. She was a mother with two children and a junior in ASU's Industrial Design program when she submitted a water-toy design in a competition. Inspired after seeing drained bath tubs strewn with wet toys, Finell's imagination kicked into gear. Rebecca and her team first created the wall-mounted Frog Pod Bath Toy Scoop and built-in storage shelf. The drainable scoop easily gathers dripping toys and they dry without scum and mildew.

The genesis of the company was serendipitous. Rebecca met Ryan Fernandez, who became the company's CEO and co-founder, at their children's nursery. Ryan invited them to a birthday party. In a December 3, 2010 interview with the *Ahwatukee News*, Rebecca exclaimed, "I overheard him saying he'd just finished his MBA and was looking for a product to take to market. I knew it was meant to be." In fewer than six years their products are being carried by Target and Babies "R" Us. They are found in more than sixty countries. The duo have designed a work environment with open, collaborative-type work spaces. They are building a day care center for all their employees' children. They provide health care coverage at no cost to the employees and they maintain a fun yet challenging work environment.

INSPIRE OR MOTIVATE

To be an effective leader, you need to have certain leadership values at your core. Answering the following questions can help you discover if and how much you have of these attributes.

"Why am I here?"

Many leaders cannot answer this question. Are you here because you want to be? Because you are leading toward a goal and mission in you believe? Why is the answer important? If you desire to optimize your energy and increase your bottom line, in other words, create optimal productivity at minimal cost, it's essential to understand what makes you tick—not only for you, but also for each of your employees. What do you choose to contribute to this world—fear or love? Would you like to leave the world better than you found it? What will be your legacy as a leader?

"How do I influence?"

Is it by showing that you genuinely care? People reject leaders whose attitude is to put themselves above everything else. When they see a leader who has the honesty and courage to take on tough political issues regardless of personal, political or career risk, they see a true leader. These qualities show you care about your employees as individuals and will stand behind them.

I have observed that good leaders lead followers while great leaders lead leaders. Good leaders add value through growth and expansion. Great leaders multiply value and drive explosive growth and exponential expansion. Taking time to invest in yourself and in building the next generation of leaders will allow you to clearly define and leave your legacy.

How do you lead? Do you drive the machine, knowing you can always replace people? Or do you foster others' success, which in turn drives business?

Do you inspire or motivate? What is the difference?

You can lead by motivating—but is this optimal? To motivate is to induce, incite, impel. Motivation is about "I get you to do what's good for me." Motivation is fear based. For example, if you don't make your budget, you will be fired (because if you don't make your budget, I cannot make mine). There may be times when motivation can be a "kick in the pants," but if there's a way to inspire the same result, inspiration works better.

Inspiration comes from a selfless place that is less about you and your ego, and more about the other person, the employee. It's about love—and if love is too squishy a word for you, try "genuine caring." The Merriam-Webster online dictionary defines *inspire* as "...to guide by divine or supernatural inspiration; to exert an...enlivening, or exalting influence on." The Latin root of the word "inspire", *spir,* is the breath, the soul, the spirit, the vigor which animates life (www.wordempire.blogspot.com). The most powerful source of energy to the body is your breath. You can live without food for many days, water for a few days, but only about three to four minutes without breath. Breathing is as important to your life and leadership as electricity is to your computer.

Inspire or motivate? Look at the difference as how you approach maintaining a healthy weight. You are motivated to exercise because you want to indulge at dinner and are afraid that if you don't, you'll gain weight. Versus you are inspired to exercise because it makes you feel better and you like how your clothes fit. It's the difference between doing something because you are afraid of the consequences if you don't do it, and doing something because it makes you feel good—with the latter, you are acting in a way that loves and honors yourself.

Great leaders who are familiar to all of us, such as John F. Kennedy, Margaret Thatcher, Martin Luther King and Nelson Mandela inspire their followers. Every great dad and mom who seeks to instill good values and moral character in their children inspires them. Every great teacher or mentor who wants his or her students to excel inspires them... then gets out of the way!

What is so remarkable about leaders like Nelson Mandela is that they're in touch with what they need to do and how to use their talents to fulfill their calling. If the movie, *Invictus*, is accurate, Mandela knew that inspiring the nation by winning the 1995 World Cup with a mainly white rugby team could do more to bridge whites and blacks than forced approaches.

Martin Luther King acted *as if there were* equality for blacks, even though blacks were being beaten by police officers in the streets while peacefully protesting.

Inspirational leaders know what they stand for. When you as a leader understand yourself, you will inspire yourself and others to realize great dreams. You will have found your scream.

How do you influence? Do you show you genuinely care? Are you lifting the hearts of those around you? Or are you a motivator, leading through threats of termination, poor performance evaluations and other punishments akin to a system to train animals, like breaking a horse? Even horse training is going through a revolution—horse whispering (showing that you genuinely care) is starting to replace "breaking" them. Can you coach without breaking an employee's spirit? Are you guiding the brilliance in your employees and helping them grow and find success? Do you lead by example?

Inspirational leadership is something you live and practice, not something you tell others to do. "Walk the talk" as we used to say at work. "An example is not the main thing in influencing others—it is the only thing," said Albert Schweitzer.

How does your mission statement read? Your company is the biggest, best, fastest, strongest, most profitable, best customer care-oriented... it goes on. Are these the words of an inspirational mission? Compare them to what Timberland, the outdoor footwear and apparel company, states as its cause: to equip people to make their difference in the world. Timberland's CEO wants to change the world by getting people into boots and outdoor gear that help them improve upon what they do. It's not to make the strongest, most profitable boots in the world. When your mission is a meaningful cause, people—your employees—want to be part of it. It's how you integrate the human spirit with the mechanics of making money in a capitalist system.

How do you move from motivation to inspiration—from head to heart? I believe true power comes from joining the desires of the heart with the wisdom of the mind. Do you recall a time when you trusted your gut feeling? The gut refers to your heart, your feelings, your intuition—not your mind.

It's now time to learn how to find your scream. The first principle you'll learn is how to find your answers within.

EXERCISES
1. What would you like your legacy to be?
2. List some actions that inspire. List some that motivate. Review the differences in how you feel about them.
3. Write a description of the type of work environment that inspires you to do your best. Describe what inspires you about this environment.

THREE

YOUR ANSWERS ARE WITHIN

The intuitive mind is a sacred gift and the rational mind is a faithful servant. We have created a society that honors the servant and has forgotten the gift.
— Albert Einstein

You have a more powerful search engine than Google or Yahoo to find the answers to your biggest questions in life—who you are and what you deeply value. You'll find the answers are not all in your mind or outside yourself, but within, in your personal answer room.

If you had a traditional American upbringing, you did not learn how to find your answers within when you were in school. Intuition 101 was not offered as a class. Intuition is defined by Merriam-Webster.com as an immediate apprehension or cognition. This direct knowledge or cognition is attained without evident rational thought and inference. (I refer not as a psychologist, but as a layperson, throughout this book, to your non-rational mind as synonymous with your gut, your heart (love), your intuition, your unconscious or subconscious mind; and to your conscious mind as an ego-based, logical and reasoning state.)

Einstein attributes his genius to intuition. In other words, to using more parts of his brain than those simply available for rational thinking. He looked at things through different eyes to find the hidden solutions to problems. A quote from Einstein condenses all the potential that he believed every individual shares and why some people never achieve their potential.

> "A human being is part of a whole, called by us the Universe, a part limited in time and space. He experiences himself, his thoughts and feelings, as something separated from the rest a kind of optical delusion of his consciousness. This delusion is a kind of prison for us, restricting us to our personal desires

and to affection for a few persons nearest us. Our task must be to free ourselves from this prison by widening our circles of compassion to embrace all living creatures and the whole of nature in its beauty."

Your rational mind limits what you understand. As I will discuss in Chapter 7, your ego guides your mind and separates you from a greater understanding. You simply cannot process the amount of information available to you, as it bombards you moment by moment in tweets, texts, voice mails or emails. You have to check in with your intuition for new insights. Learn to listen to your gut, your heart, to stay centered to what you know to be true. When you learn to listen within, you will unwaveringly know what you value and who you are at your core. You will take actions in alignment with that knowing.

HEAD VERSUS HEART

Intuition is actually the seed of inspiration. You may think of yourself as a highly analytical left-brained person. Despite that, you have a functioning right brain—because there are no intuition-deficit disorders, meaning we all have perfect intuition; we just typically don't learn how to tap into it in Western society. By integrating the right side of the brain—the feminine aspect of receptivity, the experience of insight—with the analytical left, you can flood your life with richness.

Dr. Joe Dispenza, neuroscientist and chiropractor, studies the brain process. He explains in his book, *Evolve Your Brain*, that the conscious brain's language is thought, while your subconscious, that is, your intuition, is your body's language and is expressed in feelings, beliefs, and clues. According to Dr. Dispenza, "We're all swimming in a sea of symbols; it just takes learning to recognize them."

Your conscious mind uses five to ten percent of your brain power while your subconscious, your intuition, accesses the other 90 to 95 percent, according to Dr. Dispenza. In other words, full consciousness is not your permanent mode. About 90 percent of your actions and reactions are controlled by your subconscious memory. Your conscious mind processes information at 40 bits per second while your subconscious—your gut feeling—is 500,000 times faster. Your heart's electromagnetic field emits 2.5 watts of energy with every heartbeat.

Compared to the electromagnetic field produced by the brain, the electrical component of the heart's field is about 60 times greater in amplitude, and permeates every cell in the body. The magnetic component is approximately 5000 times stronger than the brain's magnetic field. Compelling evidence based on a rigorous experimental design showed that both the heart and brain receive and respond to information about a future event before the event actually happens. New data suggest that the heart's field is directly involved in intuitive perception, and may receive this information before the brain, according to the Institute of HeartMath®.

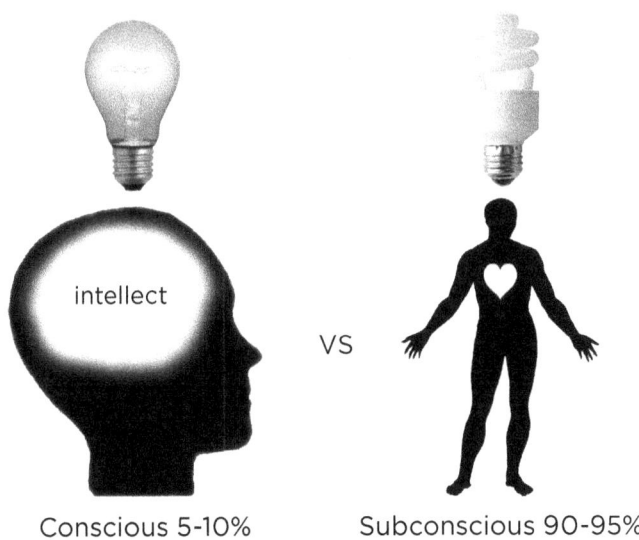

David R. Hawkins M.D., Ph.D., after years of study and millions of calibrations, also concludes that there's a quantifiable difference between using reason (head) versus love (heart) in the way you think and act. He writes, in *Power vs. Force*, that there's a defined range of values "accurately corresponding to well-recognized sets of attitudes and emotions, localized by specific attractor energy fields, much as electromagnetic fields gather iron fillings."

According to Dr. Hawkins, Energy Level 400 is associated with Reason. This is the level of science, medicine and of understanding and information. Reason, however, does not of itself provide a guide to truth. Energy Level 500 is Love, which he characterizes as a state of being that is forgiving, nurturing and a supportive way of relating to the world. It doesn't proceed from the mind; it emanates from the heart. "Reason deals only with particulars, whereas Love deals with entireties. This ability, often ascribed to intuition, is the capacity for instantaneous understanding without resorting to sequential symbol processing." Love focuses on the goodness of life and dissolves negativity by re-contextualizing it, rather than by attacking it.

If you access information predominantly from your analytic left brain, it's like relying on that old Edison incandescent light bulb to live and do your work. Your subconscious mind, your intuition, is the doorway to infinite intelligence!

So why not access all of the information you can from your intuition, your non-rational mind?

PERSONAL AND PROFESSIONAL INTUITION

In the spring of 2002, a small team at my company began working with an intuitive expert, Laura Alden Kamm. I met Laura on January 22, 2002 in Scottsdale, Arizona. Five minutes after I finished reading her book, *Intuitive Wellness*, I was so moved that I called her for an appointment.

Laura is a professional medical intuitive who reads personal and organizational energy. I did not understand exactly how this worked, but was fascinated. I did not have any serious health issues other than recurring indigestion. I was curious about where my energy and my company's energy might be blocked. My objective was simply to be "all that I can be." I was intrigued about what she might find.

Laura had natural intuitive gifts as a child, and after a near-death experience, she gained enhanced abilities. Laura works like an MRI in the way she can read congested or flowing energy at a cellular level. I approached the session with an open mind, but it was also accompanied by my healthy dose of analytical skepticism. Laura taped the session. I listened to it for the first time more than nine years later while writing this book. I was awestruck by her intuitive acumen. I'm even more amazed now that I've had the opportunity to see how the future unfolded to corroborate the accuracy of her readings.

In the initial session, I didn't tell Laura anything except my name. I withheld any more information because I wanted to see if she was the real thing. I had never been to a psychic or anything else like it. But Laura's not a psychic. She's a medical intuitive, which is different. Laura explains in an email dated November 30, 2010:

> "Psychic ability is a subset of intuition. A person with a highly developed skill of intuition has harnessed their psychic abilities; however, someone who uses primarily psychic abilities has not necessarily honed their intuitive skill. There is a hierarchy of skill sets involved in intuition; one's psychic ability is on the third of five rungs of Intuitive Perception and Intelligence. Someone who uses the term medical intuitive is someone who should demonstrate highly skilled and gifted abilities to intuitively discern the structures of the human body—from gross to microscopic.
>
> In the paradigm of Applied Medical Intuition I developed over the past twenty years, the medical intuitive intuitively scans the body's structures through one or more of their intuitive learning preferences—hearing, seeing, feeling, and knowing. They can discern details of what is occurring—physically, emotionally, spiritually and energetically—in a person's body and in the electromagnetic field around the body and all physical structures. Psychic abilities can roughly assess a region

of the body in which there is an issue and typically pick up on emotions occurring there. However, they are not able to discern microscopic components and tangential details. Psychic ability *reads* broad brush strokes of the intelligences of the body, but not the deeper individual causes, structures, or intelligences. Psychic ability does not allow for the mental intuitive movement, gathering correlations and referred data, from surface to deeper structures. That ability involves other subsets of intuitive abilities."

Laura's overall observation in my first session was that I had great balance in my energy. She scanned my entire body and all that she noted was that my right ovary was cranky due to stress. She perceived that I experienced menstrual cramps, and that my idea of a fix was for my ovary to be surgically removed as a convenience to eliminate the pain. Laura did not see this as necessary at that time as long as I began to nurture myself and committed to have more fun. She did not see a nervous system imbalance.

To put Laura's diagnosis in context, my family general physician knew that I had severe cramps and had prescribed an ultrasound to see if I had fibroids. The results found only a few small ones. My doctor advised me to take ibuprofen. My only other health issue at the time was allergies, for which I was taking Sudafed®. I wanted to quit taking decongestants and all medicines. The same physician recommended a prescription allergy medicine. I asked about a natural alternative. Her response was, "Do you want to get better or not?"

The allergy prescription only covered up the symptoms temporarily. It didn't get to the cause of the sinus issue. But eventually, by following Laura's guidance and following up with her recommendation that I visit Dr. Gladys McGarey, I ceased all medications successfully.

Laura had no background information on me, yet saw that I was a leader of a hundred or so people, but not thousands. She saw people jumping off transmission lines! (Yes, she was correct about my working for an energy company!) At that time, Laura told me to map my personal process of self-discovery and leadership to write a book to help others. As a leader, she understood that I took care of the human organism within the corporate organism. To be the best leader, I needed to observe when my ego-based mind took me off my purpose. I was advised to keep a journal and to note when I listened better to others. This process would also open my heart. I hadn't thought of writing this book at that time. I had journaled occasionally, and became more determined to do so after our session.

She taught me to create greater calm with an exercise called Run the Rainbow. It entails breathing in each of the colors of the rainbow—red, orange, yellow, green, blue, indigo and violet—with seven breaths. I explain how to perform this exercise at the end of this chapter. Laura advised that practicing this exercise would help me find my answers within.

After working with her a few more times, I realized that organizations could access the collective intuitive information from their employees to solve business problems just as individuals can.

So we selected a small willing group of computer, engineering and quantitative types to work with Laura to determine how our customers could use energy smarter. The project involved massive, mind-blowing amounts of electric meter-read data. That is why we did not want to stay in the left brain for this! We wanted to look at patterns and see information in a more intuitive way to discover new answers.

Every five seconds of every hour in every day, the interval demand type of meters that we used would measure the electricity consumed by our customers. That included the energy usage of all 33 USC and CSU university campus buildings, Albertsons and Whole Foods grocery stores, Boeing, Cisco Systems, department stores, fast food restaurants and more.

If you take the metered data from franchised fast food restaurants like McDonald's restaurants during Phoenix's hot summer months, you will have millions of points of electric usage. Since franchised fast food restaurants have the same floor plan, ovens, cooking equipment, refrigerators, freezers, lighting, etc., when you graphically overlay the hours of a day with each location's hourly usage, you might expect consumption to be the same. Not so. The considerable differences in usage were determined to be behavioral and amounted to a ten percent difference in annual energy bills!

There are not many significant operating costs that businesses can often cut by ten percent, so this presented a meaningful opportunity for savings in the franchise locations that were using more electricity.

To solve this problem and many more sophisticated ones, at GreenEnergyCo we developed a room conducive to tapping into our intuition, our subconscious, that we called the Cove. The Cove was designed with five-by-four-foot-sized touch computer screens (SMART Boards™) onto which we uploaded the data. The technology allowed us to place data in layers creating a three dimensional space for a more intuitive analysis.

With training, the team members developed the ability to get into a subconscious state through simple meditation. They then got "out of their heads" and looked at the data from a different and deeper level for answers to appear. Our team members learned to see patterns in complex data and how to get past "analysis paralysis." Interesting patterns emerged that only could be explained by human behavior. In one location, we surmised that an employee would come in at 5 a.m. and turn on everything at once. At other locations, turning on equipment was staggered as daily needs dictated. The latter practice saved tens of thousands of dollars in electric bills over the course of a year.

We also used the meditation process for more conceptual issues, such as when California was changing its market rules for how electricity could be bought, scheduled and moved over its transmission lines. As a result, the electricity had to be priced differently. Instead of the whole state having one delivery charge, it would be subdivided into smaller delivery areas based on local variations in energy costs. It was akin to the U.S. Post Office charging a different postage-stamp rate in every zip code. As you can imagine, if you were paying 44 cents to mail your product, and suddenly you had to pay 88 cents or 22 cents, your profitability would be impacted greatly. Of course, you would want to analyze the proposed changes. We used this subconscious, intuitive process to better understand the magnitude of the risks that the California market structure could have on our business.

HOW TO PUT INTUITION TO WORK FOR YOUR COMPANY

We used other simple tools to strategize business opportunities that were more intuitive than analytical.

Let's say you want to assess which customers are in your "sweet spot." As a startup, we had to grow revenue and net income quickly. Determining where we had the most success and doing more of what made us the most money with the least cost was critical. We could readily get bogged down in analysis and miss the forest for the trees given our heavily weighted engineering work force. We had to learn to step back and see in a new way.

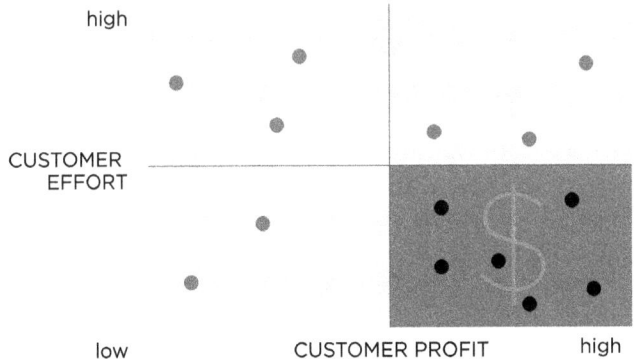

You might be experiencing the effects of the recession and need to make more money, too. Consider using a tool like the chart you see on this page. Let's say you are interested in determining your returns on the efforts you are spending on customers—which ones deliver the most net profits for you. You can combine quantitative and qualitative information and look for patterns or trends in the "picture." The vertical axis in this example represents the amount of effort you "feel" it takes to serve the customer. If you have data on cost-to-serve, you can use that, but the idea here's to allow intuitive information to flow. In the lower left portion you plot those customers who take lower amounts of effort or cost to serve. Place those who require more resources in the upper left section. Use a relative scale of most, more, less, least effort.

Next you factor in how much profit (gross or net profit depends on what you hope to discover from the inquiry) you derive from each customer. So, on the horizontal axis across the bottom of the chart, you would place a less profitable customer in the left side of the chart. You would place a data point for a customer who is less profitable and low effort in the lower left corner. If the customer is low effort and you secure high profits from serving him, you would depict that customer by placing a point in the far right lower corner. This is your sweet spot. These are the customers you want to continue to cultivate. In these times especially, you want to focus your resources on doing more of what you are already doing well.

The exercise revealed far more than identifying the type of customers who were the most profitable, for instance, "What shouldn't you do?"—expend effort on customers who are high effort, low return (top left corner). Sometimes there were marketing reasons for serving such low-return customers, but the reasons needed to be clearly understood.

Using this simple tool allows you and your leaders to step back and look at the selected problem more qualitatively, without getting mired in overly-detailed data and analysis. Certainly there's a place for analysis and we benefit from it, but the point here is to gather even more answers from less analytical methods.

As another example, consider what patterns or trends a retailer might observe. The retailer's complaint may be that profits are too low. What could be causing that? You might use the chart to examine your markdown policy. You could plot whether the particular sales item had a high or low markdown compared to the net profit you made from the sale of the reduced price item. You may gain surprising insights about which items and sales

discounts do or don't add to your bottom line and why.
This tool helps you focus on doing more of what works. Remember, work smarter, not harder, by using your intuitive knowing in tandem with your analytical mind to find your answers. Be your own Einstein.

INDIGENOUS INTUITIVE WISDOM

While I always had an intuitive "knowing," I initially questioned it as a new leader. Trained as a behavioral economist, energy attorney and corporate president, and having come from a regulated environment, I initially led from analytics, from the head. I changed that approach over the years as I saw the outstanding results I achieved from trusting my gut. And it led me to explore the concept of intuitive powers more deeply.

Let's dive even deeper into non-rational forms of useful information, intuition, for short-hand. Do you believe in something mystical? Do you believe that things can exist, even if you can't see, smell, touch, taste or hear them?

Have you seen the movie *Avatar*? If you haven't, I will give the background of how the Na'vi, the ten-plus-feet-tall, wise, indigenous blue people of the planet Pandora, access all of the information available to them. They interconnect with the wisdom of Nature. Each Na'vi has a long braid with something that looks like pistils in a flower, centered at the end. They place the end of their braid on a plant or creature and the answers from all of Nature, from the past and into the future, upload to the Na'vi. There's some kind of electrochemical communication between the roots of the trees—like the synapses between neurons. Each tree has 10^4 connections to the trees around it, and there are 10^{12} trees on Pandora. That's more connections than the human brain. In the movie, this is portrayed as a network—a global network. And the Na'vi can access it—they can upload and download data—memories—from any plant or creature anywhere on Pandora.

While the Na'vi are fictional characters, their views are not too far off from those I experienced with indigenous people in South Africa and Peru. These people accessed information from our ancestors and through divinations. Today's indigenous people are the descendants—spread across the world from the Arctic to the South Pacific—of the original people who inhabited a country or a geographical region at the time when people from different cultures or ethnic origins arrived. Although the new arrivals later become dominant through conquest, occupation, settlement or other means, in many cases the indigenous people have retained much of their distinct traditions and social, cultural, economic and political characteristics.

This quote by Robert Ingersoll captures some of my observations: "In nature there are neither rewards nor punishments; there are consequences." In ancient cultures, nothing was intrinsically good or evil; it was simply a matter of how one stood in relation to it. Our ancestors were aware that their senses were made for interacting with Nature much like the Na'vi in Avatar, and today's South African Zulus and Peruvian Q'eros communicate with trees and all of Nature. According to our Peruvian translator, Alonso Mendez, Mayans knew of the black hole at the center of the Milky Way Galaxy, yet from a modern astronomical perspective this is only a recent discovery. I learned from the current day indigenous people that they still view Nature as a necessity of life and I learned that organized religions sought to draw people away from their sacred connection with Nature. As I describe in later chapters, our separation from Nature as a people has contributed to the imbalances within us.

It's also intriguing how the indigenous people who I have observed access information using intuitive wisdom that has similarities from tribe to tribe. One of my most confirming interactions occurred when I visited the indigenous Zulu-Sangoma healers in South Africa. While I didn't experience a download through a braid, I did learn how to find the perfect balance between power and peace, and head and heart. I learned how to better access that 90 percent of subconscious (intuitive) information I had not been tapping into as much as I had the ten percent in my rational mind.

LEARNING FROM ZULU SANGOMA HEALERS

I highly recommend that if you are experiencing a major transition in life, the best medicine is to disconnect from your immediate surroundings and open your heart and thoughts to new opportunities. That is exactly what I did on October 1, 2007. This was forty-eight hours after we commenced the shutdown of the commodity business line. I numbly packed up the boxes in GreenEnergyCo's office with my career documents and mementos from the last ten years. I had worked for the sister utility company for fifteen years prior to that—a total of twenty-five years in that particular corporate family—more than half of my life.

I stashed the boxes in my garage and turned my attention to packing and repacking the few items I would have to fit into one suitcase for an entire month in South Africa. I next found myself sitting on a twenty-four-hour flight from Phoenix to Johannesburg. I arrived at the airport knowing only one of the fourteen people on our month-long journey—my college girlfriend, Becca, who was a critical care nurse in Seattle, Washington. She, and other nurses and medical professionals she knew, were going to live and study with the Zulu Sangoma traditional healers. They had discovered that by combining Western-style medicine with healing touch, their patients were recovering more quickly. Their goal was to learn more.

I originally spoke with Becca in early July about her upcoming adventure. I already knew about the parent company's decision to change strategic direction and shut down GreenEnergyCo's major commodity business line. Despite our success, we had become a "mis-fit" because our business was not related to the core utility business, as I explain in chapter 5. I was working discreetly with the parent company's executive management on a wind-down plan. I couldn't imagine a better way to transition from my twenty-eight-year business career to what the future would hold than to leave the past behind.

"I will join you!" I told Becca. She couldn't understand how, given the intensity of leading the GreenEnergyCo, and on such short notice. I told her I could make it happen. To give you some sense of how keenly intuitive the group's leader was, she had told Becca that she knew one more person would accompany their group, even though the departure date was drawing close.

I recall the experience with crystal clarity as I noted in my journal, which accompanied me on my trip:

> Once we arrive in South Africa, we fill two vans outside the airport. We look at each other and wonder what the other is thinking. On the two-hour drive to the Ecabazani Zulu Cultural Preserve through the grasslands with their signature canopy trees, we pass through a game preserve. I ask our leader, a nurse and intuitive named Nancy Rebecca, if we'll see wild animals. "Only if you hold your energy in and keep that intent in your heart," Nancy advises. Sure enough, within minutes, outside the left window about ten yards away, I see three fifteen-foot-tall giraffes lumbering along gracefully like three wise men.
>
> "Look!" I exclaim to the stranger next to me. I have never seen a black rhinoceros, and there one is outside the front of the van with a baby that appears to weigh about five hundred pounds. Next we come upon a herd of the most exquisite animal, the kudu. Brown and bigger than an American elk, kudu have twisted horns that are three feet long, and white markings under their eyes and across their nose, like painted warriors.
>
> "This isn't Kansas anymore!" I tell myself.
>
> We park on a dirt road, high above a big lake surrounded by dirt huts. At Ecabazani, the sign in the dirt parking area says, "Hoot Upon Arrival." So our driver honks, and CJ and David, who founded the preserve, climb many rock steps to greet us. There are no electric utility poles to be seen, nor would there be for most of our trip.
>
> The Zulus have a self-sustained environment at this cultural preserve. The chickens eat the weeds out of the organic garden. The chicken manure and all other garbage/compost are put in a big hole to capture the methane, which is used to

run a small cook stove. Lanterns light our way.

A Zulu man runs up to me with an innocent smile and says, "Makhosi (pronounced "Micose"). It means "uplifted or raised spirit" in Zulu. It is directly connected to honoring the presence of our ancestors and is used in a heartfelt greeting. I respond with a bow from my heart to your heart, "Makhosi." The young man grabs my bag, throws it on top of his head and hikes it down a steep stone path. At the bottom, outside a thatched hut, he sets down my bag. I push open the wood door, flop down on the cot and light the oil lamp. I see cattle penned right outside my hut's front door. I lay there in amazement at how different my world has become in just three days, as I hear the cows mooing and pooing several feet away. My headlamp comes in handy for any late-night visits to the outhouse.

Later that evening, I begin my great adventure by participating in a traditional dance in a sacred ceremony, after eating a dinner of goat cooked on a wood fire. I no longer focus my thoughts on the work-filled world I left behind. Such a vastly different environment must certainly be accelerating my new vision. I could feel the positive energy of these indigenous people and their connectedness to the Earth. Check out the picture in the hut—you can see the energy orbs, captured by digital photography. Hot and sweaty from dancing into the night, I return to my cot and the mooing of the cows.

A few days later we would travel to Karkloof, South Africa, where the traditional Zulu Sangoma healers will "throw the bones" and intuitively access information from our ancestors.

Sarah and Muvo, who are both acknowledged Sangoma healers, will demonstrate their natural and honed gifts. They studied more than two years to develop their intuitive skills. To be inducted as healers in their culture, one of the tests they had to pass was to find goats and cows that were hidden miles away. The book I was advised to read prior to our trip, by Nicky Arden, *African Spirits Speak: A White Woman's Journey into the Healing Tradition of the Sangoma*, describes this practice. So I was somewhat prepared.

I approach the throwing of the bones experience with great skepticism. The next day, in Karkloof, I awake anxiously—not with the kind of anxiety I used to experience driving seventeen miles in rush hour traffic to my office on the twelfth floor of a downtown high-rise, but with excited anticipation. I wear a shawl over my shoulders and a long one around my waist out of "respect for the ancestors." I sit uncomfortably with legs crossed on the dirt floor across from Muvo, a twenty-six-year-old South African man with a traditional beaded headdress. I place my coins, as I was advised to do in advance, on the floor as an offering.

Muvo bows, says "Makhosi" and asks only my mother's maiden name and my father's surname. From a special cloth, he throws a collection of bones, some with red or white beads wrapped around them, and some shells. A large, long bone rolls toward me and lands on top of a larger clamshell. It unmistakably looks like a large angel! Muvo, wearing the traditional beaded headdress, lowers his head and goes into a trance. He chuckles as if in conversation with someone. After a few minutes of awkward silence, he looks up at me, and in broken English tells me what my ancestors have to say.

My husband's grandfather had wanted his grandson, Jeff, and me to come together so I could "help Jeff find his heart." This was as good an explanation as any, frankly, for our serendipitous meeting at age twenty-six on the deck of the Flagstaff Arizona Snowbowl ski lodge. Maybe this explained how two logical, sensible attorneys got engaged in twenty-one days and were married five months later!

Muvo explains that my husband is a very clever man but lets "his good energy be swapped with those of the bad people." This actually makes sense to me. Jeff has been a career major-felony prosecutor and spends many days dealing with murderers, child molesters, thieves and their victims. (Nonetheless, I'm still reserving judgment about the legitimacy of all Muvo's intuitive powers.) Part of my purpose, Muvo says, is to protect Jeff from this energy drain each day. I should envision a mirror in front of him as he leaves home to deflect the bad energy. (Much is said in metaphor among indigenous people.)

Muvo could see that I was in the midst of change. Things will shift with Jeff when I make my change, he says. Not because I cause Jeff to change, but because I will no longer respond in the same way. This will create a new set of choices for how Jeff can respond.

Muvo queries the bones further and shows me four positioned close together. He describes what a close family I have by looking at the order of these bones. He tells me about my two children and their paths and not to worry about them. The large clamshell that lies atop a bone represents Michael, the archangel, who is looking over me. (Subsequent readings by other intuitives confirmed this same detail.)

He reveals many more personal details about the need to balance my red (male/anger) energy and white (female) energy. Having just left GreenEnergyCo, I am sure my red energy is flaming.

Muvo states that when I was very young, my parents firmly taught me what they thought was good and bad, right and wrong. My hypercritical father meant well. He thought he would protect me from the cruel world by toughening me up so I could withstand the criticisms. "Do not judge," Muvo says! Let being right go.

Muvo tells me that I "keep looking for answers in my mind. I keep questioning my knowing—my intuition." I must trust my intuition and not try to change the outcome when I "know" of things that are likely to happen. He tells me not to be frustrated when I cannot prevent things from happening. As I receive information, I am to convey it to the recipient without judging it or trying to use it to change an outcome that I see.

Muvo compassionately says to me, "You have faced many hard things in life and no longer have to defend yourself."

Muvo tells me to listen to the arches of my feet—when they ache, my body is talking to me and telling me I am out of balance. My stomach energy is way too high, he says. I need to take muti for three days to rid me of what ails me. It will help me regain balance in my red and white energy. This muti is an indigenous remedy made from the bark of native plants. The prescription was to vigorously stir the muti in a bucket of water with a hand-selected stick and drink it.

What I learned about Sangoma traditional medicine is that whatever you need to rid yourself of, vomiting is the preferred way to expel it! I was more reluctant to ingest this muti than to go to the reading of the bones. But what did I have to lose (except fluid)? For the next three days, I drank excessive quantities of water with bark and other floating objects in it. Goal achieved—because once ingested, my body wanted to rid itself of it! Metaphorically, I hurled out other things with it, too. That was also the goal. Purge the old and make room for the new. Muvo had encouraged me to clearly visualize what I wanted to refill the space with! I decided to refill it with balanced energy, and renewed trust in my intuition. I would continue to make life choices that honored "my scream."

At the end of the reading of the bones, Muvo tells me to write down all of the things for which I want to forgive myself or others. Write the patterns I want to change or release. Ask your ancestors for help and they will answer. Tomorrow, when I am in the river during the cleansing, I must shout and scream and let out the angry red energy. He bows his head and says, "Makhosi."

That next morning (after taking my muti remedy), with an elevated heartbeat, we hike for about thirty minutes on the tree-lined trail to the Kusane River. It's about seventy-eight degrees Fahrenheit outside, so I opt for sleeveless. I carry my list of patterns that I want to change, a coin and a blanket. I knew the water was far colder than the outside air.

As we approach, I hear screams. Screams of release? Of the water being shockingly cold? As unsettling as it is, I nervously take my turn. I wade into the river and bow my head in preparation for the cleansing. My heart beats in rhythm with the beat of the drum being pounded on the shore. I then feel the icy river water pouring over my head. (I guarantee you it was more shocking than a Gatorade cooler being dumped on a coach after a game!)

As I stand in the frigid water, my feet are unstable. The right feels solid but the left lighter. At first, to the beat of the drum, I feel joyful, and make low, *awww* sounds. Sarah sees a big release. I throw a coin far away, tear off each of the written phrases that I want to release from my list, and throw them in the water. They dump more icy water on me. My arm tingles and both little fingers go numb. Then the rain begins, adding to the buckets of water being poured. Unsure of how you call for your ancestors, I silently requested that my deceased father and Archangel Michael help me release the past. I feel a huge shift in energy. I can feel my hands releasing negative energy.

Sarah encourages me to really connect with the ancestors. She explains as soon as you make a request, your ancestors respond. Be conscious of what you are asking. "Today my intention is _____ and I would like you to help me." Continue to engage with your ancestors when they don't seem to respond. This practice may seem similar to prayer in many religious faiths; this is just the Zulu version. I scream with the surprise and the release of toxic energy as they continue to dump bucket after bucket of river water on me. This continues until my arms go limp and I have no energy left to scream.

It's effective. There's an expansive calm, a peacefulness. A river cleansing sure beats a hospital bed and drugs to cure what ails you!

During my visit there are many other lessons on how to best live "from my heart." I buy a Sans necklace from Zens Zenkozi Mbelu. The Sans were among the earliest indigenous people, so their tribe is called "the first people." Zens explains his work philosophy. He wakes up every day and gives thanks and asks, "Who will I make happy today?" As he goes to sleep, he gives thanks.

I learn the significance of what sounds like he is saying "honopouopo." I am told it means, "Heal the thing within myself to help others." I learn from the many wise indigenous people I meet to set my intent to transform and to take what is love and leave behind what is not.

I continue my adventure in South Africa by staying in rustic cabins in the National Park in Ukhahlamba's Drakensberg Mountains.

There, one of our medical professionals offers to give me an Acutonics® session. I have no idea what that is. She assures me it won't hurt, so I agree. She uses a tuning fork around my body. The areas where it does not vibrate soundly are out of balance, so she works on those areas to achieve balance. I think it works something like acupuncture without the needles. It felt good.

I decide to work on balance through the way I feel love, and that is by hiking in Nature. I also find that while walking, I often get downloads of intuitive information. The grass-covered mountains where I'm taking my walks inspired some of the scenes in Tolkien's Lord of the Rings, and I can see why. On a long, solitary hike several miles away from our cabins, I walk down the dirt path and turn the corner by a large rock outcropping. Suddenly, I come between members of a baboon family. On the right side of the path, the large male snarls his teeth and barks at me. I turn on my video camera and leave my family a final message in case he attacks. I'm undecided, should I walk slowly backwards while keeping my eye on him, or run? I hold my fear-energy in, and slowly, but confidently, turn around and walk away with the barking still ringing in my ears.

After several calming breaths, I remember what I hoped to see on this hike. (It wasn't baboons in the wild). I long to catch sight of the mystical eland creatures that few have ever seen. They reportedly look like a strange horned antelope. I hike out to the vista point, World's View, singing *The Sound of Music* to myself. I twirled a few times like Julie Andrews, too. I strain my eyes looking for the elands. Out of nowhere, it was as if a voice said, "Look up." There on the rim at the top of the mountain, I see them. Immediately, I click a photo and in that blink, they are gone. (Since learning to listen to my intuition, I have experienced innumerable synchronous events like this one.)

After a month in South Africa, feeling relaxed and clear about where I am heading, I completely lose my voice on the plane as we fly home. I have no voice for four days. Conferring with medical intuitive Laura Alden Kamm upon my return, she says it's akin to a hairball in my throat. The loss of speech is a metaphor for the angst of what is still unsaid—my embedded and still unreleased feeling of abandonment—of my Mother dying when I was young and of the parent company unwinding a portion of GreenEnergyCo. As that angst is working itself out, the energy I'm releasing blocks in my throat. The parts of me that have been

stifled are at last coming to the surface.
I began to see with greater clarity that my scream included writing about my journey to help others. I felt vulnerable. I had to overcome the feeling of vulnerability to complete this book. I realized that my purpose was to awaken other leaders to the power of their own intuition. I had the privilege of incubating the Scream to Dream principles. That privilege would be wasted if I didn't learn how to convey them to others.

CONNECTING AND BRIDGING CULTURES

I learned from Sarah and Muvo that within Zulu culture it's very important to honor the elders and their stories of the land, as keepers of the memory of its nature, reverence and sacred connection to the people. My journey to South Africa piqued my curiosity to continue my exploration of the connectedness of all people and of intuition. It wasn't long before another series of synchronous events led me to the 14,000-foot-high indigenous villages in Peru's Andean Mountains.

Upon my return from South Africa, I began speaking to community groups about my personal and leadership experiences. I joined the National Speaker's Association (NSA) to "up my game." I would be starting my part-time executive director energy job in January 2008, but I had time to initiate my commitment to writing the book.

In February, 2009, I happened to scurry into an NSA event in Tempe, Arizona, just minutes before the program began. I sat in the only remaining seat, in a room filled with 100 people. A tall, attractive woman about my age was sitting next to me. As she nodded during the talk, she appeared to be interested in the same topics that I was. At a break, we introduced ourselves. What a coincidence! Kimberly had worked at my former utility company in the marketing department. She had been on a personal journey of her own and was writing a book on how to prosper in these economic times. Kimberly was also debating whether to go to Peru in a few months. She contemplated joining a group led by a Prescott, Arizona, woman, Carla Woody, MA, CHT.

Carla founded Kenosis, LLC to instill values often forgotten in Western culture—the appreciation of our environment and all beings. Carla's belief is that by bringing all cultures together, we can create a renewed sense of honor, create a shift in consciousness for us all and heal our world.

Carla sponsors trips to promote the sharing and bridging of beliefs between indigenous cultures. The group that Kimberly was thinking of joining would live and study with the Peruvian indigenous people, the Q'eros.

The fee for those who joined the tour would also cover the cost of three others—two Navajos, a mother and young son who performed the traditional sun dancer rituals, and a Hopi woman, who otherwise could not afford to make the trip. The interpreter/guide who would accompany the group is a respected Mayan archeo-astronomer, Alonso Mendez.

I met Kimberly for lunch. She and I had a few other conversations about the trip. It felt right. I would join this newfound friend. I had only one intent for my adventure in Peru—to clear the space inside me for the new. I would leave past judgments behind. I was transitioning to a new place in life and must make room for my new "way of being." Again, I journaled the experience as follows.

On May, 25, 2009, Kimberly and I fly from Phoenix to Lima, Peru. We lay uncomfortably on the Lima airport chairs for six hours, then fly to Cusco, an almost 11,000-foot-high city. After landing in the Cusco airport, we need a cab driver. I sense that the ones in the airport who are yelling for us to join them are a scam. Kimberly and I carry our bags outside, and it becomes evident that no one speaks English. Using my limited high school Spanish, I speak to a pleasant young man. In Spanish, he said his name is Norel. He swiftly rattles off in Spanish something about taking us on a sightseeing trip on the way to catch the train to our destination, Machu Picchu.

The serendipitous selection of this angel of a cab driver, Norel, on May 26, 2009, becomes clear. Norel was studying to get his college degree. To fund his schooling he created a travel service. He picks up people at the airport and offers to conduct private tours through the Sacred Valley on the way to the popular tourist train stop in Ollantaytambo. The train leaves there and winds through the vertical mountains to Machu Picchu. He warns us that a labor strike is set for the next day. The strikers sometimes lay their bodies across the tracks and it's likely the train won't be running. We have to be back in time to join our group the next day, so we decide not to risk it. We will go on a whirlwind trip there and back in the next eight hours. That means we will need a cab ride back from Ollantaytambo to Cusco very late that same night. Norel agrees to stay the entire day and wait for us.

When we finally arrive at Machu Picchu, we have been traveling from the United States for about thirty-six hours. First a plane ride from Phoenix to Lima, then a flight to Cusco, a several-hour scenic cab ride, then a train ride through the mountains and finally a windy bus ride up the mountainside and to the top, to Machu Picchu. When the bus arrives, we have a total of two hours before Machu Picchu closes. The 15th-century pre-Incan site is far more amazing than I expect. I do my best to absorb all the energy of that sacred place in the 120 minutes before it closes. The magnificence of what people created 600 years ago far surpasses what I had seen in schoolbooks and in pictures on the Internet! These were an inspired people with knowledge of how to construct water and sewage systems, cultivate vertical mountainsides and read the heavens. It is breathtaking in more than one way!

Back at the train station we wait for six hours— the strike seems to have started early and is backing up 400 other grimy hikers. We return to Ollantaytambo at 11 p.m. It is pouring rain, and chaotic with all the latecomers trying to figure out how to get transportation. It is pitch black as we run up and down the unlit roads yelling, "Norel." Out of the darkness and rain we hear "Beeckie!" (Vicki). There is our angel, Norel, with all our bags. He has even found us a hotel room in Cusco through a friend. We reach it at 3 a.m.

The next morning, somewhat groggy still, we join the rest of our travel group and participate in a blessings ceremony high on the mountainside outside Cusco. We board a bus again and with fifteen other people ascend the vertical mountains. Dirty, ragged, unsupervised young children run freely up and down these steep mountains with big smiles on their faces. They give me flowers picked about two feet away from me, hoping I have candy from my pack to give them in return.

Our Mayan translator, Alonso, accompanies us. Alonso interprets the Spanish spoken by Don Americo Yabar. Don Americo is an internationally-renowned Peruvian guide who was initiated by the indigenous Q'ero as a young man. Designated as a living bridge between cultures, he has helped many Westerners open their hearts. He teaches that by listening to your heart you have more power over your life.

Considered the last of the Incas, the Q'eros call themselves the children of Inkari, the first Inca. The Q'eros live in isolation at 14,000 to 17,000 feet in the Andes, as they have for hundreds of years since the arrival of the conquistadors. The most untouched by Western culture of any indigenous people in the Americas, the Q'eros preserve their ancient traditions. From them, you can learn about *pachacuti*, i.e., stepping outside of time, and living in *ayni*, sacred reciprocity with all things. Their diet is corn, potatoes, guinea pig, alpaca—lots of carbohydrates. Yet these very small people are not overweight because they climb the steep mountainsides all day and generally eat only what they need.

Alonso, being of Mayan descent, explains the connections

of the traditions of many different indigenous peoples of the Americas, including non-Maya groups such as the Hopi, the Aztecs, and the Incas. Sacred sites such as Machu Picchu, that was a royal estate of the Inca empire, are built with stones that foretell a prophecy of great changes in the world in 2012. These include a new era where we bring balance and beauty back to the Earth as peoples. The Hopis have similar prophecies about the era we are entering as a planet Earth.

During the blessings ceremony, the *despacho*, Don Americo translates the Q'ero's language into Spanish. Then Alonso translates the Spanish into English. I am instructed through three languages to put the items I would like blessed on the woven rug. I place the outline of this book on it and a drawing of my family, because I have no pictures with me. During the ceremony the elders chant, sing and spit tobacco on the items to be blessed.

I quickly learn these indigenous people's beliefs. Their close connection with the *Pachamama*, Mother Earth, as it is called in their original Quechua language, and the dramatic mountain spirit, *Apu*, is clear.

We leave Cusco the next day to stay with the indigenous Q'eros. Don Americo travels with us to the vertical mountains of Salk'awasi, a very special place, at about 14,000 feet.

Salk'awasi is located in the tiny village of Mollomarqa, in the Andes. This is where the Q'eros train new teachers in their original, ancient ways of being.

"Salk'awasi" means house of undomesticated energy. The Q'eros symbolize it as a totem of the eagle, puma and condor. Salk'awasi refers to the right, or creative, side of the brain. This is where "intent lives," our undomesticated energy, *salk'a*, creativity.

Domesticated energy—ordinary reality—is where most of us place our attention. It refers to the left, or analytical, side of the brain. The Q'eros symbolize domesticated energy with the cow and the dog. Any construct of the mind or ego comes from the analytical side.

Don Americo explains that we must have both sides working in harmony to be in alignment.

Don Americo begins to lead our group in a Q'ero traditional meditation. As a very active person and one who meditates best while moving, I'm apprehensive. Fifteen of us stand shoulder to shoulder, feeling the connectivity and energy transmitted within and between us. The Navajo mother and son, the Moenkopi Hopi woman, two doctors, an architect, a midwife, Carla, Alonso, Kimberly, myself and all the others come from diverse personal and professional backgrounds and reside in places scattered throughout the western United States.

Don Americo instructs us to first take our right hand and scoop the energy from Mother Earth, the Pachamama. Take a deep breath and bring that energy into your heart and hold it there. Next take your left hand, and reach way up into the sky, and scoop the energy from the Cosmos while taking a deep breath. Have both hands full of the energy from Heaven and Earth meet at your heart. Do this three times. Everything is connected with Nature. You learn to open your heart and soul. Next, you work with the wind and the sun.

A funny moment breaks up the meditative spell. A surprising sound is emitted from behind one of us. Gas. (Not from me!) When head, heart and stomach are not aligned, digestion issues abound, Don Americo chuckles.

Then he sends us off to find a spot in Nature that calls to us. At first I have difficulty seeing, hearing or relating to this hour-long meditation assignment. But I find a large fallen tree on which I lay. It reminds me of being a kid. I loved building forts outdoors and would use a large log for a bed in my fort. From this vantage point, I look down from 14,000 feet, to far below at the grand river that looks like a trickle from up here. I gaze up at the branches of the huge cottonwood tree that is next to me. The leaves look like black cutouts against the darkening, clear blue sky. The sun had almost set.

In my meditation, I ask about creating this book. I close my eyes and breathe very deeply. Intuitively, what I hear is to find my answers within and the rest will come. I ask myself how to be rid of frustration, and the answer—an immediate knowing within—is to not push, be vulnerable, and let life come to me. An inner voice challenges me to find that perfect balance between power and peace.

After what seems like a long time, I open my eyes and I look up to the sky. By now, the sun has set. The sky is full of stars and I immediately feel that I can see those who watch over us. The tall tree beside me is shedding its old rough bark to reveal the smooth new skin underneath. Again, I have this knowing within that I need not be frustrated. I must be patient. First, I am to clear the critical space within myself. Second, I am to fill the void with a perpetual observation of all the joys surrounding me and with love for myself.

Don Americo calls us all back in the darkness at the end of the hour. He challenges us to live in full color. When you feel the texture of each moment, even the struggle is an experience of beauty. Live in the texture of the moment and embrace each person. Often those who frustrate you the most are a reflection of something you don't like in yourself. Speak your truth from the heart.

I understand as it applies to me personally that there's no space left for judgments. From now on I vow to take time before speaking to phrase my comments objectively—something I had not been taught in law school, certainly! (I learned how to cross-examine, though. I was never as good at direct testimony). I will ask and listen instead of telling. I understand that all the answers are available to me if I just learn to listen within and trust my intuition without second-guessing myself.

The next day we begin with a meditation session outdoors. Don Americo challenges us to be creative. Creativity is a link to the Divine. "Live in metaphor," he says. "It allows us to see and think in beauty. Electricity kills the night. Grammar kills the poetry." (Funny. I notice that when I slow down and listen, my writing becomes effortless.) "Don't complicate life," he says. "It's simple. Don't be too serious. Go to the wind, then the tree, then the water. The only serious thought," he adds, "is a dead person." He laughs and his eyes twinkle like those of a mischievous child. "When there's a cloud by your head, think of the wind and have it blow the cloud away. When you see your family, blow in their face and let them know you are blowing their worry away with the wind of love." (Now, how can it hurt for you to try this at home? Give advance warning before you blow in your loved ones' faces, however, and preferably try this after brushing your teeth.)

Don Americo continues to guide us. "Play a game and detach. If one angers you, leave, and then no one is home to be bothered. Laughter is like a whole yoga session," he says. He reiterates, "we must live in harmony with Nature." The Hopi woman with us tells us that her people always make an offer of gratitude (cornmeal) before eating. Her philosophy is to take only what you need from the Earth.

"*Deseo illuminado ahor?*" ("How many times a day are you illuminated?") Don Americo posits. "Live in mystery, *eres tu, eres todos*. Words can touch, sky can touch, moon can touch." He tells us to connect to love with battery cables, where you generate great energy, creative energy.

On the subject of balance, harmony and integration, he tells a story. "A master ate the sun and his body hurt. The older master opened him up and said, 'You have too much sun inside. Eat apples instead, so you don't directly consume the sun; the apple consumes the sun first.' Some eat the stars. You can partake of others' energy but not all of it, as it creates imbalance. Some mothers eat their kids' energy and vice versa. It's not good or bad; you just need to understand your diet.'" Don Americo impishly smiles.

At the next dawn we begin our bus ride over dirt roads that are narrower than the bus, up to the Q'ero indigenous village at almost 15,000 feet in the Andes. I learn the rule of the road: when two vehicles come head to head, the winner is the driver who stares down the other, causing him to back up until a spot in the road is found where the aggressor can pass. Usually this occurs when we're overlooking a vertical cliff.

When we all arrive, it's obvious that Don Americo is loved by the villagers because they run up and embrace him. The community is closely connected even though their small adobe houses are spread across the mountainside. The tradition when the Q'eros meet is to ask that they meet in harmony, and they invite, with great respect, Mother Earth, Pachamama, and the mighty mountain peaks, Apu, in their greeting.

After I smooth out my sleeping bag under the stars on the 15,000-foot slope, we attend an evening village celebration. The Q'eros value celebration and ritual. They celebrate weekly. The youth play traditional instruments and the ladies dance. Don tells us that we have lost connections in the West. The West's toxicity "relates to separation."

The celebration concludes with Don Miguelito, a ninety-five-year-old intuitive healer, performing divinations with coca leaves. Coca leaves are a native agricultural and ceremonial plant. The Q'ero use them in a non-narcotic form for divinations, and in tea to help your blood oxygenate so you can adjust to the altitude. They served it all the time.

Miguelito wears the traditional dress of hand-made woven shawls, all eighty pounds and four feet of him. He climbs the steep mountainside with ease and agility to greet us. Villagers light candles and place them on a table in front of him.

At the divination, he asks only my name. Don Americo translates. I'm chosen to be first for the reading because of the eager energy I exude. Don Miguelito readily senses it.

I kneel on the ground before him and lay a coin on the table (sound familiar?). He throws fresh coca leaves from a woven bowl onto the table. He says I have the strong, keen character of a cat and that I have a good soul.

As in Karkloof, South Africa, where the traditional Zulu Sangoma healers "threw the bones," my husband (who was not there) was again the subject of the reading. Two coca leaves lay side by side, aligned perfectly. Don Miguelito says that my husband and I will have many deep discussions upon my return. He says to keep the Southern Cross in the sky in my heart. He opines about a surgery that I am debating having (and since have had). He says that I am strong and that it will go well. He also foresees that I am in for very big changes ahead.

I listen to the thirteen other divinations that follow mine, noting how different and insightful they all are. He divines the essence of each person that I have come to know.

The rest of our stay is in the jungle of Manu. We sponsor the travel of four of the Q'ero leaders who never had the opportunity or gift to leave their village high in the Andes. We again brave the narrower-than-one-lane-road in our small bus for a day and wind around the hairpin curves and plunging mountainside to the headwaters of the Amazon River. Two men jump out of the bus and place two-by-four "bridges," one under each front wheel, across the continuous ruts in the road made by the water gushing down the sides of the mountain. We cross, they pick up the two-by-fours, and pull them out at the next rutted turn. We play the game of "pass-or-not-pass stare-downs" with the oncoming drivers. Finally, we see water. We load up into two long, old wooden boats and motor for miles and hours down the river to our eco-camp huts, Pantiacolla Lodge. This is a green, all natural, ecological camp. All you can see is the verdant green of the jungle riversides and the mighty waters.

The huts in the eco-camp have mosquito netting around the beds and the familiar oil lanterns beside them. After sitting for so long, I need to move! I jog down a narrow jungle path on the Capybara trail. I am startled by how close and loud the howler monkeys sound.

That evening, Don Americo has us gather and shares that

we are only the masters of ourselves, no one else. When the master within is awake, when the awareness is aflame, we become the master of our own destiny. To do so, we must dis-identify with our mind. Only then will our life become a work of art. He challenges, "What has fire for you? Fire that takes no wood? Opportunities will come to you that match your intent, so you must be aware of what will lead you further on your desired path."

The next day, late in the afternoon, I jog down the same Capybara path to reflect on Don Americo's message. I have a small camera to capture pictures of those big howler monkeys. I note each turn, but the path drops into darkness an hour earlier than I expect. Clouds blow in overhead, and with the tremendous height and depth of the foliage, there's no light from above. I use my camera flash sparingly to see if any turns in the path look familiar. At dinner the night before, there was talk of a jaguar spotted close by. I know that if I become fearful, not only will the animals sense that energy, but I will also waste the very energy I need to get back.

I try to maintain faith that I will find my way. I don't panic. I start to jog faster. I hold up my camera light and the vegetation and small rivulet along the path don't look familiar. I estimate that I ran the wrong way for over an hour. It is getting much colder and is pitch black. I stop, breathe and collect myself. I turn around. I cannot get discouraged. About an hour later, I recognize the fork in the path that is marked and closest to camp. As I approach camp, I see a search party is forming. Carla nervously jokes that I should go to bed without dinner for worrying them. Don Americo says he knew I'd be OK because I was strong and did not have fear.

On the last night in the jungle under a full moon, we build a roaring, six-foot diameter campfire on the banks of the river by our camp. I have my tennis shoes and knee high socks on under my pants and plenty of mosquito repellent. The six-inch bugs come out at night. This moment takes me back to the joy of camping as a child—to the simple pleasures. But this experience is much more universal. With a group embracing more than three generations and five different cultures and languages, we take turns playing music and singing songs in our native tongues. This includes Q'ero flute playing, Navajo songs and chants, Mayan songs, Spanish songs, and good old Beatles songs in English, which almost all of us know. Yes, this truly is a *kumbayah* moment.

I grasp the implications for today's global economy: we need to better understand how to connect and bridge worlds. We need more collaboration and cooperation in how we live and lead. We are more alike at our core than we are different.

As we say our goodbyes, Don Americo leaves us with a message.

You come into the world pure and knowing who you are. Then responses to your family turn into beliefs. Some serve you purely, others don't. Some beliefs are very heavy, like you are not safe or you are not good enough. Yet within, you have a knowing that you deserve the best in the world and that it exists for you. To care for anyone else, you must first care for yourself! As you return to your families, don't let your ego create fear within you to return to ways you have decided to leave behind, in the soil of Peru. Keep the peace within you through practice. *Be released from the expectation of others. Live life consciously, non-judgmentally, with unconditional love, forgiveness and patience. Live in full color; live in metaphor.*

He winks.

WAYS TO ENTER YOUR ANSWER ROOM

Good news. You don't have to live in huts without electricity or running water to access your intuitive information, your answer room. You enter into a non-thinking state. It's easier than you think. Here's how.

There are many simple ways to enter your own personal answer room.

To do so, you only need to turn off the chatter in your mind. The method you choose to turn off the chatter depends on what works best for you. Because I like movement, walking or jogging puts me in a state where my mind quiets down. You may want to walk, run, bike, journal or meditate. Prayer may work for you. Perhaps you can access your intuition during yoga practice. Yoga breathing emphasizes focusing solely on your breath in the moment.

Walk on the beach or down a wooded path. Slow down to enjoy life and take more time for quiet contemplative and relaxing moments where you can be immersed in Nature's healing vibrations. After all, "Every major faith teacher found enlightenment while outside—on a mountaintop, in the desert or under a tree," advises Rabbi Jamie Korngold in an interview in *USA Weekend* (April 2-4, 2010).

Try "zoning out" in the shower as the water pours over you. Or soaking in a bath. Or welcoming that quiet, mindless time on the toilet. We all spend time there. You can even receive intuitive "downloads" during rote activities, like cleaning out the clutter in your closet (not something I'm going to do). Sweeping the floor. Washing the dishes.

Maybe you already journal. Thomas Edison and Albert Einstein are great examples of journaling geniuses. I find by journaling, I can release things that are on my mind. It can be an amazingly helpful release and de-stressor. You don't need to worry about complete sentences; just write whatever comes to you. Try doing so with your left (or non-dominant) hand to get out of your everyday head.

When I read my journal to write this book, some of the most beautiful thoughts came when I was on vacation. From an entry made while sailing and diving on a forty-seven-foot catamaran off the coast of Belize I wrote, "…and when we feel the Earth, the Universe's rhythm, and let loose our own will, then indeed the dance begins." I suspect many of you feel much more at peace when you are on a relaxing outing or vacation. The challenge for all of us is how to carry this sense of wellbeing into everyday life.

Looking back, I see how important it was to capture the observations while in the moment. Through the act of journaling I now see that I set specific intentions into motion through my words.

Your best ideas may come to you in the middle of the night, after you awaken from a dream. Recall that neuroscientist Dr. Joe Dispenza explains that your subconscious, your intuition, works in feelings, symbols and clues, not as rational thoughts. The indigenous cultures we visited taught us that instructions from the heart can come to you as metaphors, too. That's also how dreams work. When you journal about your dreams, you often find that they convey your most important messages through symbols and stories.

The language of the subconscious, of intuition, takes some training to understand. For example, water in a dream is all about emotions. Rooms are often metaphors for examining conflicts within you. When your feet are central to the theme of a dream, it often means you are struggling with understanding something that's important to you. Hair can often be a symbol for thoughts. Your back, the past; your front, the future. I've included resources for dream analysis in the Resources section at the end of this book.

I once wrote about a dream that I'll relate to you, because it offers a good example of understanding instructions from the heart through metaphor. The dream took place on June 12, 2003. The eighteenth-century wooden ship on which I was traveling neared land after crossing a rough ocean. I jumped into the rowboat and headed to the shore. A gigantic, five-story-high double-headed green and blue snake guarded the entry to a castle. I skillfully made it past the snake sentry and made my way up to the castle tower where I confronted my next challenger. It was a man, but his face was not clear. He was standing to my left. A long white snake lay across the entire room beside my left foot and between my challenger and me. I was paralyzed. What should I do next? I had been so brave and already survived the other snakes. Why another? I launched myself over the snake, and I awoke. It was so vivid.

I wanted an explanation. Many epic changes were happening at work. A fairly new executive had joined the parent company and was gaining influence. It was becoming obvious that he did not favor subsidiary company activities that were unrelated to the core utility business, such as the commodity business in GreenEnergyCo.

I was referred to someone who could help me interpret this dream—Gladys McGarey, M.D., M.D.(H), the co-founder of the American Holistic Medical Association. At the flourishing age of ninety she lives and works in Scottsdale, Arizona. You will learn much more about this pioneer of "living medicine" in Chapter 6. In her book, *The Physician Within You*, she highlights the importance of understanding dreams as they relate to your own health. Dr. Gladys shares many of her patients telling dreams. She paints clear pictures for you about the instructive information that the dreams contain. Write down your dreams before you get out of bed, before they evaporate. You may be surprised at the answers they communicate to you.

Dr. Gladys held weekly coffee meetings for anyone interested in learning about dream interpretation. I attended the next session. She was not aware of what I did professionally. Nonetheless, her interpretation of my dream was that I had already swum the sea of emotions and already conquered the big challenges of my career. Now at the top, I had to deal with the white line of integrity. It was telling that the snake was on the left side of my body, as that represents the feminine side. I had accomplished what I needed to with the male side. I needed to honor the integrity of who I am and what I believe. The type of corporate environment I was in had paralyzed my intuition and me. I was living in conflict with myself. When I step over the white line, I will be free.

Another way to tap into the power of your intuition is to practice being quiet. There's strength in calmness, and inner peace is the source of wisdom. I am slowly learning this. You may have a meditation that you practice. What meditation is all about really, is not chanting a mantra, or repeating an affirmation, but just watching as if your mind belongs to someone else! You detach and step outside yourself.

You can access your intuition through meditation at work. A group of us decided to hold self-led meditations during lunch. Our days were so hectic that it really helped us catch our breath and get clearer. Those on our team who had worked with the intuitive expert Laura Alden Kamm to develop personal and professional intuitive problem-solving capabilities shared some techniques with all of us. In her book, *Intuitive Wellness*, Laura offers, "If you are not happy with the way in which your life is going, start trusting that deeper intuitive truth that is within you. It takes trust to listen when your life has been dominated by your mind and ego. When you let go of them you will come to realize, as I have, that you have the ability to solve any issues in your life."

EXERCISES

1. A simple tool that I learned from Laura is to "run the rainbow." It's a quick and easy favorite of mine that I mentioned earlier in this chapter. I have taught it to my friends, children and employees. It helped my friend's high school son who was nervous about taking tests. He used this exercise right before exams to calm himself. It worked. I would "run the rainbow"

prior to meetings with our parent company CEO or board of directors. I knew I was prepared, and used the exercise to either consciously or subconsciously possess information so I could respond successfully to any surprising or difficult questions. My goal was to insure that both channels were available to me so I could access the power of all information, cognitive and intuitive.

Here's how to Run the Rainbow, step by step:

- Sit in a comfortable chair with your shoes off and your feet planted on the ground. Rest your arms in your lap.
- Minimize external noise.
- Calm your mind through seven deep breaths. Do this by going through the colors of the rainbow (ROYGBIV).
- Close your eyes softly and sit tall but comfortably. Visualize the color red. Have your feet ground to the earth by seeing roots grow out of your toes and heels into the earth. Bring the color red up through your feet that are so deeply grounded in Mother Earth. As you bring up the color red, take a deep breath. As you breathe in, see and feel and hear the color red coming up through your feet, into your calves, thighs, hips and up through your tailbone and spine, up your back into neck, and completely fill your head with a big red ball of energy. Then blow it out strongly. When you breathe out, see and feel and hear the red ball of breath roll through your arms and shoot out your fingertips.
- Next, bring the color orange up through the earth just like you did red, then yellow, then green, then blue, then indigo (like eggplant color), then violet.

This exercise only takes about two minutes. I used to modify it by doing it while walking over to the corporate office from our building next door, and it worked! It quickly cleared my mind and I was calmed by my breath, so I could think and act clearly in a demanding situation. Running the Rainbow is adapted and printed here with permission from Laura Alden Kamm, *Intuitive Wellness*.

2. You can add another breathing exercise to Running the Rainbow if you have time. After you run through the rainbow's seven breaths you can breathe in gold light from above you. See yourself outside your physical presence, which helps prepare you for the next exercise:

- Visualize a space twelve inches above your head. See yourself as a third party witness from that vantage point. Look down on yourself sitting comfortably below in a chair. Take a deep breath and run the color gold or see gold light from the heavens run down through you from above as you sit in the chair.

- Pick a spot in the sky and look down at the Earth as if you were an astronaut. Repeat seeing the gold light as it continues to emanate from that spot and run through you as you continue to sit in the chair. Take a deep breath.

- Now pick a location way out in the galaxy and do the same.

By Running the Rainbow, all the energy of the Universe is available to you from above and from the Earth below. This technique is much like what the Q'eros do, but I learned it before I knew anything about the Q'eros. You may want to scoop the energy from the Earth and Sky and bring it into your heart while you take a breath, as Don Americo guides you to do.

When you get out of your head and into your heart, you will have access to much more information that provides all the answers you need. I learned to follow my heart and to trust that I would not be led to the wrong place. I know that if I were supposed to be somewhere else, I would be there, and that the Universe (God, Source, Spirit or Divine, depending on your beliefs) inspires you and me to move at the right time and manner.

3. Here are more exercises to help you find your answers within.
   - When have you successfully listened to your gut, that is, your intuition?
   - When has your head "gotten in your way?"
   - Think of and write down as many ways as you can to enter your answer room. Pick at least one to get you into a non-thinking state at least three times a week for ten minutes.
4. Calibrate your breath. See if you can inhale deeply and slowly through your nose for a count of at least ten. Hold it for ten. Exhale very slowly through your mouth for at least ten counts, or longer than your inhale count. Take note throughout your day as to when you breathe deeply or shallowly and try to increase the times you breathe deeply.
5. When you see your family, blow in their face and let them know you are blowing their worry away with the wind of love. "Remember to give warning!"

FOUR

EXPLORE YOUR CORE

Today you are You, that is truer than true. There is no one alive who is Youer than You.
— Dr. Seuss, American writer and cartoonist

The second truth to finding your scream is to become keenly aware of who you authentically are and what you deeply value by exploring your core. Self-awareness is integral to finding your scream. You will achieve this in part through intuition and in part through examining data-driven information. Again, you integrate the wisdom of your heart with the power of your mind.

Exploring your core leads you to understand your natural strengths and interests. (You actually already know where you excel and what you value, but you may need to rediscover and unearth it within you). With this knowledge you become an incredibly effective and fulfilled person, employee or leader because you are aligned to take actions every day that honor who you are and what you value.

CHILDHOOD PLAY

I shared with you my marble victory at age seven when time stood still. A time when I was in a heart-felt place.

What did you play that gave you your greatest joy, when time stood still for you at age seven? Where did your dreams and imagination take you? When the sheer thought of such play lit up your eyes and your whole body was jazzed with vibrant energy.

Spend a moment right now and write down what pops into your head—without over-thinking it. What did you choose to do with your free time when you came home from school and no one was nagging you to do your homework or practice piano or clean up your room?

Did you play with dolls or trucks or Matchbox cars or micromachines or sticks or guns? Did you read or draw or color? Did you play imaginary games, possibly dress-up? If so, what shoes did you wear? Did you make things out of Play-Doh? Did you cook with an Easy-Bake Oven? Or build with Legos® or Lincoln Logs? Did you play in nature? Build forts? Collect baseball or Pokémon™ cards, or play with a deck of cards? Were you a sports nut?

What came easily to you? What did you passionately love to do? See it. Feel it. Hear it. Taste it. Why did you like it so much? What about it resonated with your very core?

In my case, in a neighborhood of all boys, not only did I play (and win at) marbles, but I also played with the ninety-nine-cent bags of plastic olive-green army men. (If you remember those, your age is showing!) I remember that the lemonade stand was not entrepreneurial enough for me. Nor did it "make enough bank." As I already mentioned, I would create things—paper flowers, clay objects, jewelry, painted rocks, you name it—and sell them. Sometimes I would see an incredible deal on something, so I'd buy and resell it. Or I would trade for something that I had, that a friend wanted. (Hey, is there anyone out there who wants to trade their timeshare in the Caribbean for one in Puerto Vallarta —and cut out the middleman exchange)?

Your childhood delights and adult values may or may not be aligned with your current work or lifestyle. Ego and economics cause many people, especially in our society, to become doctors, lawyers, executives, managers or someone with a title or perceived stature.

Reflecting back, I began to see how I got out of alignment. I went to law school on a dare from my boyfriend who planned to attend law school. And it met my mother's expectations of me being a star.

However, Dr. Vernon Smith, my Nobel Prize-honored economics professor, was disappointed with my decision to go to law school. He encouraged me to get a Ph.D. in behavioral economics, markets and trading. This area truly is a passion of mine, the one I actually lived from the heart when I was younger. I found the road back to it when I found my scream—when I left the practice of law and became the president of a commodity marketing, trading and green energy company.

I view my circuitous journey not as a waste of my time or energy, but as my path. I was destined to go down that road so I could experience it fully—so I could explain the process clearly, and now help you find your scream.

Remembering what you enjoyed as a child is a significant clue to the type of work or lifestyle that may be the most fulfilling to you now. The activities you loved provide insights into what you value in your heart and soul and dreams. Maybe work is great, but other aspects of your life are not as you dreamed them, or maybe it's the other way around. When you understand what creates fire for you, fire that takes no wood, you are in touch with your core.

Has your favorite playtime been lost in your hectic life? Have you left behind your true self? I have seen it happen so early with our youth. I taught as a volunteer an hour of Masterpiece Art once a week for six weeks, for nine years. This was at both of my kids' grade school classes each year from kindergarten through sixth grade. I observed as early as the second class I led, that many of these beautiful young kids had already lost themselves and their creativity. By the third grade, the majority would only color within the lines. For example, when one assignment required students to draw a picture of their pet or favorite animal from a photo—without making a hard outline—many students were stumped. I suggested using hatch marks for feathers, for example, but the kids defaulted to drawing outlines.

Your childhood games or hobbies may or may not be your life's work, but just reflecting on what you liked to do provides insights into your scream. There's something about what you loved to do and why that's at the core of what will fulfill you now. It's a shaping impulse.

"Bear" Grylls, the star of the television show, *Man vs. Wild*, said, "I've got a dream job. If someone had told me when I was five years old, when I was climbing trees and caked in mud, that one day I'll have a job doing the exact same thing, I would have thought it was heaven," in a May, 2010, interview with *Outside*. Bear concludes that he would be unemployable at anything else. The cameraman calls him "almost childish," and explains that this sense of juvenile spontaneity has been the real secret of the show. The shaping impulse of Grylls' life appears to be boredom avoidance. His indifference to eating horrible food like a live bullfrog and leftover neck meat from a lion-killed zebra carcass was cemented by his mother, a rubbish cook. She "pulled pork chops out of the dustbin that were three weeks old and covered in silvery green mold and asked, 'Who threw these out? They're perfectly good.'"

Remember the stories you loved as a child. What about the tale, or the hero or heroine, resonates with you and why? What clues can you explore for insights to your scream? The stories you couldn't get enough of as a kid are very telling about who you really are and what mission is at the core of your life's purpose.

I love the children's book *Verdi* by Janell Cannon. I didn't want to grow up to be like my parents. I resolved to honor who I was and to stay fun loving and young at heart. Here's a short synopsis of the story of Verdi, a young python, who didn't want to grow up to be like the older snakes:

> When Verdi's mother told him to grow up big and green, Verdi didn't want to, because he was young and yellow with sporty stripes. Why grow up like the big, green, lazy, boring and rude snake he saw lounging on a high branch? No, he would stay young and yellow. Verdi would foolishly grab a tree branch and whip himself through the air for a grand thrill, twisting his body into a sporty-looking figure eight, forgetting he would fall back to earth.
>
> Verdi lay crumpled on the ground from his inevitable fall when two old green snakes dragged him onto a branch and splinted him straight onto it so he could heal. While recovering, Verdi turned very green, although he didn't know it.

Two young yellow snakes saw old green Verdi in the tree and mocked him and questioned whether he ever moved. A sudden realization hit him. "They're just like I used to be, and I'm now what I was afraid to be."

He looked at his big green body and slowly smiled. "How would you like to climb trees with me?" The young yellow snakes were astounded. Verdi taught them how to fling themselves from the tree in a perfect figure eight. Leaping and looping with his little striped yellow friends, Verdi laughed. "I may be big and very green, but I'm still me!"

DATA-DRIVEN ASSESSMENT TOOLS

You benefit from the power of more in-depth information about yourself when you integrate what you intuitively know about what you love to do with information derived from data-driven assessment tools.

I found at work that many people were not in touch with the areas where they excelled. The first week anyone worked for GreenEnergyCo, they'd be offered the opportunity to take an assessment tool that illuminated their natural strengths and values. No one refused. The results were confidential. According to the experts with whom we worked, who I mention below, 80 percent of who you are is what you *value*, not what you show outwardly as your personality. Understanding what values drive you is elemental to self-awareness.

As I mentioned in Chapter 1, we originally used the DISCProfile and Motivation Insights for frontline employees. We always used them in combination, so I will refer to them as DISC/MI. We used the DISC and Core Values Index™ (CVI) for leaders. With some expert help, we mapped each leader's CVI values and DISC traits for comparative information. We looked at it as an investment in helping our employees and leaders understand themselves better. It was a very inexpensive investment at that— less than $100 to $200 per employee, that included a one-on-one debriefing session with an expert. The returns dwarfed the cost. My belief, which the results confirmed, was how critical it was for each person to understand his or her self. With this information, we could best align our people with work that optimized their strengths.

If someone were hired in a capacity that initially wasn't the optimal match, we worked toward a best-fit over time. Having everyone take the same assessment also created a common language through which we could all communicate.

We used these tools for team integration and to evaluate the best position for each leader, based on those who scored highest on the profiles for the positions we needed.

For example, I moved a key leader out of his former position as the head of sales because he was a more exacting professional engineer who was not as natural a fit for a sales leader. I later "re-fitted" him again by offering him an assignment in an emerging area. Ultimately this led to a position as the head of the energy asset-based business at which he truly excelled.

You are probably familiar with profiling tools such as the CVI, DISC/MI and Myers-Briggs Type Indicator® (MBTI). These assessments measure some of your most defining characteristics, from outwardly observed personality styles to your innermost values. I will briefly describe some of these assessment tools to give you an idea of what these assessments tell you about yourself. While I prefer some assessments over others, any of them provide useful information to enhance your self-awareness. Just by reading the categories you can glean information about yourself. The best way to learn more about yourself, however, is to take one or more of the assessments.

The References and Resources section at the end of this book lists some resources for you to consider, including free on-line tools. (Make sure that whatever assessment you use has been validated to ensure it really measures the traits it purports to measure. Assessments that may intuitively appear valid but were never validated statistically may provide only entertainment value).

Once you are aware of your signature strengths and values,

you can determine if you currently live, lead and work in alignment with them. You can also apply the "explore your core" principle to your overall company or organization. I describe that process in the next chapter.

THE CORE VALUES INDEX™

The *Core Values Index*™ (CVI) assessment tool is based on a very simple concept: people adapt their *Core Values Nature*™ into a personality behavioral system that causes them to make certain decisions and judgments, which causes them to take certain actions and use certain behaviors that cause certain results. Put simply, by understanding someone's *Core Values Nature*, we can predict their actions. It's not a personality or behavioral profile instrument, *per se*.

Mr. Lynn Taylor is the developer of the *Core Values Index* and the *Human Operating System*™, which provide an understanding of how we as people operate at the conscious and unconscious levels. This has led to his development of *Core Values Consciousness*™, a new pathway to higher consciousness for all people. He first developed a computerized pattern recognition algorithm in the early eighties in his work for an echocardiography company.

OVERVIEW OF THE CORE VALUES INDEX™ *(CVI)*

My company worked with a professional consultant, Sandy Kohlberg, Ph.D., to apply the CVI assessment results to our leadership team. The CVI measures a person's innate, unchanging nature, our individual capacities for being a unique presence in the room. The CVI consists of an objective test that measures four *Core Value Energies*™, based on forced choice responses to sets of tactical value words. Taylor Protocols, the company that publishes CVI, has used the CVI successfully to help more than 700 clients realign positions, people, duties and responsibilities over the past twenty years.

The following basic review of what the CVI assesses can help increase your self-awareness. However, you'll need to take the full assessment for a complete analysis of your core values. The tool categorizes individuals, according to their values scores, into one of the four work-related *Core Values Energy* profiles: *power (builder), love (merchant), wisdom (innovator)* and *knowledge (banker).* The following chart summarizes the typical workplace performance characteristics for each profile.

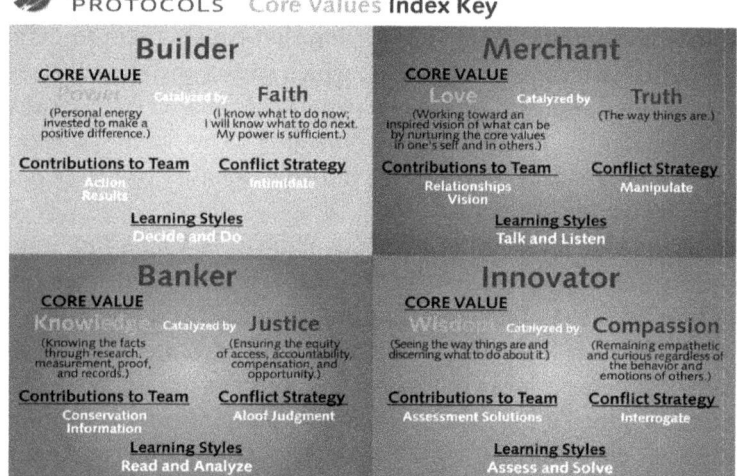

Note: All content about the CVI, including graphics may not be reproduced by any means, written or mechanical, or be programmed into any electronic retrieval or information storage system without permission in writing from Lynn E. Taylor. This information is intended for use in this book only. Any repetitive use of the CVI™ assessment and training information by companies and individuals requires a license from Lynn E. Taylor and Taylor Protocols, Inc. All graphics and Trademarks used by Lynn E. Taylor, and Taylor Protocols, Inc. are considered intellectual property of Lynn E Taylor and Taylor Protocols and may not be copied or re-distributed.

In addition, the CVI assessment evaluates what you value by measuring your capacity to operate intuitively or cognitively; whether you are more practical or creative, and more independent or more community oriented.

- Intuitive type: Has a knowing as an instinct with sharp, eclectic insight.

- Independent type: Has a desire and ability to act autonomously, without supervision or significant restraints.

- Practical type: Has a preference to rely on experience, practice or use, rather than theory or speculation.
- Creative type: Has originality, expression and vision and imagines what can be.
- Community type: Believes in teamwork and organizations of individuals as strategic tools for success.
- Cognitive type: Has the process and faculty of knowledge and reasoning.

Although everyone is a blend of all four *Core Value Energies*, we each have a dominant core value. When we are performing at our highest and best level we start from our dominant core value and move through the other values as needed in a particular situation, sequentially, according to our strengths. For example, if you are a builder, when you are in conflict mode your dominant response will be to intimidate.

Here's how Lynn Taylor summarizes each core value:

- The *Builder's core value* is *power* supported by the *Catalytic Value* of *faith*. *Power* is the personal energy used to make a difference and create a positive result. Faith is the confidence a person has to say, "I know what to do. I know that what I am about to do is right. I will know what to do next." *Builders* drive toward results by taking the aspirations of the *merchants*, the ideas of the innovators and the facts from the *bankers*. They lead by example. The learning style is to decide and do. When confronted, they tend to fire back in an intimidating way. There's a strong independence based on intuition and a practicality.
- The *Merchant's core value* is *love* supported by the *Catalytic Value* of *truth*. *Love* is the nurturing of the *Core Values Nature* in one's self and in others. *Truth* is the ability to see the way things are. *Merchants* are amazing relationship people, risk takers and visionaries who see

endless possibilities. They foster the pursuit of wealth, art and beauty. *Merchants* are team builders and deal makers who inspire the best in others. They lead through love and excitement. They ask others to help them achieve their unique vision. The learning style is to talk and listen. When in conflict, they tend to cast the situation in a manipulative way. They rely on intuition and creativity and support community.

- The *Banker's core value* is *knowledge* supported by the *Catalytic Value* of *justice*. *Knowledge* is the how and why of things. It's the fair and equitable way. *Bankers* gain and preserve the most important *knowledge*. They collect and preserve the most important resources of society and organize thought and information. They keep balance in the system and protect others from unreasonable risk. They conserve, analyze and inform. They constantly gather *knowledge* so that when the time comes, they will have the answer. The learning style is to read and analyze. When pushed, they may become passive aggressive, "fight out of sight." They tend to react in an *aloof* manner. *Bankers* are driven by values of practicality, community and cognitive processes.

- The *Innovator's core value* is *wisdom* supported by the *Catalytic Value* of *compassion*. *Wisdom* is the ability to see the way things work and know what to do about it. This enables them to understand why other people react the way they do. They observe and solve problems. They ask, "What if?" They keep projects rolling by providing alternative solutions through a better way. They lead through brainstorming, strategic thinking, questioning and observation. From a place of understanding, they are able to provide wise solutions and effective strategies. The learning style is to assess and solve. When pressured, they tend to fire back lots of questions in an *interrogation* style. If you are this type, you will operate from a place of independence, creativity and thoughtfulness.

Where are you on the four quadrants of the chart above? What resonates with you the most?

- Are you a builder who seeks results and takes actions based on faith? When pressed, do you fire back in an impatient, intimidating voice?
- Are you a lover of people who likes to talk and listen and who values relationships? Do you have an inspired vision of where and how things can be? When pushed, do you play "nicey-nicey" and try to coax or manipulate others to see your way?
- Are you a banker type who values justice, objective knowledge and presentation of information (ah, like my husband, the prosecutor)? And when challenged, are you indirect or not available and aloof?
- Do you love to innovate and seek solutions to many questions and problems? Do you seek wisdom and when confronted, interrogate the offender?

Let me share a personal application of how you explore your core by connecting what you played when you were little with what your assessments reveal.

It seems it's always easier to see the "scream" in others, especially those close to us, isn't it? As parents, my husband and I naturally observed our daughter's strengths and interests as she grew. When Shelby was twenty-four months old, she was sitting in her car seat in the middle of the back seat. She had her little legs spread out, reaching to the back of each of our front seats. There was a console in between our seats. She looked down at the space that was created by her two outstretched legs and the console and said "triangle." We knew then she had spatial recognition like no other! A triangle was exactly the shape of space created between her legs and the console. She also loved to color and draw as far back as we can remember. Sometime later she began to cut out magazine pictures that showed the latest fashions and makeup designs, and she kept them in a little notebook.

Shelby played soccer since the time she was three. She and all the other three-year-olds would glob onto the ball and run in a pack with it. Over time, her skills grew because she enjoyed the game so much. When she was a sophomore, Shelby became captain of the junior varsity soccer team at Mountain Point High School in Ahwatukee, Arizona. She could consistently kick the soccer ball from midfield into the goal. Instead of doing so, she chose to kick it three feet to the side of the goal to her teammate, another forward, who had the hunger, heart and desire for the reward and responsibility of scoring. Shelby never booted that ball with the intention of getting on the scoreboard. Instead, her gift was to support others for team success.

While we could see this, her coach didn't. She expected Shelby to be a scorer. Shelby quit playing soccer the next year. Good for her. The coach's relentless expectation for her to score didn't align with who Shelby is or what she values. As a parent, after watching Shelby grow and improve through thousands of soccer games, at first this choice was disappointing. However, we quickly endorsed her decision—one that honored her and was healthy for her.

Because my family is among the guinea pigs (at least I didn't say experimental rats) for the Scream to Dream Approach, Shelby took the Myers-Briggs, CVI, and DISC/MI assessments when she was in high school and college. In fact, it's an excellent idea to have young people learn about themselves early so they can become aligned with their scream and live their dream even sooner!

Shelby is a Merchant/Innovator under the CVI tool and at the top of the creative value scale. According to the DISC/MI assessment that we will go over next she is a 100 percent influencer/people-person and a high supporter, someone who values aesthetics more than most other people. According to Myers-Briggs, her type is the introvert, intuitive, sensing, feeling. This makes perfect sense, and her profiles are consistent across these instruments. They reveal her natural talent and interest in creative problem solving and love for beauty. She is a people person who likes to work in teams and who thinks before she speaks.

You can see the connection between her profiles and her career when you understand where her core talents and values have taken her so far. Shelby graduated with a 4.0 GPA from Arizona State University (ASU) with a degree in graphic communications. Her desire to help others become successful is apparent in her ability to help people portray their messages visually. She listens intently to what the customers want to communicate and puts it into a picture message, or package, or website so that they can win by gaining sales. She still is not a happy camper when she is the frontrunner. But you would want her as an invaluable member of your team!

TTI'S DISCPROFILE AND MOTIVATION INSIGHTS

At GreenEnergyCo we worked with Dr. Joy Schwertley to administer the DISCProfile and Motivation Insights instruments through TTI Performance Systems, Inc.

DISCProfile measures behaviors and communication styles and categorizes them into behavioral styles:

- D (dominance): How you respond to problems or challenges.
- I (influence): How you influence others to see your point of view.
- S (steadiness): How you respond to the pace of the environment.
- C (compliance): How you respond to rules and procedures.

As with all of the assessment tools we used at GreenEnergyCo, DISCProfile isn't meant to be judgmental. It helps people understand their own and others' behavioral styles to improve communications and interactions.

TTI's Motivation Insights assessment measures the interests, goals and preferences that guide our lives and careers. Joy's experience is that the motivators tell far more about an individual than their observable behaviors. The Motivation Insights assessment measures:

- Theoretical: a passion for discovery and knowledge.
- Utilitarian: a passion for power over your life and money, bottom line orientation.
- Aesthetic: a passion for balance and harmony in one's own life and to protect Nature.
- Social: a passion to eliminate hate and conflict and for service to others.
- Individualistic: a passion to achieve an influential position.
- Traditional: a passion to pursue life's higher meaning within a defined system.

Joy found over her thirty-year career in administering more than 22,000 DISC and Motivator assessments that ALL seven hundred respondents who were CEOs, business owners or high-level leaders scored first as Utilitarian and second as Individualistic. But just because your scores don't happen to be highest in these two motivators, it doesn't mean you can't be a leader. It may very well indicate, however, that you are not living your scream and that you may be out of alignment as a leader.

Similarly, Bill Bonnstetter, founder and chairman of TTI Performance Systems, Inc., researched serial entrepreneurs. He concludes that while many fail, 88 percent of those studied began dreaming about starting their own business before the age of 25, and 42 percent were imagining it before the age of twelve (*Arizona Republic*, Oct. 24, 2010).

Here's an example of how these instruments applied to me. I had already started on my leadership journey at GreenEnergyCo when I took the assessments, but my profile summaries will show you how accurately these instruments capture core values and motivators.

According to my CVI profile, my most dominant motivation is a practical builder. A close second is a visionary merchant who loves to accomplish results through people. These motivations explain my desire to build GreenEnergyCo and inspire individuals to be their best. They explain through data-based results why I tend to use power for the good to bring results; the fact that I have faith and know how to proceed; why, when pushed into a conflict mode, my natural response is to react with an intimidating voice or manner (which I learned to recognize and to purposefully respond differently); and why I use vision to accomplish the desired results through a team.

My DISCProfile and Motivation Insights scores also affirmed that I was a natural fit to lead GreenEnergyCo. My DISC scores were high in dominance and even higher in influence. They confirmed that I want to create my own destiny and that I can direct others to accomplish my vision. I am a people lover and choose to influence them.

My Myers-Briggs Type (I discuss the Myers-Briggs Type Indicator assessment later in the chapter) is extrovert/intuitive/thinking/judging (ENTJ). I find this assessment most useful to describe external behaviors.

My top Motivation Insights values are typical of a natural leader—Utilitarian and Individualistic. These indicate that I value financial freedom and want to chart my own path rather than have others do it for me. Note that as you proceed on your life's journey, your values may change. Once I secured financial freedom, for example, I focused more on my social value of helping others.

What about you? Are you a forward with the hunger to score? Are you cheering on the sidelines as a team supporter? Are you a sweeper in the backfield? Or are you coaching the team?

As you examine how these values apply to you, exploring how what you played when you were little also provides telling insights. Consider how well your childhood delights and adult values are aligned with your work or lifestyle now.

THE DISC AND MOTIVATION INSIGHTS AT WORK

Learning their individual DISC and Motivation Insights allowed all the employees at GreenEnergyCo to understand their personal strengths, interests and challenges. One of the ways we used our understanding was to work toward better resolutions to conflicts or disagreements.

For example, I became aware that my enthusiasm could become a limitation when I'd get excited and interrupt people while they were talking. I chose to change my behavior by writing in a notebook at my desk each time I interrupted. I decided to listen more and to wait before responding, to honor the other person. After a few weeks, I noticed a behavior change. So did others.

When you know yourself, you are also better at recognizing and understanding others' behavioral differences. This allows you to create more win/win situations. We used our understanding of behavioral differences to build better teams. People naturally like people who are similar to them. However, many years of team research shows that the most effective teams are comprised of diverse individuals. Sometimes it is not as easy to communicate nor understand people who are very different from you. As employees at GreenEnergyCo, we learned the DISC/MI language so we could communicate with the diverse members in our teams from a common platform. This was a huge factor in creating community and driving high performance.

Another important way that we used the DISC/MI assessment was to identify adaptive versus core behaviors. The questions posed by the DISC/MI instruments distinguish between what you show others (adaptive) versus who you really are (your core).

For example, GreenEnergyCo employed an individual whose DISC results revealed a serious skew between who he was versus what he showed the world. A private intervention prevented initial disaster. This person became aware of his issues, which saved him from getting fired and the company from potentially having a lawsuit filed against us. Ultimately, he realized he was not a best-fit for us and voluntarily moved on to other employment.

Another of my leaders and I "tested" these tools. The leader was a young, bright man of Asian descent. He and I had different conversational styles and constantly talked past each other. We both became frustrated with one another. I asked a facilitator to intervene because it's much easier to direct one's perceptions about an interpersonal conflict to a neutral third party. (I strongly suggest tapping a respected, objective person to act as a referee or mediator—perhaps a human resources person—within your business for an early intervention and to enhance productivity.)

Our facilitator taught us how to take the emotion out of our communication impasses and to laugh when we began our dysfunctional pattern of conversing. We identified that we started our discussion from different points, one of us from a conceptual level; the other from the ground up with all the gory details. While we usually ended up in the same place, getting there was ugly. (Frankly, I also had to overcome his strong cultural bias against an assertive, tall, female, non-math-major leader.)

So just appreciating our diversity was not enough. The next time my fellow leader and I had a conversation and I started to feel red-faced, I realized what we were doing, laughed and started the discussion over.

I also learned to look beyond a person's behaviors that annoyed me. I now ask myself why I become annoyed at the behavior—is it a trait similar to something I don't like in myself? I search to see the true nature of the other person, to better understand his or her intent to get beyond the external behavior. If you can do this and use a neutral referee when needed, many hours of non-productive time and negative water cooler gossip will be eliminated.

Another beauty of the DISC/MI assessment is that you can explore the core of a company's values as well as an individual's. We did this by aggregating the individual DISC's into a total company view. We also compared our company's collective DISC/MI profiles with those of our parent and sister utility company. The dominant characteristic of many employees within certain areas of the utility company was a high compliance/low risk-taking trait. It made perfect sense. Of course you'd want nuclear plant personnel "to color within the lines" and closely adhere to safety procedures. You expect mistakes to be made and employees to learn from them; but mistakes are not always tolerated in a highly-regulated world.

Our startup company needed some personnel with resourcefulness and prudent risk-taking traits. We would explore an area of potential opportunity and at the 60 percent risk mark, say, abandon that investigation. We continued to do so until we found our best opportunity. We were thin on personnel resources so we filled our "gaps," be they people or systems, only when the market conditions required it. Whereas in the regulated world, it may be deemed to be too risky to not be fully resourced. These are very different approaches with very different results.

Some excellent utility workers were perceived as mis-fits by some of my former colleagues because they were low-compliance individuals trying to fit successfully into a high-compliance world. They felt like square pegs being forced into round holes—ouch! And people who work in environments where they are not the best-fit often are made to feel like failures, or at a minimum, mis-fits. Some of these were the talented people I wooed over to GreenEnergyCo from the utility. I knew in our environment that who they were at their core would be a best-fit for us.

Trying to adapt by contorting yourself can be stressful. That's why exploring your core is so important to your health, well-being, personal and professional success. You must first become completely self-aware by exploring your core and listening within in order to identify, pursue and live your dream.

MYERS-BRIGGS TYPE INDICATOR

Another assessment that can help you explore your core is the Myers-Briggs Type Indicator (MBTI). It's based on Carl Jung's psychological types. His theory is essentially that behaviors are the result of basic differences in the way individuals instinctively use their perception and judgment.

Perception is how you become aware of things, people, happenings or ideas. Judgment is how you draw conclusions about what you have perceived. If people differ systematically in what they perceive and in how they reach conclusions, then it's only reasonable for them to differ accordingly in their interests, reactions, values, motivations and skills.

The MBTI categorizes people into one of sixteen different types, depending on how they relate to the world. Each of the sixteen types represents a different combination of the following categories. The descriptions are based on information from the *MBTI® Manual: A Guide to the Development and Use of the Myers-Briggs Type Indicator®*.

- Favorite world: Do you prefer to focus on the outer world (extrovert) or on your own inner world (introvert)?

- Information: Do you prefer to focus on the basic information you take in (sensing type) or do you prefer to interpret and add meaning (intuitive type)?

- Decisions: When making decisions, do you prefer to first look at logic and consistency (thinking type) or first look at the people and special circumstances (feeling type)?

- Structure: In dealing with the outside world, do you prefer to get things decided (judging type) or do you prefer to stay open to new information and options (perceiving type)?

This assessment instrument can also be helpful to students. For example, my daughter's graphic communications instructor used it to create multi-disciplined teams in her class. She intentionally mixed up students with different types so they could learn how to work with people who have different styles than they possess.

When you integrate what you intuitively know about what you love to do, such as your beloved childhood play, with information about you that you derive from data-driven assessment tools, you have it all at your fingertips. By exploring your core, you have the power of all information available to you to guide you in living and leading a fulfilled life—one in alignment with your scream.

EXERCISES

1. Write down in as much detail as possible what you liked to do when you were young, say, age seven, and why. Visualize yourself playing and use all five senses. Write what you valued about that type of activity.
2. Take an assessment that reveals your values. You can try the free on-line ones at http://www.authentichappiness.sas.upenn.ed or contact one of the resources in the References and Resources section of this book to take the CVI or DISC and MI.
3. Consider what you played as a child and what the assessments reveal about your values. What do these indicate about your best-fit type of work?

EXPLORE YOUR ORGANIZATION'S CORE

Just as your car runs more smoothly and requires less energy to go faster and farther when the wheels are in perfect alignment, you perform better when your thoughts, feelings, emotions, goals, and values are in balance.

— BRIAN TRACY, INTERNATIONAL BUSINESS SPEAKER, AUTHOR AND TRAINER

You have seen how the Explore Your Core principle of the Scream to Dream Approach works for you personally and professionally. A company or organization is the best version of itself when a work environment is created in which company leaders and employees are the best they can be. When each one of you is aligned to optimize your signature strengths and values and to derive meaning from what you do for your customers, the organization cannot help but excel.

Just as you, as an individual, become awakened with self-awareness, so does your organization. You look at your company internally, its collective strengths, values and fears. We saw earlier that you can intuitively discern where your company is succeeding, for example, by using the qualitative chart. Sometimes it's as simple as just asking what goods or services you excel at providing through your people, and doing more of it. For example, initially the purchase of commodity electricity seemed risky to the customer because of the price volatility. With some classes of customers, we found we had the best success selling to consultant-experts who had existing relationships with them. Our action plan included targeting these consulting professionals through industry associations instead of selling directly to the business customer.

By taking time to clearly identify what strengths you need in key positions and hiring and retaining best-fit employees, you create alignment and increase productivity. I empowered my leaders to make many decisions without me. The decisions had to be within their defined job responsibilities and within the established guardrails, such as their contract signing levels. I defined certain areas where I would be included, such as participating in key executive-level customer accounts and in key hirings—the major revenue producing aspects. We identified our top five risks and I stayed more closely involved with those activities—our liabilities. Focusing inward on your company's strengths and those of your people is equally as important as focusing externally on customers, suppliers, bankers and the marketplace.

By aligning people's strengths as leaders, you also reduce turnover. You have probably experienced at some point in your career not being able to work for a particular boss. Did you know that the number one reason why workers leave for another job is a poor relationship with their immediate boss? Our human resources director reminded us of this. Sure, sometimes it's a matter of you changing your perception, or it could be that the boss is not living his scream by leading. She would encourage us to take a moral and caring route, which is a profitable course for any company. Nobody cares how much you know as a leader or employee until they know how much you care. Real caring is the giving of time, attention and support! It happens one on one. And it applies equally to personal and professional relationships.

The assessment tools you reviewed in the previous chapter help you determine whose values align with leadership. We have all seen superior performers who demand a leadership title but it's obvious that they are, instead, a best-fit technical person. Once their ego gets out of their way, you can craft the optimal position for them to utilize their natural gifts and talents.

Some of the best practices that worked for the GreenEnergyCo leaders included: provide the necessary resources to accomplish the job; provide the room (the employees' defined sandbox) to do their jobs; clearly state expectations; and design recognition that matches the individual employee's values with the organizational goals. We helped everyone learn their strengths through assessment tools and a culture that encouraged introspection, as I mentioned earlier. Of course, you also need tools, skills, training, support and assistance to reach your stated and measurable goals.

We spent very little time focusing on our limitations. Don't misunderstand; it's critical to be completely aware of your limitations. Otherwise you can get into trouble by taking on tasks that are outside of your expertise. With self-awareness, you can consciously plug your gaps. But we did not try to completely sandpaper our employees into fitting into that round hole.

It's a universal truth that all people want to know what's expected of them, feel valued and be given the opportunity to succeed. That opportunity is effectively denied if you don't receive timely, honest feedback on your work. I insisted on meaningful, ongoing performance reviews with objective metrics as well as qualitative measures. The individual then had a chance to make corrections before it was too late. This approach was unlike other performance review processes I had experienced.

To recap, we also enabled better communication through such things as having a common DISC language among employees since everyone was familiar with the tool. We minimized downtime that resulted from miscommunication by utilizing neutral third parties (either our human resources leader or an outside professional) to intervene, if two people weren't communicating well. This was a highly cost-effective process. The lost downtime was far offset by a modest expense for the assessments, evaluations and occasional consulting call.

Hiring, placing and retaining best-fits fostered team morale and our environment motivated our employees to create our company's success. Each employee understood how he or she contributed to the overall purpose of the company—just like a goose knows its position in its V formation. What, you ask, does a goose's V formation have to do with contributing to the company?

Geese may not be the most inspiring creatures to you. However, I find the following analogy of great companies and a flock of geese instructive.

When a goose flaps its wings, it creates an "uplift" for the following bird. By flying in a V formation, the whole flock adds 71 percent more to its flying range than if each bird flew alone.

What we learn from the geese is that when the leaders and their people share a common purpose, commitment and passion for their company, they can get where they are going quicker and more successfully because they are traveling on the thrust of one another.

The geese in formation honk from behind to encourage those up front to keep up their speed... If a goose falls out of formation, it suddenly feels the drag and resistance of trying to fly alone. It quickly gets back into formation to take advantage of the "lifting power" of the birds immediately in front.

The leaders need to make certain they are "honking" from behind the group to encourage and empower others.

When a goose gets sick or wounded or shot down, two geese drop out of formation and follow it down to help and give protection. They stay with the goose until it is able to fly again. Then they launch out on their own to catch up with the flock.

If employees follow the good example of the geese, they stand by each other through the most difficult of situations and trying times. There is magic when all work together to further the company's mission. (Paraphrased in part from the "Lessons From Geese For The YMCA" from Jerold Panas, Linzy and Partners.)

Another analogy that exemplifies highly effective teamwork is a cycling team. As a long-time cyclist, I have experienced the real support of other riders in a pace line. This occurs professionally in the peloton, as you may have seen in the Tour De France. There's an advantage of 20 to 40 percent more efficiency when you tuck your front wheel tight in behind another rider's back wheel and it increases if several riders are around you. (For more on this topic see Livestrong.com on drafting when cycling.)

This team acts much like the geese flying with a common purpose. You get where you are going by traveling on the thrust of one another. When you draft behind a leader and when in a group, a turbulent wake of air is made creating a vortex. If you are the rider behind the leader, the low pressure created moves you forward and the eddies push you forward. You learn to go in the flow of the path with least resistance. Watch out if you are behind the group for the occasional nose blowing. I have gotten quite a "bath" being in back!

In a professional race, you take turns expending 100 percent of the effort leading so you can all go much further together. And you learn to "spin" which is about 80 to 100 rpms (rotations per minute, or how fast your turn your peddles). At the ideal speed, and when your foot stroke becomes a smooth circle, you are the most efficient. You work smarter, not harder. You expend less energy to go the same distance. This is what winners do.

When you need nourishment, three riders drop behind, with one securing the food from the support vehicle. The one carrying the food tucks in behind the two other riders who take turns sprinting their way back to the peloton. If one becomes injured or needs a bike repair, two drop back again to help that rider get back into the group. The strongest sprinter pulls the leader, such as Lance Armstrong, to the front and "slingshots" him into the lead. And, of course the crowd cheers you on.

WHAT'S MEANINGFUL ABOUT YOUR BUSINESS?

Every organization that has a prepared business plan will find they have three common elements. Here's what they are and why they're important to helping your organization find its core.

- The Why (vision/mission).
- The What (goals).
- The How (values).

THE WHY

At GreenEnergyCo we existed to make a difference in the health of our customers' business and our world by offering customized commodity and green energy solutions. This was our organization's scream, in effect. I was fortunate at GreenEnergyCo to see the incredible results, like growing from negative income to $220 million a year, through the alignment of our leaders and workforce. These material results were a by-product of what we did well. We felt that we were pioneers in being the first to bring businesses the power to choose. With a monopoly utility provider you take what's offered. But we were different. We offered a choice to the business to procure and manage its energy, and to match how green—how environmentally friendly—its purchase was compared to its corporate goals. We had a solidifying strength of purpose in creating this change for companies.

For simplicity, I have combined the vision and mission. You can have a separate vision from a mission statement. If you do, the vision is the overarching summary of the mission, goals and values. Your vision will state why, how and what you intend to accomplish over a specific period of time.

The vision and mission must resonate with your heart and inspire your associates to want to contribute to your meaningful cause. The kind of alignment that produces optimal results requires diving into the right brain, intuitive, softer stuff. This is the solidifying sticky glue. It's the spirit of the organization. It's the responsibility that people will choose.

Recall the mission of Timberland, the outdoor gear company, which is to "equip people to do what they do best." It's not to make the most profitable, strongest, best footwear, for example. The point is, when you re-examine what your business does, there's likely to be some *meaningful* aspect to which your people want to contribute. Timberland's mission fulfills its employees' need to contribute to something with meaning. That's why it's ranked #31 in *The 50 Best Places to Work* by *Outside's* May 2010 survey of phenomenal companies.

In a successful business, company or organization, the leader's values and the business's mission must be aligned, also. Timberland's CEO, Jeffrey Swartz, describes the importance of this alignment in a family-owned business: "Families are also communities, and they are also organized around values and mission. When you come from a context of family—I'd come to work and my dad would be here—it forces the integration of personal values and mission into the workday. That's a powerful way to think about organizing the business."

If there's incongruence between the leadership's ideals and the business mission, it will become unfavorably transparent. My educated guess is that it will drag earnings.

THE WHAT

Your goals need to balance the possible with real stretch goals. If you set the bar too low and reach it, then what? Well, of course, celebrate the success, reward appropriately and raise the bar. But if the goals are perceived to be impossible, your people will see them as disingenuous and discouraging. Keep the goals few, simple and understandable. I typically see way too many goals listed to get any accomplished well. This is done out of the fear of leaving out something. But it will backfire.

My experience with goal setting from GreenEnergyCo's startup to our peak growth over ten years shows one thing is clear: focus on what's most important.

Also, focus on no more than three top-level goals. Expect what you inspect—that is, expect to see the results of what you inspect, or measure. Your return on investment, your ROI, is where you focus your lens, in other words, your time, energy and attention.

Setting the top three goals is as basic as:

> Goal 1: Pick the most important goal that distinguishes you and keeps you in business.
>
> Goal 2: Pick the second most important goal that keeps you in business.
>
> Goal 3: Pick the third most important goal that keeps you in business.

If you strive and achieve your top three goals, your business should be 80 percent along the way to success. Focus is foremost. Make space for succeeding at the most important objectives by letting go of some subordinate objectives. This will free up the resources that are distracted by the less important work. It's just as important to agree on what you will NOT do as what you will. You also must align each division and individual's goals to support the overall organizational goals. All the pieces should create the unified mosaic.

GreenEnergyCo's three top corporate goals were known as **RSVP**:

> R: Reputation: weighted 25%.
>
> SV: Strategic Value: weighted 25%. (Strategic value of the competitive changes we made in the marketplace and in the growth of our people.)
>
> P: Profitability: weighted 50%.

Our goals were intentionally prioritized in the RSVP order. Reputation came first, in order to provide clear guidance to our empowered employees in the field that no corners were to be cut in making a buck. Our reputation would distinguish us. Enron had begun damaging the image of commodity trading. We were different and could be trusted. Several general contractors were known to perform incomplete work. That would not be GreenEnergyCo. For example, the City of Phoenix had to trust and have confidence in us to hook up to our downtown district cooling system. Instead of upgrading or installing air conditioning in City buildings, they would need to rely on our system for thirty-plus years! Without cooling in the heat of Phoenix summers, work cannot continue.

We measured the success of our reputation through a defined process of surveying our customers.

We offered strategic value to our parent company through an advance preview of the competitive challenges to come in Arizona. This measure was more qualitative in nature. We secured our Board of Directors' approval of the action plans to support this goal. We developed our people in a fast-moving environment and exposed them to diverse learning opportunities in different states. We measured growth and development of our people in a variety of specified ways.

Our actions that supported the strategic value bore out as a true value to both our people and the parent company. In effect, this was an employee development program paid for through our profits and ultimately, many of these talented people were re-deployed into the sister utility company after the shutdown. Many have become stars after reintegrating into the utility because they had adapted to so many marketplaces and gained so much responsibility in GreenEnergyCo. Their contribution to the parent company provided a significant return at no added cost.

Obviously, you need money to succeed. Money comes from what you do really well. But it's not the driver. The profitability goal and its 50 percent weight acknowledged that profit is what funded our mission. It's key to paying salaries, and the level of profits affected our potential for offering incentive payments and bonuses. If the minimum level of profits weren't achieved, there'd be no incentive payouts. (I describe the payment philosophy below in the incentives section.)

It's important how you communicate "the what," the goals. Dr. Joy Schwertley, who had helped our leadership group understand our DISC/MI and values, also helped us understand effective communication. She explained that there are personal

and practical aspects to consider. In any communication, people need to feel as though they are:
- Treated with dignity and respect
- Listened to and understood
- Involved in a meaningful way
- Trusted and valued
- Supported

To set the stage for trusting relationships, communication needs to address both the personal needs above, as well as the practical needs, which are the company goals. When personal needs are met, the discussion will be more open, and you will garner more support for the goal. All people want to do well and feel good about themselves, to be asked their opinion and be involved in decision making. This also strengthens your people's belief that you value them. It encourages them to work with you to accomplish the goal.

It's also critical to align the individual's goals in his or her performance plan with the corporate goals. Even our data entry people knew which of the four RSVP goals their job meaningfully impacted. I set forth expectations I had of our employees to be active managers of their own career as well.

Here are the expectations I enumerated for our employees. I asked them questions, and in italics are my answers.

What do I expect from each of you? *Do your balanced best.*

What is "your balanced best"? *Use self discipline and time management to balance family, health and work.*

What else do I expect? *That you have a positive attitude, confront inconsistent actions, have enough trust to respectfully disagree, and have the highest personal and business ethics. This will create success for our customers and us.*

Who is responsible for your career? *I also expect that you take responsibility for your career. Understand your gifts; know where you fit. Feel safe and secure by knowing you are valued for your creation of talent and strategic knowledge. Believe in our track record of seizing opportunities as they come. Continue to satisfy our customers with the innovative solutions they want.*

Where do you fit? *Finally, understand your role and how you make a difference in achieving GreenEnergyCo's goals (RSVP).*

When you achieve your goals, celebrate your successes. Note that individuals differ in how they want to be recognized. Some dislike being in the limelight and prefer the leader to honor them in private. Tailor the reward to the individual whenever practical, for the most meaningful impact.

THE HOW

After you are clear on what's meaningful about why you are in business and for what, that is, your focused goals, you need to establish how you will "win." In other words, what values will guide how you execute your work. Much like the alignment required to be balanced in mind, body and spirit as an individual, alignment of the organization's mission and values is critical for success.

The values governing our work at GreenEnergyCo were the **Four "I's:" Integrity, Intensity, Intelligence and Impishness.**

- **Integrity:** Our word is our bond. We value our diversity and trustworthiness.

- **Intelligence:** Our thoughtful solutions must be insightful, and beneficial to our business and our customers.

- **Intensity:** Our work ethic and focus on our customers must be relentless.

- **Impishness:** Our behavior should reflect the joy of life and respect for others.

Integrity describes the way in which we would perform all our work and making sure it aligned with and supported the RSVP goal of Reputation. Intelligence is the value showing how we stressed thoughtful and insightful approaches to problems in creative ways that integrate "head and heart."

The Intensity of focused work was critical, given that we had very limited resources and stiff competition. Productivity was incredibly high and contributed to profitability.

And impishness meant that as hard as we worked, it was also important to have good-natured fun and gratitude for the simple joys in life. This was the balance for the intense work ethic.

We had many impish moments in the workplace that contributed to our sense of community. It was also a de-stressor, given how full our workdays often were. Many of our employees were very competitive with each other. A small woman was bragging to her larger male boss about eating one-and-a-half times the amount of food that most men eat. In disbelief, her boss wagered that he could eat one-and-a-half times as many hot dogs as she could. They got the two-foot-long hot dog called the Big Unit, named after Randy Johnson, the Diamondbacks' baseball pitcher. (The Diamondbacks baseball stadium was a couple of baseball tosses from our offices.) The loser had to pay for lunch and wear a full body hot dog costume for our Halloween party. The woman lost. She looked lovely as a five-foot-tall hot dog!

There was a sequel to that bet. The friendly "retaliation" for losing the hot dog eating contest was to fill the boss's convertible Camaro with three four-foot-tall bags of packing peanuts. When the boss opened his car door, packing peanuts flooded the parking garage in front of a grimacing maintenance worker. We quickly gathered the hiding onlookers into a cleanup team.

To give you another glimpse of our impish environment, I will relate the office furniture incident. The parent company's corporate support group advised me that to efficiently maintain office furniture, it must all be the same. Well, we didn't have thousands of people, so maintenance wasn't a significant cost, and I allowed individuality. There were some novel paint schemes and cubicle decorations. Some shopped for furniture on eBay to upgrade the desks they'd inherited. Two mid-level leaders who were in need of upgrades had, on numerous occasions, asked about better office furniture. Their direct leader was too preoccupied, so I purchased the furniture for them as a surprise.

On the afternoon that the furniture delivery was scheduled, I called a meeting with them so their team members could secretly set up the items. They removed their leaders' old furniture. But the new furniture was late. I couldn't detain the leaders any longer. The team improvised by placing a box for a table and a conference room chair in their offices. When the two mid-level leaders left my office and entered theirs, their faces turned red. They thought it was a bad joke at first. Within an hour, the new furniture arrived and the mix-up made the eventual surprise even sweeter.

DEFINING AND ALIGNING INDIVIDUAL ROLES AND BOUNDARIES

A most important and difficult part of establishing individual roles is to define clear, empowering boundaries that don't overlap with other people's responsibilities. Empowering boundaries are ones that have the proper relationship between freedom and restriction. Because all work places are different, I will use a parenting analogy for boundary setting.

Would you allow a three-year-old to cross the street alone? How about a thirteen-year-old? What would happen if you didn't say anything to your teen when she came home an hour later than curfew three times in a row? In my experience, if you allow your child to come home late one or two times without a consistently enforced consequence, you have lost your credibility. The boundaries are breached.

When my kids fought in the backseat of the car, it only took two times for them to get the clear message. If they didn't stop after the first warning, both would have to get out of the car and walk. I drove around the block—within a safe range—before picking them up again. After that, if a friend started acting up in the backseat they would say, "Stop, or my mom will make you get out and walk."

Another analogy for boundaries is to visualize canyon walls. If they are too narrow, you can only advance as fast as the horse in front of you. If they are too wide, there can be chaos with horses running in circles or running over each other. Because GreenEnergyCo was proceeding into uncharted territory, strong, independent, stallion-like leaders were on my team. They earned their freedom by respecting high and exacting standards. Once they proved themselves, they were free to gallop within the canyon walls.

As I learned from an American Management Association course, if roles and responsibilities overlap, someone might be making a mess in your sandbox! The sandbox is bound by four boundaries: External, Systems, People and Processes. The External side represents the rules outside the organization or company, those bounded by society's laws, ethics and morals. The Systems side is bound by company policies and procedures, such as signing authority for contract values. The People side is bound by job descriptions and performance standards. The Processes side is bound by company budget and plans. As long as decisions are made within these confines, there's freedom to do your job in whatever manner works best for you.

While empowerment requires freedom, we had monthly measurements to alert us if we ventured off course. As the leader in charge, I would abdicate my fiduciary responsibilities to our shareholders and the board if I granted unfettered freedom. We created an instrument panel—our dashboard—to illuminate ahead of time if we were on the path to achieve our RSVP goals by year-end. We determined which leading indicators best predicted profitability.

For sales, predictive indicators were the number of bids we were winning, or qualified sales leads we had in the queue. For our asset-based business, preventative plant maintenance was an indicator of whether we might experience a premature outage that would cost us profits. The measurements allowed us to take corrective action if we were not on course. The dashboard measured the indicators monthly and the RSVP goals quarterly with a simple green, yellow, red system. We focused on the goals in the red zone. With this tool, I could see where my leaders were flying from "ground control." By adhering to the measurements, in effect, my leaders gained their freedom flight.

Leaders also need to take care that they don't create overlap and a collision course for their people. As a former strategic planning leader for the parent company, I was responsible for coordinating our five-year business plan. Whenever there was more than one vice-president or leader listed as responsible for a project, inevitably there were problems. To be most productive, authority, accountability and responsibility should be all housed within one leader's "sandbox."

Don't misunderstand—there are always other areas supplying you with goods and services on which you can rely. I'm distinguishing when it's not clear who's ultimately responsible for the end goal. When two high-level leaders are responsible for one end goal, you have confusion. If you "borrow" people who are reviewed by and report to someone else, it can conflict with and be difficult for them to give priority to your assignment.

As a leader, if you can be the consummate presence who sets clear goals, expects high standards and establishes non-overlapping boundaries, you can establish an environment for optimal productivity.

INCENTIVES OR DISINCENTIVES?

Part of my job as president of GreenEnergyCo was to design incentive plans. This is key to aligning rewards with desired actions. You really can design incentives effectively to encourage and reward your employees for extraordinary results. However, incentive designs can be full of pitfalls as well as promise. What I learned in a nutshell is that an incentive goal cannot be too heavily weighted in favor of a single individual because it can incite that person to become a renegade.

Sales incentive design could be the subject of a separate book, frankly. Everyone figures out how they are paid—just like kids readily understand allowance and cell phone payment plans. When motivated, anyone can "game" a plan and it can lead to perverse results. The incentive can fuel a personal agenda. That's how incentives became disincentives, in some cases, for achieving GreenEnergyCo's corporate objectives and can become disincentives in any organization.

In one case, a salesman succeeded in making a multi-year contract with a large institutional customer. Contract people, pricing, customer service and construction supported him. There was a "debate" about the percent of the incentive that was his personally. However, the sale would not have been made without the team, so with the intervention of management discretion, an agreed appropriate split was mutually decided. Consequently, the team was there to support yet another deal.

Governing boards or leaders should retain discretion when making incentive payments. Circumstances always change a year later when payments are to be made. In the rare instances that there are windfalls or unintended consequences, discretion may need to prevail. This must be balanced with ensuring that you honor your promises to make payments if specified results are achieved. It's just that not every circumstance can be contemplated or described in a simple plan a year in advance. In this litigious society, the discretional language may prove helpful, although honesty and doing the right thing should prevail. (As a skilled former contracts attorney, I will be the first to tell you that a contract is only as good as the morality and integrity of the person signing it. I don't care how skillfully it's drafted. It may help in the rare case you can afford an expensive litigation, is all.) We experienced some challenges to our plan and ultimately worked out the different interpretations.

Our most effective incentive design plan was based on the achievement of one-third corporate earnings; one-third employee business line goals; and one-third individual goals. Nothing was paid out until both our parent company's and GreenEnergyCo's minimum profitability levels were attained. The profitability above the threshold earnings level funded the stretch payout and we shared our success with our employees. The first one-third of the incentive award opportunity was paid on the overall corporate profitability level achieved above the threshold RSVP goals; the next one-third was based on the employee's business line reaching threshold goals and increased up to a percentage based on the level of stretch goals attained; and the final one-third was based on the specific individual goals achieved. For example, a leader's incentive might be a threshold of $20,000 up to $60,000 maximum payout. GreenEnergyCo's threshold earnings goal might be $10 million. If we made $12 million, the extra $2 million would fund incentives. Let's say $12 million was the maximum corporate payout earnings level, so the leader was awarded the first $20,000. If the leader's business line made its goals, another $20,000 would be warranted. However, there might have been some individual development or stretch goals that were or were not achieved. Based upon the results, the last $20,000 or a portion thereof would be paid. It is important to have a floor and ceiling level for extraordinary personal performance. I have experienced uncapped plans and care needs to be exercised in establishing such a plan. You can always do the "right thing" as a leader in awarding more if unanticipated superb results occur above the stated cap.

Organization or company plans all differ. The industry may set competitive benchmarks for your incentive level to compete for talent. Some of our competitors had high base salaries and lower incentive payments and visa versa. Merit increases were handled differently. Each employee's performance was compared to every other employee. Our top leadership ranked each employee as an A, B or C to determine the level of merit pay. We calibrated these rankings collectively for consistency in grading. (I discuss this process in more detail later in this chaper.)

Disincentives can sometimes dwarf the effect of incentives. Maybe you, like I have in the past, cringe when you hear the corporate-speak, "walk the talk." But overused as the saying is, employees really do observe your actions and compare them to what you say. It will backfire if you, as a leader, don't follow your own mantra. If you don't endorse and aren't willing to champion the idea, don't do it. Just like when a parent says, do what I say, not as I do, the kids observe the parent's actions. When a leader sets lofty goals and then doesn't adhere to them, everyone sees the emperor without his clothes.

For example, when you are challenged to excel, only to learn that those with mediocre performance are rewarded equally, this is a real performance de-motivator. This is more de-motivating than not getting acknowledged in any fashion, monetary or otherwise, when you excel. However, at GreenEnergyCo, it was our clear policy that those who did excel were rewarded accordingly.

Many times, the best "incentive" for exceptional performance is to immediately acknowledge a job well done. A thoughtful, specific compliment or hand-written note is as effective as some incentive plans! I experienced great success in customizing rewards for my leaders in cases where I had discretion. For example, my controller did a stellar job during some difficult budget planning. He was getting married and outside any formal incentive plan, we paid for a very nice honeymoon to Bora Bora. I tried to determine what each employee valued and the best way was often to just ask. A frequent response was flexibility, such as in their daily work schedule.

FLEXIBILITY IN THE WORKPLACE TO ALIGN WITH INDIVIDUAL PREFERENCES

To the extent business objectives are not compromised, providing flexibility in the workplace is a top incentive. Individuals vary considerably in their most productive manner of working. Trusting your team to manage their own hours—for example, to allow them to come into the office after their child's school performance at 10 a.m. and stay until 8 p.m.—may not seem like the best way to get the most productivity out of your people, but I saw it create a willingness to overachieve! Some people work better from 6 a.m. to 10 a.m., others from 10 a.m. to 2 p.m. and some from 2 p.m. to 6 p.m. We recognized this and accommodated it. Many other successful companies apparently do the same.

LiveStrong was ranked #32 in *The 50 Best Places To Work* survey conducted by *Outside*, and reported in the May, 2010 issue. LiveStrong's management believes in flexible hours and allows employees to take unlimited paid time off with the understanding that they won't abuse the privilege. "This is a results-oriented workplace," says Mona Patel, the executive VP of people and organizational development at LiveStrong. Mona reports, "Nobody has abused the privilege." Many of the top 50 companies let workers take off time for family or to make "fresh tracks in the snow." I agree wholeheartedly that it keeps workers energized.

My key leader, Roberto, who, through his team delivered more than $100 million in revenues per year, valued tradition and family foremost. I mentioned earlier that he longed to be near them in Minnesota. GreenEnergyCo management trusted him to commute one week a month to Phoenix and work the other three weeks from his Minnesota office. Because my expertise in the commodity electricity arena could back him, and I was willing to do so when needed, it worked wonderfully. His team was exceptionally productive. Productivity was our focus rather than the hours they worked or where they were located.

Telecommuting was common at GreenEnergyCo because the resources in our office were not essential to performing the work. But communication is central because you must make the expectations known; no matter what hours and where your employees work! If the expectation is $100 million a year in sales, let them know it. If the expectation is that they show up in the office at 9:00 every morning, so be it.

BEST-FIT HIRING, PLACEMENT AND RETENTION

Great workplaces align hiring and firing with the organization's mission and goals and send clear messages to the workforce and the community about exactly who the company is and what the company stands for. Clear messages to your employees raise productivity while mixed messages dilute it. Picture rowing teams. The ones that win inevitably are those that row in alignment, not the ones with several stronger members who are out of synch with the rest of the team.

We have already explored how mis-fits become best-fits through the use of assessment tools and intuition to become self-aware of natural strengths and talents, and then by aligning their strengths with their work. These tools also help you better place and retain your current employees and build teams. They can be used to hire and retain new employees more optimally.

Certainly, finance and computer systems are critical to your company's performance, but don't underestimate the importance of hiring the best-fit people the first time around. Hiring mis-fits is costly to the company's finances and to morale. Because we largely avoided hiring future mis-fits, we reduced turnover costs. Also, with best-fit employees, team productivity improved. Our experience, backed by a variety of studies, demonstrated that the cost of not hiring non-performers saved multiples of times the cost of hiring a new employee.

Our uses of the DISC/MI for self-awareness and team placement among existing leaders and team members didn't require scientific test validation to comport with Federal anti-discrimination laws. However, when we used the CVI as a pre-employment test to hire sales candidates, we had to first show that what it measured statistically actually predicted successful performance in the specific sales position functions. We also tested it internally to determine the optimal characteristics for the position.

We created a Top Performer Profile. All of my leaders took the CVI assessment as if they were the candidate. Because the actual candidates took the same CVI, we could compare their answers to our ideal before we met them. So when I interviewed a candidate I felt as though I could "see into the interviewee's soul." The assessment showed if he or she matched the "sweet spot." Based on their responses to the CVI, we teed up key questions to ask the candidates. Through their responses, we could assess if they knew themselves and could identify traits that didn't serve them well. Those who were more self-aware were more ideal candidates because they'd taken personal measures to identify and "plug the holes."

For example, the lead salesman Top Performer Profile yielded target characteristics of a high Merchant on the CVI. To put it simply, one of the weaknesses typical of a Merchant can be a lack of organizational skills. One interviewee brought in a loose-leaf notebook with papers falling out and a calendar consisting of scribbled dates—in this day and age! Another had a Blackberry to organize himself. While this one characteristic could not determine their eventual success, knowing the attributes to seek overall helped us select salespeople who would likely be the most successful.

So while I trusted my gut in hiring, I also found that using pre-validated assessments is worth it in filling key profit-producing positions like sales. Identifying the most important characteristics of the position may be just as beneficial in many cases. The added cost of validating the tool ahead of time was worthwhile only in specific instances. Don't underestimate your intuition in hiring though. If something doesn't feel right, listen to that inner leader—as long as it's not based upon a bias, belief or non-objective perception. Hiring best-fits includes identifying the traits that fit into the work environment and culture, too.

ACCOMMODATE FOUR GENERATIONS, FOUR PERSPECTIVES

Our leaders and employees ranged in age from the twenties to the sixties. It's very possible that your workplace consists of four generations of workers, too. You also have your own organizational or corporate culture. Do you effectively and optimally assimilate and accommodate all generations? Are you aware of when your perceptions from your generational perspective color your communications with other generations? We will go into greater depth on how perceptions can distort otherwise neutral situations in Chapter 7. As you may have observed, each generation views the world very differently.

It can feel like four different cultures are working for you: the silent generation (born between 1930 and 1945, with about 63 million still in the workforce); baby boomers (born between 1946 and 1964, with about 78 million in the workforce); generation Xers (born between 1965 and 1976, with about 48 million in the workforce) and generation Yers or Millennials (born between 1977 and 1990, with about 80 million in the workforce).

You can see the gap in workforce members with Xers numbering about 40% of baby boomers. The boomers are retiring at a rate of thousands per day. Thus, the Millennials are gaining in size and influence in our workplaces. Understanding them will be critical to hiring best-fits and optimizing productivity.

When you think about it, each generation's members were reared in a different historic and economic context and were raised with a different general parenting style. Consequently, each generation has different personal work ethics, values and expectations from their leaders or employers. Still, the best can be brought out in each generation to the benefit of all.

Differences in comfort levels with digital technology also contribute to the somewhat cavernous generation gaps. People who are in my baby boomer age group, for example, learned computer technology later in life and many are amateurs compared to people who are under thirty. I remember about twelve years ago when a twenty-year-old was building our first website and asked me to demo it. I didn't know how to navigate and he said, "Well you just click on our logo, which is the home button, Ms. Sandler."

Then there's my godchild who picked up a Nintendo controller for the first time at age four and beat me at the simple Mario Kart video game. On the other end of the spectrum is my kids' seventy-eight-year-old grandparent who can only turn on a computer and send basic emails, while the eighty-year-old one can run circles around me. She plays online games, makes computer-generated cards, etc. So it really varies.

While not being that interested in technology, I personally want the results you can get from it. I decided to go where many of the Millennials are heading in the world. With a push from my adult children, I got an iPhone and MAC computer, not because I innately value gadgets or computers, but because I desire to communicate with my kids and our world. No matter which generation to which you belong, whether you've kept up with technology or not, is often a product of your values, drivers and interests.

Look at the dramatically different way younger generations communicate with each other: they text, twitter and use Facebook messages. Nowadays, I make sure I ask what a person's preferred communication style is, and it's surprising how many parents and business leaders are great texters because they want to stay in contact with their teens.

Relationship status is expressed differently by different generations. I remember, if you were female, angora string wrapped around a promise ring in high school meant you were "going steady." Or you would wear your sweetheart's varsity sports "letter sweater." In college, you might wear your fraternity boyfriend's pin. Now you only have to look at the self-declared Facebook status to know whether someone is in an exclusive relationship or single. You know the breakup is official when their relationship status has changed!

Work ethics differ between the groups, too. If we just look at history and what was happening during each generation's youth, there are telling generalizations. At GreenEnergyCo I reported to officers and a board largely made up of the silent generation or older baby boomers. Twenty-eight years ago there was an unwritten cultural rule, but an obvious one, that loyalty was expected. It makes sense that the silent generation would respect hierarchy in the utility industry, given that several leaders served in the military where they'd learned loyalty and obedience.

Most of my leaders were very conservative and fiscally responsible personally and professionally. I also heard my own parents from this generation describe what it was like for their parents and for them as kids to survive the Great Depression and the impact it made on them. As early as age five, when I went grocery shopping with my dad, I could see how the fiscal lessons he learned affected the way he spent money. He taught me his belief that a generic brand is a better value and to read the labels showing the cost in cents per pound or unit! I look back at my boomer generation, and while I was twelve in 1968, the social revolution was a part of my life. John F. Kennedy's and Martin Luther King's deaths (1963 and 1968 respectively) made lasting impressions about the risk of and need for change. I remember crawling under my desk in grade school to prepare for a Cold War air raid. My male friends were deciding if they would move to Canada and avoid the draft (if it were still in effect when they became age eligible) because they did not believe in the Vietnam War. No longer was hierarchy something to be followed without questioning. But the American Dream was still a promise that if I played my cards right, worked hard, built up a resumé, grew up to be a lawyer and such... .

Many in my generation have been accused of being ambitious, materialistic and greedy. Many like challenging assignments and are considered workaholics. While stereotypes are stereotypes, I actually do see peers who fit this description. While there's an expression that baby boomers live to work while Millennials work to live, I see this changing some. But only a few years ago I witnessed boomer leaders making judgments about their millennial employees. They accused them of having a weak work ethic or an unwillingness to work long hours and pay the same dues those boomers did to climb the corporate ladder.

Communication differences that aren't recognized and valued without judgment by members of different generations can create unproductive results. When in opposition of a proposal, the silent generation might hold their tongues, boomers might openly disagree and Millennials might respond "whatever." Of course, judgments can be due to diverse cultural perspectives and many other situations, not just generational differences. What is important is to pay attention to when you are being judgmental, whether it comes from your age or life circumstances.

The generations Xers were right behind me in the workplace. I noticed that when their kid was sick the dad might stay home instead of the working mom. Watergate happened in their era, which left a bad taste about the honesty of politicians. Statistics show that many of them come from dual-income or single-parent homes. Somewhat like my situation, many grew up taking care of themselves at an early age, which created high independence among many of them. Perhaps that's why the generation Xers seemed less willing to wait their turn to lead. (GreenEnergyCo had a very flat organization, so I gave them chances to at least lead projects when no formal leadership positions were open.)

I have observed that my children, Millennials, are accustomed to working in teams with shared rewards. While these traits of wanting to be respected and involved are shared by all generations, Millennials seem to want to be respected and involved to a greater degree. I've recruited youths this age to serve in a non-profit capacity such as representatives on YMCA boards. At least in these particular instances, they want to take part in determining what their YMCA facility does, the programs it offers and assist in fundraising.

Perhaps this involvement is a result of being the center of their parents' lives? If you are a baby boomer parent, how many soccer games and band performances did you attend, or similar kid events, like my husband and I did? I see many of the Millennials wanting to make a difference and turn around what's "wrong" with the world. I frankly have not observed that body art, tattoos and piercings correlate negatively with work ethics (although I did have to coach our Millennial-aged receptionist to not wear flip-flops or bare midriffs on casual Fridays).

Flexibility in how Millennials want do their work is a requirement in today's workplace! The young people I'm familiar with from work and the young adult children of my friends want a work-life balance and don't want to miss their children's lives when they have them. In pre-hiring interviews, young interviewees often displayed a keen interest in whether GreenEnergyCo had flexible work hours, child care facilities, a gym (or a paid membership to one), comprehensive health care coverage, a balance of work and personal life, social responsibility and meaningful work. In pre-recessionary hirings, GreenEnergyCo competed for talent on this basis. Millennials looking for work now may be less choosy, but the top performers are still as discriminating. I know my daughter was impressed by many of these attributes that her new employer, Boon, Inc., created in their workplace, that I described in Chapter 2.

When you consider it, many of the Millennials experienced their parents being down-sized or forced to retire early. So it's not surprising that there was plenty of discussion about how GreenEnergyCo would help them build skills during hiring interviews. I always advised all my employees to focus on development. This ultimately is their protection against an employer laying them off and even if they are, it gives them an advantage in being rehired.

The degree to which some young interviewees asked about what GreenEnergyCo could do for them, not what they could contribute to our mission and goals was almost presumptuous!

We addressed many of the younger generations' values because of our rallying mission to bring choice in how businesses procured their energy; how much of it was green energy; and by pioneering new marketplaces and rules. We were making it up as we went along which allowed fertile ground for creativity. We worked on some fascinating renewables projects that helped our customers and our environment. We recognized the need for contributing to our communities and shared in it through corporate volunteering days, like when we helped renovate the Salvation Army's transitional housing, offered flexibility in our work environment and discounted health club memberships. We worked intensely while at work, punctuated by an occasional playful moment. I encouraged the workers to do their "balanced best" and to not be workaholics.

I see work-life balance in a corporate culture as advantageous to young and old, perhaps for very different reasons. Be creative in using workers from all four generations. I know of seasoned workers who desire to work part-time or desire flextime rather than being fully retired. We hired some semi-retired experts cost-effectively on a project basis to coach and train our younger workers. Some of my acquaintances who retired early have become very depressed; although clearly it varies according to their outside interests and financial circumstances. If you offer flexibility in work schedules, the silent generation or boomers can enjoy the vacations and downtime they have earned, while still contributing meaningfully to your workforce.

Catering to the work-life balance needs of workers is central to treating the employee as a whole person. It fosters the integration of mind, body and spirit that is essential to employees living their scream. To the extent this promotes a healthier, less stressed individual, you will experience greater productivity and reduced health care costs. Despite our very hectic, full workdays, I encouraged people to take time off and not work weekends—to re-energize. Or to go sit in the massage chair during a stressful day. Or join our lunch hour meditation session. Or work out at lunch with me. When you work smarter, not harder, and focus on work-life balance as a priority, it doesn't mean less work gets accomplished.

Inspired people need inspired surroundings as well as a proper work-life balance to succeed! For example, Timberland allows forty hours of volunteer time a year. The company rates its apparel according to a green (eco-friendly) index. Also among *Outside's* greatest places to work survey are many dog-friendly offices, and organizations that offer telecommuting, flex-time and unique celebrations. These companies also focus on adopting honest strategies for environmental responsibility, whether the emphasis is on energy use in their own buildings, their supply chain or what goes into their products.

There are many other perks that can attract different groups and show that your company cares. I find the following perks particularly interesting: besides providing employee gyms, some of the organizations in *Outside's* survey fund wellness programs, offer ski pass reimbursements and race entry fees, and build cyclo-cross tracks. Eddie Bauer took its company back to its roots by training and funding an ascent team that climbed to the summit of Mount Everest. Clif Bar & Company offers personal training, massages, nutritional counseling, a spring-loaded wooden yoga floor, thirty-two other classes and two-and-one-half hours of paid workout time per week. If you have flexibility to tailor benefits such as these, it can be a big advantage in attracting workers from different age groups. Moreover, it supports the company value placed on the health and wellness of their greatest asset—their employees. A cafeteria-style plan can appeal to all generations. Older generations may be more interested in assisted living care whereas the younger generations find daycare assistance more appealing. The younger workers may opt for a medical plan with a high deductible because of their good health. Longer vacation time, job-sharing opportunities, training and development appeal to all the generations though for different reasons. As I mentioned, with training and development, the older generations want to keep up with the younger generations while the younger generations are looking for ways to develop personally and professionally.

What is important about four generations is that all four perspectives can be valuable to creating the optimal organization. However, if your organization's core culture has a strong bias against any particular generation, you may not attract the talent you need. Examine and explore your core—your culture—in effect, to determine if any perceptions or biases are preventing you from creating the optimal organization.

ALIGNED ACTION

Earlier, I gave examples of where GreenEnergyCo was screaming with success. As it became more obvious that the parent company (our sole shareholder) was embarking on a "back to core utility" strategy, I knew it was imperative that we increase earnings contributions, which were falling off in the commodity business. A key market in California had changed and it became riskier to profit there. We needed new sources of revenue. We began all-day intensive strategic planning sessions. The goal was to leave with a common view of a company vision that best served our customers and shareholder, and that each leader would agree to back. We were going to continue our planning sessions until we agreed to agree to something.

Agreement is aligned action. I learned to secure buy-in, and it was best done through asking questions that resulted in mutual sharing and discovery. Command and control leadership would not have worked. It pushes and uses persuasion. Advice-giving assumes the leader knows all the answers—and I certainly didn't. I needed the best creativity from each of my leaders. Aligned action pulls: it assumes the team can find the answers. By asking open-ended questions, my intent was to have everyone relate to a higher purpose, to connect you and me, to honor and listen—not to let the ego rule. When we, as leaders, are inclusive and appreciative, share and connect all with a sense of wonder, we can create an environment of innovation.

I asked my team leaders:

- What would we love to create for our company?
- What does success look like together?
- Describe what your area will be doing and look like five years from now.

We would re-convene our strategic planning with answers that we could all share and discuss to find common ground. We set Rules of Engagement for our next session, such as we were to confront one another's behavior if a comment were based in persuasion and ego, not in sharing and discovering. We had already learned that the human pattern of conversation is to first feel, and then have thoughts, just as Dr. Joe Dispenza explains. These feelings and thoughts then congeal as beliefs (we will discuss this more in Chapter 7) and finally result in conclusions. As a team's feelings and thoughts solidify into consensus and direction, it leads to action.

Some of the five-year scenarios that we produced for our three main business lines were visionary. They were also full of specific information and hypothetical financial *pro formas*. We were setting our intent to create our future. We actually got part way there before the parent company shut down the commodity business line and then sold off the district cooling business.

Fortunately, the energy efficiency and renewables business line remains and is growing.

NON-ALIGNMENT IN AND AMONG TEAMS

I've focused on many of the exceptional things that worked at GreenEnergyCo with the hope that some of these ideas will work for you in your business or organization. Not everything was perfect there, of course. We had our growing pains. We painfully, yet gratefully, learned that despite meeting RSVP goals, if a particular leader possesses core values that are fundamentally incongruent with the organization, that leader no longer fit. And allowing that leader to stay could do more damage than good.

Two years prior to closing, along with our strategic planning, I instituted an initiative of "One Company, One Vision." The leader of one business line was acting so autonomously that it was causing a separation in how we brought the best energy solution to our customers. That stallion was running wild and too free. There was also a question of integrity. This leader used deception to make it look like the canyon walls were being honored.

I couldn't put my finger on it at first. Two business lines' employees were at odds. It was critical that we share a common vision and pull together to increase earnings.

I decided to gather a baseline on what was and wasn't working. Also, interviewing employees in a non-threatening manner might reveal the source of the disharmony. This may be impractical if you have thousands. I spoke to about 100 people, including the night shift. (If you don't have time to interview everyone involved, you could interview a sampling of leaders and groups.) The goal was to look for recurring themes or issues in the information disclosed. I ensured everyone that all communications were confidential and that it was in their best interest to help our company.

I asked everyone the same five simple questions:
1. What do you like to do best?
2. What do you do well?

3. What does the company do best?
4. What can we do better?
5. Do you have any advice for me as the leader?

Generally, people like to be asked to give their opinion. By asking open-ended questions, the information may be more forthcoming. That is, unless they fear retribution from the discordant leader. Common themes emerged, even though many people were careful about what they said. The most problematic theme was fear, a lack of trust in the renegade leader, and a perception that his team had been "brainwashed."

I wanted to make sure this was the main issue impairing our ability to act as "one company." I infrequently and selectively used consultants, but this was a tough nut to crack. Also, I wanted to be neutral with my leaders and I wanted to discover if I was doing something that contributed to the problem. I hired an organizational and development expert facilitator, Sandy Kolberg, Ph.D.

I read the *Five Dysfunctions of a Team* at her suggestion. This book identified common problem areas in organizations and the corresponding signs or signals of dysfunction:

- **Inattention to results.** *Status and ego (personal results are put above needs of the team) building walls and empires.*

- **Avoidance of accountability.** *Low standards (lack of high standards of performance without confronting it) or high standards that are allowed to be ignored.*

- **Making and keeping commitments.** *Ambiguity (people are hiding out and not seeking clarity of goals and tasks).*

- **Fear of conflict.** *Artificial harmony (conflicts always taken off-line so things look nice).*

- **Absence of trust.** *Invulnerability (people are not willing to be vulnerable or show their true selves).*

In contrast to these dysfunctions of a team, a fully functioning one produces results, takes total accountability and commitment, has open discussion and constructive conflict, and has trust. The group's success takes precedence over the individual ego. The team works to the highest accountability. Goals are clear without hidden agendas. There's passion but respect in dealing with conflict. People are willing to be vulnerable, to seek and search for help.

After examining the problems with our leadership team facilitated by Dr. Kolberg, assimilating the information from my employees, and listening to my gut, I confirmed that we did not pull together as one company primarily due to an absence of trust by my leaders in the one problematic leader.

The true profitability on certain jobs had been cleverly obfuscated for a few years and despite a multitude of accountants, the truth was not revealed. Without expensive forensic accounting, it would be difficult to prove. Nonetheless, I knew I had to take corrective action.

I confronted him and asked that he work with an executive coach. He pretended to agree. The deceptive pattern of behavior continued, as validated by the coach. After several chances with no appreciable change, I asked him to leave. He was in disbelief that I would stand up to "HIM."

He had "brainwashed" his team by planting notions that the parent company was going to abandon this line of business. (This was not and is not the case with the energy efficiency business line). When he left, he convinced several employees to go with him. The departure of several key people within a few weeks was very disruptive. If they valued his leadership style, however, I was supportive of their leaving our culture. They did not share our company's values or scream.

This experience also taught me the importance of non-compete covenants, which we did not have in many instances. While courts don't like these covenants because they restrict an employee's movement and ability to gain new work, if compensation accompanies this restriction it can be enforced. Probably six months worth of a non-compete would work in our business because information becomes stale. This would have allowed for a smoother transition when he and several employees left. We did have an employee code of conduct that was violated, but legal recourse based on this alone would be costly and time consuming.

There's a very fine balance between "being right" and pursuing that claim or other business claims legally. On the one hand, much like your kids' curfew, if you don't enforce consequences, it sends a message to the marketplace that employees can take advantage of your company or organization and get away with it. This can cost you in the long run. On the other hand, we had a leader pursue a claim against a contractor who was clearly responsible, and yet when the legal fees consumed one-third of the potential award amount prior to the trial beginning, it's time to settle! Judges and juries are hard to predict. Two businesses in litigation often don't create an emotional swing for either side. There are usually mistakes (at least in perception of who is right and wrong) on both entities' parts that are revealed in a trial, thereby making it risky to litigate. Not only that, but depositions, document retrieval and case preparation are a huge drain on managements' time and this must be weighed in.

The episode of involuntarily separating with my former leader undulated into an unsettling fear for those who remained in his business line and for the other two business lines. It was the fear of change and uncertainty. Calm communication was essential at this point to allay the distress. I set up weekly brown bag lunches for employees to ask me their burning questions. I initially explained to all of the employees that we were co-creators of our business strategy and we would rebuild the group that remained in a manner that best utilized our strengths. (And in fact, the energy efficiency group remains today!) Each of us could rely on our resourcefulness as individuals.

I told them that opportunities could come in the form of surprises. Much like surprise parties can throw you off schedule, there can be gifts in the surprise. New ideas can be developed, and their ideas could help create our success. At transitional times such as these, fears should be expressed but it's important not to dwell on this negative emotion. What's the biggest fear? The fear of failure. Our antidote was to rally. Together, we would create a new direction.

We revisited our five-year strategic plans and decided to invest more in green energy solutions. We developed one of the early carbon footprint models for our customers. We demonstrated to our customers how they helped the environment so they could communicate to decision makers, for example, how many cars they would take off the road in the form of reduced emissions. Our green and energy efficiency sales increased.

While this transition was messy, we did not view it so much as a mistake as we did an outcome. The renegade leader's departure solidified our leadership. Now that the thorn was out of our foot, the trust level increased among the rest of us. The crisis actually brought an unparalleled level of leadership unity. We had new opportunities to again align our talent and optimize our resources by doing more with the best. New positions and open spots emerged so that our remaining employees could gain new work experiences. I urged everyone to be self-inspired. This was a cataclysmic learning moment.

There are some people in most organizations who are not committed to the mission and values, and all the employees know it. Terminating them can be cathartic to the whole organization. Don't wait too long! Free them to be a best-fit where their values match the new organization. Understand that this is not the same thing as having everyone think the same way or be "yes men." Healthy disagreement and exchange of different ideas is essential and should not be discouraged if you desire to create the optimal team.

We had an earlier instance of non-alignment with a leader in the commodity business line that had less dramatic results. We discovered moral infractions between a male leader and his female employee. We confronted them separately about the conduct and neither one was forthright. Ultimately, both were terminated. Again, it presented an opportunity to promote and re-align others. It sent a clear message to our workforce that our values would be honored.

Immediately after the terminations, as you can expect, employee morale in the commodity business line sank. Rumors, politics and negativity pervaded for a while. Management attempted to restore our four values in the workplace: the Four I's (Integrity, Intensity, Intelligence and Impishness). We attempted various initiatives to rebuild teamwork, inspiration and the positive energy that previously prevailed. But without success. Management realized that the front line—self-named "the empowered employees"—should develop the plan to restore the Four I's. The empowered employees established the ground rules for the initiative, called "The I's Have It." The rules included the goal of rebuilding teamwork, how to measure success, establishing the budget, and how to make it fun and not distract unnecessarily from daily work. The empowered group desired to restore trust and close the chasm that had developed between them and management. They also secured management buy-in on their work plan.

The I's Have It succeeded in bringing all the people of the commodity group together to see how working collectively and cooperatively toward a common goal could help us achieve more as a company. The motto of the group was that the ability to direct individual accomplishments to meet organizational objectives is the fuel that allows common people to attain uncommon results.

MERIT REVIEW AND SELF-SELECTION IN OR OUT, USUALLY

In GreenEnergyCo, part of our continuous feedback was an annual merit review. As in most companies, the review is necessary to fulfill corporate requirements to offer merit increases. If an increase were warranted during the year, we would implement the reward outside the annual process, however. To ensure consistency and fairness in ranking individual performance annually, all leaders met and we calibrated our ratings. Some leaders were more lenient or used different criteria so we discussed our reasoning together.

We kept it simple and made columns on the white board for an A, B and C group. We did not address the Bs, but focused on what made a performer a "star" (A) and what qualified as underperforming (C). The leaders explained why the named individuals were an A or a C.

The Cs typically would not be a C in another six months. We believed in giving everyone who didn't measure up a chance to improve and stay. Those who didn't meet improvement expectations usually chose to leave. Because of the respectful feedback we gave them, they were often prepared to separate. Voluntary separation, rather than firing, boosted everyone's productivity. It respected the individual who could then take ownership about moving to a better fit. At first this may not sound compassionate, yet that's exactly what it was. If you continued to perform at a C level, you likely were not living your scream and should move on.

The real injustice would be for mis-fit individuals to not learn why they weren't performing up to the company's expectations. We worked with these individuals to self-discover their scream, but not everyone chose to do so. Among the most difficult employees are those who live in their own reality, meaning, if you asked ten people what the situation is, only this person would have a different view. Sometimes we would encourage them to find another job prior to requiring them to leave. We allowed them to bid on other jobs throughout the enterprise. They deserved to find the place where they would be a best-fit.

For the company to excel, we knew we needed a disproportionate number of As, that is, exceptional contributors. Our company was very lean, so if someone did not carry their load we all felt it. The C individual typically knew this and decided to move on without our initiating any action.

As I mentioned earlier, in our ten years, there were a few involuntary separations. But this was the exception. With my legal background I was very familiar with the drain on energy to contend with firing documentation, depositions and equity hearings. Voluntary separation was far better for everyone's morale. Previously, as the attorney for the utility, I spent a year in the employment arena handling equity disputes for management. I quickly saw that disgruntled, litigious, fired employees typically knew exactly why they were let go, but they sued on principle—because they were treated with disrespect. This wastes so much time and money. Avoid it.

If you have to fire someone—after reasonable attempts to coach him—look the employee in the eye and explain why he's not performing his job successfully. Don't go behind his back, surprise him or publically announce the separation without first having a face-to-face, heart-to-heart meeting. Unless, that is, you have time and money to burn on a lawsuit. Give them a warning and a measurable benchmark that must be achieved to keep the job. Then if they don't reach it, they, in effect, fired themselves.

Funny—I've seen a subconscious desire in some individuals to get fired. They know they don't want to be there but are afraid to make a change. Their subconscious guides them when they're not living their scream, but they don't always realize it. In 1925, Florence Scovel Shinn, quoting another metaphysician, summed it up, "'If you do not run your subconscious mind yourself, someone else will run it for you.'"

Once you are aware of your subconscious, intuitive calling, you can consciously act in alignment with it. When aware, you won't be surprised by firings, nor will you be fired, because you'll have moved into a position aligned with who you are.

THE FLIP SIDE OF THE SAME COIN—CHANGE 10 PERCENT TO GAIN 90 PERCENT

When you are truly self-aware, you understand that the flip side of your dominant strength often creates a limitation. GreenEnergyCo's culture, starting with me, demonstrated that we were not afraid to learn about ourselves. We became more open to what was and what was not working for us individually, as leaders and as a company. We learned that often, the roles or patterns of which we're afraid to let go are those that have contributed positively to our past success. But these past successes may be unrelated to our current situations.

For example, you may pride yourself on being a super-mom, a great provider, a leader or a caregiver. But such roles are masks—

they can hide all that we can be and actually limit us. (More on this topic in the following chapters.) I clung to my tenacity trait because it had successfully pulled me through my challenging times in my twenties. The flip side of the tenacity coin was impatience and perceived pushiness. While my tenacity was a positive strength, if I toned it down just ten percent I would be ninety percent more effective.

Because I had a very strong competitive, high-achieving survivor trait, and came from a German hard-working upbringing, I assumed struggle was the natural course. I persevered, and successfully so, by most Western standards. Some executives called me the "bounce-back kid." I kept finding new ways, along with our team, to profit.

Through use of the DISC/MI, CVI, looking within and personal exploration, I awakened to the fact that my perceived strength of determination had become a detriment. The higher I rose up the corporate ladder, the more politically correct I had to become to fit in the environment. Pushing too hard against the parent company's culture to get what I perceived GreenEnergyCo needed would backfire. The overall corporate parent's credit was becoming more limited, and I fought for "our share." However, stockholders were not rewarding the enterprise for our profits because they weren't as consistent as those of the regulated business.

My interactions with some executives at the parent company became ones of constant conflict. With twenty-five prior years of successful interactions, this was a disturbing trend. While credit was necessary for GreenEnergyCo's growth, there were higher priority utility or parent company uses for it. When conferring with banks to secure our own credit, the banks indicated our parent should know us best and provide the lowest cost of capital. Yet the parent did not view it this way. No matter what successes we would continue to have, we no longer fit.

We became that square peg trying to be shoved into a round hole. It's a blessing that we were "freed" when the parent company shut down the commodity business and we were forced to leave! It wasn't healthy for most of us to stay, although some of

GreenEnergyCo's employees in the energy efficiency business line did stay and thrive, as I mentioned before.

FREEDOM

And so it was. My departure was amongst the first of many. As it turns out, it was our destiny. I cannot blame my departure on anyone else. I could no longer remain, nor could most of us, in a corporate structure where the parent was not enlightened regarding the way to inspire and treat people. The entire top leadership with whom I had worked my entire career in the parent company was changing. Many of the individuals were real stars and deserved to be in an environment that honored and appreciated them. As we all do. Being released enabled us to find new best-fit environments.

It was very painful to address the employees once the parent company decision had been made. I applauded our people for being *The Little Engine That Could.* Despite our small size compared to our competitors, the ever-changing marketplace and market rules, we always said, "I think I can, I think I can." We reached the apex of our mountain, and our "toys" were all delivered, just like the little engine that could. As I broke the news to our people and the reality of our closure sunk in, the large room went dead silent. You couldn't hear a breath. If you are familiar with the Harry Potter books or movies, I likened the feeling to that of the death-eaters sucking all the oxygen out of the room. It was a sickening silence.

Yet it was a very humane event. Everyone affected came together to hear the news. They were able to feel emotions together. We were fortunate to have a staggered shutdown and the team worked on the plan. They were given time to bid on other positions, look outside the company or take a severance package. Because of the diverse skill sets they had developed and the reputation we had for excellence in our workers, our sister or parent company hired many. Those who chose to leave moved on to successful careers with other companies. ALL of them were able to pay it forward wherever they went. Some have reinstated many of the leadership policies—the Scream-to-Dream Approach—in their new companies.

About two months after the closure announcement meeting and after I had left GreenEnergyCo, I had a prophetic dream about twin towers collapsing and burning like those hit in New York City on 9/11. However, the towers in my dream were those of GreenEnergyCo and the utility company. Our buildings happen to stand twenty stories high, next to each other. In my dream, I planted flower bulbs all around the black and burnt-out buildings and watched them grow into a beautiful garden. I realized that I was done grieving, and that my dream symbolized the celebration of rebirth and new growth.

Without any "push" on my part, I was offered a part-time energy executive director position that was perfect for this phase of my life. It allows me time to speak and write while staying active and influential in the green energy arena. I did not have to fight for the right to claim my space and be there like I did in the later years with the parent company of GreenEnergyCo. I remember when I got the call about becoming the executive director of the scheduling and transmission energy association. There were complications with the outgoing leader, so the board was unsure when and if they could offer me the job. Unlike much of my past behavior, I said I was interested, and if it worked out, then it was meant to be. I was patient. I had learned to let the pieces fall as they will, and I have enjoyed this position now for several years.

JOINT VENTURES AND PARTNERSHIPS

I want to add just a few perspectives on joint ventures and partnerships for my readers who are leaders. When you explore your organization's core, you should be able to identify partners that are good matches for what you value. At the inception of GreenEnergyCo, I inherited many of the miscellaneous other competitive businesses held within the enterprise. They were all losing money, which is part of the reason we dug out of a negative ten million in revenue before growing to several hundred million per year. The parent company decided to house them all in our new subsidiary.

After a few board meetings with our joint venture energy services partner, my gut said that we were not best-fits. Our joint venture partner appeared to have accepted a B-level quality of engineering. Coming from a high-compliance, perfectionist-oriented utility culture, I was used to engineers who were A to A+ types.

Our quality differences created constant conflict on every job. Moreover, to be consistent with GreenEnergyCo's highest performing culture, we believed in delivering A-level work. In less than six months, I decided to break up the partnership and buy our way out of the relationship so that GreenEnergyCo could perform the jobs using our own team. Fit matters, in terms of consistent values. Whether in marriage or business, it goes to the core.

I learned that when you enter into a partnership or joint venture, you need aligned values for sustained success. Also, there's the philosophy of "eat or be eaten." This means that unless both organizations are equals in terms of resources, capital, and people, one entity will typically "take over" the other. You need to enter the relationship with a tight "prenup" that fairly allocates the risks and rewards of the relationship while you are both communicating positively and openly in the early stages. Once different directions arise, communication can become strained. You want the breakup fee, division of customers and territory all clearly spelled out in advance.

SUMMARY OF THE BEST OF EXECUTIVE LEADERSHIP PRACTICAL PRINCIPLES

- Connectivity, collaboration, co-creation and community are building blocks of future successful companies, their employees and customers.

- Great organizations' missions, and for that matter, great company brands, inspire and create a heart-felt emotional connection.

- A company or organization is the best version of itself

when a work environment is created in which company leaders and employees are the best they can be.

- Be true to yourself by discovering and living in alignment with your scream. (You have to first know yourself. That's why we all did DISC/MIs; and the leadership group also took the CVI).

- Help your employees find their scream; then best-fit your employees' strengths with their job functions. (You cannot infuse passion intravenously.)

- Identify your personal and corporate strengths and opportunities; also examine and understand what the biggest risks to your success are, quantitatively and qualitatively.

- Expect what you inspect. Limit your company or organization to three to five measureable goals that distinguish you and keep you in business.

- Great leaders focus on the most important priorities; the tough decisions of what to do and not to do have to be made and clarified continuously.

- Put most of your resources on what you do best and do more of it.

- Provide an environment with a sense of community where the greatest human potential can be achieved; where each can succeed; where it's meaningful and fun; and where success is celebrated!

- To co-create, listen! When people are heard they feel understood and valued.

- Collaborate and share information for efficient, autonomous decision making.

- Ensure that individual roles, responsibilities, resources and incentives are aligned with the organization's goals and that each person understands how he or she can affect the achievement of the goals.

- Routinely clarify expectations and consistently apply natural consequences for failure to meet them; non-performance cannot be tolerated. It's the biggest de-motivator.
- Separate quickly and respectfully. (It's always HOW you fire, not whether the person should be let go.)

EXERCISES

1. Explore your organization's core: Have each leader draw a car or transport that represents your business. Explain why you chose this vehicle and how it reflects your company.
2. Review your organization's mission, goals and values: Does the mission resonate with your heart and inspire your associates to want to contribute to your meaningful cause? Are your goals simple? What are the top three most important goals and why will your business succeed if you achieve them? How will you accomplish your mission and goals, meaning what aligned values drive you and your business?
3. Shared strategic goals: Write a letter dated five years from now describing where your business is in terms of product or service offerings, financial measurements, culture, etc.
4. Shared vision: Create a vision board for your business, using the work done in the exercise above. Glue pictures on a big board or create a computer screensaver showing the joint vision of you and your other leaders.
5. Write down three actions that you will take this month to assert responsibility for your own career path.

HOW DO YOU KNOW IF YOU HAVE FOUND YOUR SCREAM?

Pain is good! Pain is not your real adversary, but fear.
— Dr. Gladys Taylor McGarey, M.D., M.D.(H)

You have learned how to listen within and explore your core personally, professionally and as an organization. But how do you know if you have found your scream?

You may have discerned it already by listening to your intuition, or from the information you garnered by exploring your core strengths and values. However, if you are still unsure, listen to your body. It will not lie to you.

YOUR BODY DOESN'T LIE TO YOU

Listening to your intuition is intangible and invisible. How can you be certain that the clues you are picking up from it indicate if you are in or out of alignment? Listen to and feel your body! Your body's communication is tangible. You know when it's not in balance. Just as a healthy spine is one where each vertebra is in alignment, a healthy, fulfilled person is aligned when balanced in mind, body and spirit. When you are not in alignment with who you are and what you value, you are not living congruently with your heart's desires—your scream. You may be walking in too small of shoes—ones that stifle you and create pain. Your body will let you know when you are not living your scream through pain and disease; that is, "dis-ease."

You saw what an aligned person or small group of aligned workers can do when our GreenEnergyCo team outperformed Enron. In contrast, nonalignment makes everyday life harder, more painful and a struggle. Instead of living, leading and working from creation, destruction can result. In this chapter you will learn how to tell, from your body, when you are not living your scream. Once you identify where your body is out of alignment you can release your fear of change and move into alignment. In the next chapter, you will learn how to do so. This chapter focuses on the identification process only.

I learned about the close connection between body, mind and spirit more than 30 years ago. Remember when Muvo, the Zulu Sangoma healer told me that I'd faced many hard things in life and could now let my defenses go? I realized that he was referring in part to my mother's early death. On March 9, 1979 at the age of forty-seven, my mother died from breast cancer. I was twenty-two and in law school at Arizona State University (ASU). I recall as clearly as yesterday, at the moment of her death in the hospital, I dropped to my knees in despair and coldly stated to myself, "I'm all alone now." I never looked back at my childhood until many years later, when I began to find my scream. I put the full force of my abundant energy into looking forward and solving the many challenges that lay ahead for my family.

After my marble-playing days, when I was ten years old, my parents divorced. When I was fifteen my mother remarried. We became a dysfunctional stepfamily, like so many American youths experience. My mother had returned to college after the divorce. She wanted to grow and what, I now call, find her scream and live it. My birth father had been insecure. He did not like my mother's independence and wanted her to be happy as a stay-at-home mom. When I was in high school she succeeded at her dream. She became a college English literature and writing professor at Scottsdale Community College.

My mother married my stepfather when I was a sophomore in high school. He had two daughters about my age who did not live with us. My mother was attracted to him because he was clever, macho, talented at building things, played music, painted, and shod and trained horses. He was the opposite of my birth father in most ways and he also did not possess any of his good qualities, like being a loving, Christian man. I had an intuitive feeling that I should stay away from him, and as soon as I could, I did.

When my mother had been trying to build our new family, she had us take our stepfather's last name. We used it on our school papers, etc., as an a.k.a. (also know as)—not as a formal adoption. She pushed very hard to make this marriage work. We did not see our real father except for a few times over the ten year period after their divorce.

My mother, stepfather, sister, brother and I moved to five acres in the desert at the end of my senior year of high school. Our family hand built a Santa Fe style ranch home with open breezeways between rooms on a dirtroad in a rural area at Usery Mountain Pass, outside of Phoenix. We built stalls and had five horses. We had no city water or well, so we bought a 1,700-gallon milk truck to haul our water to our home each week. That summer I left and started college at the University of Arizona in Tucson, two hours away. My three-year-younger sister and seven-year-younger brother stayed with my mom and stepfather until our mom's death.

About seven years after they married, as my mom's impending death neared, my intuition about my stepfather was confirmed. He slept with another woman in our house in the room next to where my very ill mother was asleep from all the morphine. My stepfather was a liquor distributor and after years of seeing him drink at least two bottles of wine every night, there was no doubt he was a functional alcoholic. It became apparent that he was also a con artist. My mother had worked all their years together to bring assets into the relationship. He didn't contribute any physical assets. All of my mother's assets were held as community property and became my stepfather's.

My brother turned sixteen just before my mother's death. My stepfather realized he could collect my brother's social security checks if he secured custody of him. My sister was nineteen and attending Scottsdale Community College. My sister recalls, when our mother was jaundiced, dying and needed to go the hospital, that she wanted to call an ambulance. Our stepfather didn't want to incur the expense, even after she offered to pay for it so that our mother would be more comfortable on the ride to the hospital.

Instead, he put our mother in his rough-riding truck and drove up and down the dirt road to the hospital.

My mother was conscious enough to make it known just before her death that she wanted me to be my brother's guardian. However, she was too sick to sign papers to legalize this desire. My brother related to me:

> "I remember making the decision of whether to stay with our stepfather or not when I faced him in their bedroom. I told him I could not respect him. He said, 'That does not matter as long as you fear me.' That was enough for me to leave. Then our stepfather added, 'You are not going to get anything from this house.'"

My stepfather had signed on as a former Cleveland Browns football player in the days when they wore helmets without face masks, and he was not to be reckoned with. He never actually played because on the way to report in to practice, he drag raced his car, rolled it, and tore up his shoulder so badly that he couldn't ever play pro ball.

After a probate battle, my mother's wishes were honored for me to be my brother's legal guardian. Even though our natural father was alive and lived in Kentucky, he hadn't been part of our lives for many years and I didn't want to take my brother out of his high school to live with our father.

Accompanied by my second-year law school buddies, I retrieved my brother and a few of his personal possessions from the ranch home. With the aid of my "bodyguards" I was able to take my brother's bed, the china from my mother's first wedding and the twenty-five-year-old piano that my brother loved. That was about it.

I rented a trailer in Mesa, Arizona near ASU with a bedroom at either end where my brother and I lived. I essentially became responsible as the head of the family for my sister, brother, grandmother and myself. My sister stayed with us when not away at college.

By the way, this was the second time I lived in a trailer. When my mother divorced my father, the four of us moved into my grandmother's trailer in Northern Phoenix. My husband says the reason that I am the way I am is because I inhaled too much oxidized aluminum when I was younger!

As you can imagine, I craved for an explanation of why a good mother died and left us all alone. To try to help me understand, I read about the relationship between our thoughts and our illnesses. Eventually, I read cancer surgeon Dr. Bernie Siegel's book, *Love, Medicine and Miracles*. Dr. Siegel went beyond the surgeon's role of removing the cancer from his patients. He also worked with the families to figure out what underlying feelings and beliefs contributed to the cancer. He would have them paint or draw pictures to try to engage the subconscious to see what the stories they told might expose about family relationships and the patient's underlying emotions. He showed how deep, seething resentment in his patients ate at them internally for years, eventually displaying itself as a cancer.

This made sense to me. My mother was bright and must have noticed that something was wrong. Yet she waited until her breasts were concave before she saw a doctor. I realized that my mother's squelched dreams caused her to want a way out of her situation. She desperately desired to be the same star that she wanted me to be; yet she was on her way to a second divorce. She realized he was the wrong man before she became deathly sick. She couldn't accept what she perceived to be utter disgrace. Her deep resentment and grief were eating away at her. It was an early wakeup call for me to see what someone's un-confronted fears and unresolved issues could produce in his or her body.

I learned that your fears manifest initially through pain. When you are out of alignment with who you are at your core, you will have physical pain. To live congruently with your scream, you must first identify where you body hurts, and then why. Next, release any fears that are causing the pain, including the fear of change. For if you don't change and realign with your scream, eventually dis-ease will catch up to you.

What do you choose? Spending your time learning how to

feel great and living comfortably in alignment, or hours driving to and waiting in doctors' offices, pharmacies or medical testing facilities trying to feel better?

WHERE DOES YOUR BODY HURT?

Where do you typically get aches and pains? Head? Neck? Heart? Gut? Feet? What is giving you a pain in the back, or causing you to eat too many TUMS? Write it down. If you choose to journal, record this over a month and then reflect on your entries. It will be very telling. Your body won't lie to you.

The body is a metaphor. It mirrors your beliefs. It gives you clues about where you are not in alignment and what fears may be blocking you, so you can release them. In this chapter you'll learn how to interpret those clues, to feel and hear what your body is telling you. Are you tired with the weight of the burdens that your body's carrying? Or are you light and energetic, filled with gratitude for your magical, mysterious life?

For more than thirty years I've paid acute attention to my body's signals and have studied the mind-body-spirit connection. Your body knows what it needs. You just need a translator to interpret its language. I'll now share how some of the experts and resources that have helped me may help you.

I am basically physically very healthy. When I notice an imbalance, I seek corrective action, preferably through natural means. Through referrals over time, I met an amazing physician.

I first had the privilege of working with the co-founder of the Holistic Medical Association, Gladys Taylor McGarey, M.D., M.D.(H) in 2002. Eight years later, on October 29, 2010, my husband and I joined her friends and fans to celebrate her ninetieth birthday in a gala affair in Scottsdale, Arizona. Diane Ladd, the actress, was the master of ceremonies. TV's 1970s bionic woman, Lindsay Wagner, also honored her. For her entrance, Dr. Gladys popped out of a life-sized cake!

Dr. Gladys was raised by medical missionaries who worked in the Himalayan Mountains and in the dark, steamy jungles that were rife with malaria. Gladys mingled with the Hindu and

Moslem children as if they were her own family. All six of her children are doctors or in healing professions.

This incredible pioneer of "whole person" medicine is still vibrant. She established her nonprofit organization to promote Living Medicine and continues to write about her work. Part of the proceeds from this book will be donated to continue her legacy.

Initially, as I mentioned in Chapter 3, I consulted with Dr. Gladys about my insomnia through her dream analysis gatherings. It was during the peak growth of GreenEnergyCo and there was more on my mind than I could digest. I am sure that insomnia is a common complaint of many of my readers. I tried biofeedback and it helped, but only modestly. She suggested that I put a pad and pen by my bed and jot down what kept me awake. Take deep breaths to clear my mind of clutter. Visualize a treasure chest and put my written notes into it. Lock it up and read them in the morning.

I follow this advice to this day, and it still works. Funny, when I'd read what I scribbled the next morning, it seemed so irrelevant most times. If it was worth remembering, I usually did remember the important stuff anyway. I wondered how I let my "to do list" keep me awake for hours!

Dr. Gladys also coached me to write down my dreams immediately upon waking, as I mentioned in Chapter 3. She showed me how to find useful clues from my dreams about what was keeping me awake at night.

WHAT YOU CAN LEARN FROM DR. GLADYS

Here's what Dr. Gladys can teach you: "Pain is good! Pain is not your real adversary, but fear." Pain is usually temporary—but fear resides within you until it's released. She explains in *The Physician Within You* that the most common medications are painkillers and tranquilizers.

Dr. Gladys observes that the warlike metaphors we use to describe illness and treatments undermine our health. Medicine, she was taught in medical school, is "against life; a war against disease... We talk about antibiotics, antidepressants, antacids and even anti-aging." She cites women saying that they "fight" osteoporosis—as if they'd want to fight their own bones! Using warlike metaphors to describe disease causes us to want to destroy the disease process with more and more medication ammunition!

As Dr. Gladys observes, some people think if they don't deal with pain it will go away. (But we all know that what you resist persists!) Dr. Gladys advises that you work with the pain, breathe with it, flow with it and understand that at times it's necessary. It will subside in due time.

Fear is the real problem. Fear sits in judgment in the adrenal glands. You have to confront what is going on within you. Examine and face the reasons for the imbalance. Learn how to move your own healing energy out of the adrenals into your loving heart where, as Dr. Gladys says, "perfect love cancels all fear."

Dr. Gladys' legacy of Living Medicine is based on the perspective that we must approach the patient as a whole person, one who's a spiritual being, not a disease. Healing the entire person is the goal, not simply curing, alleviating or destroying a disease. "Because an individual has a purpose for living, the whole person—his or her past work, emotions and thoughts—all are part of the illness that exists," Dr. Gladys philosophizes in her newest work, *Living Medicine, The Dwelling Place*. Living Medicine aims to bring an integration and balance of the body, mind and spirit. She identifies many ways to work with a person's spiritual nature, including surgery. A surgical procedure conducted in a manner of caring and understanding can be an awakening experience, for example.

WHAT YOU CAN LEARN FROM YOUR BODY

To understand what your body is telling you, consider the *function* that the painful part of your body performs. You will glean insights into what's not aligned in your life. When your head hurts, Dr. Gladys might ask, "How are you putting pressure on yourself?" Or if it's your shoulder, "Are you shouldering too much?" If it's your neck, ask whom are you allowing to give you a pain in the neck or what are you being a pain about? Use these clues to explore what your underlying resistance may be. Then you can deal with whatever it is.

I've listed resources in the back of this book that can give you further insights into what your body may be telling you about non-alignment. The important thing is to pay greater attention to your body's messages. Of course, these mind-body connections are not absolute. But they may help point you in the direction of the underlying emotion that's contributing to your dis-ease. The information is worth consideration, in my opinion. It has helped me maintain excellent health.

Let's play with this mind-body method of discovering where you are out of alignment. We'll start at your head and work down your body.

YOUR PERFECT HEAD, EYES AND EARS

The function of your head is to think. When your head hurts, are you overthinking? Perhaps you are invalidating yourself in some way. Do you think you have to be perfect? You may need to release that fear. (You'll learn how in the next chapter.) Migraines can also come from perfectionism and putting pressure on yourself, but with an "extra helping" of suppressed anger.

The ears' functions are obvious. Ears represent the capacity to hear. When you have trouble hearing, what do you not want to hear?

Sight represents the capacity to see. If you have eyesight issues, what is it that you don't want to accept or see? (I have worn glasses since I was eight until I had Lasik eye surgery when I was forty-eight. I see clearly now. I am still pondering this possible connection.)

LOSING YOUR VOICE

One purpose of the throat is to enable speech. Do you get chronic sore throats? When do they occur—after certain recurring situations? Perhaps you withhold self-expression, and don't speak up for yourself or ask for what you want. What words are you swallowing? Maybe you were taught that being direct isn't being nice. What's going on in your life when you get laryngitis? Are you pleasing others while you are so angry inside that you can't speak? Are you not speaking your truth? (Early in my legal career, vocal cord nodes developed and impaired my speech. I had them removed. After I left the practice of law I never had them again! And recall, upon my return from South Africa, I lost my voice for four days. The loss of speech was a metaphor for the angst of what was still unsaid—my embedded and still unreleased feeling of abandonment—of my mother dying when I was young and of the parent company unwinding a portion of GreenEnergyCo.)

SHOULDERING OR CARRYING THE BURDEN

The function of the shoulder in conjunction with the arm is to carry and lift. If your shoulder hurts, what burden are you shouldering? (My left shoulder was tight and tense for thirty years. It's raised higher than my right one. It is partly due to past years of holding the old-fashioned receiver phone on my left shoulder while I talked, and walked around multi-tasking. Metaphorically, however, it represents how I was lifting a heavy burden and carrying it always. That is not from lifting weights in the gym, though. It was from carrying the responsibility of putting myself through college (maintaining a 4.0 and graduating Phi Beta Kappa in three years); and then caring for my family while putting myself through law school at age twenty two.

Years later, I had twelve acupuncture sessions over several weeks, and consciously worked on releasing my survival-based fears that were related to the past. Only then did most of my concrete-tension knots disintegrate. I continue acupuncture to keep energy flowing and to prevent congestion from building up in that area, as I describe later.

Working down your body, think about the function of your arms, elbows and hands. They bend, hold and embrace—the experiences of life. Past emotions that are stored in joints and elbows represent your inflexibility to change directions. Hands grasp, hold, clench. Grasping hands can be related to a fear of loss or of not having enough. If your hands hurt, it can signify a lack of willingness to passionately embrace life and to actively create your desires.

That which belongs to you cannot be taken from you, so relax, advises Louise L. Hay in *You Can Heal Your Life*. I read her work in the 1980s. Louise adds that hands can be knotty-knuckled from overthinking or gnarled with arthritic criticism. In her view, arthritis is a dis-ease that can emanate from a constant pattern of criticism—of self and others. Your body parts actually "bend" from the weight of the burden of perfection. A similar view that dates back to 1925 is that continual criticism produces rheumatism because critical, inharmonious thoughts cause unnatural deposits in the blood that settle in the joints. Such was it expressed in *The Game of Life: And How To Play It* by Florence Scovel Shinn.

My human resources director had many issues with her hands in her previous work environment. She discovered she has "healing hands." She is a natural empath and consults and guides people in a compassionate, healing manner. Her previous position didn't allow her to live her scream. At GreenEnergyCo, she had more freedom to guide our group and when she used her gifts, her hands felt better. When she is stifled in her work or her fears and stresses flair, so do her hands.

Let's continue. Look at your fingers. According to Louise Hay in *You Can Heal Your Life*, each has meaning that shows where you need to relax and let go. She and others who look at mind-body connections say that a painful thumb signifies mental over-thinking, worry and impatience; a painful index finger is about ego and fear; a painful middle finger relates to sex and anger; a painful ring finger represents unions and grief; and a painful pinkie holds information for you about issues with family and pretending. (The same interpretations go for toes.)

It could be coincidence, but the only finger that has given me recurring pain is my right thumb. I fell on it and sprained it while skiing in Jackson Hole, Wyoming, years ago. Now as it aches while I type, I'd like to blame it on the old injury and using the mouse to write this book. However, there's a suspicious link to my past pattern of overthinking and impatience.

Dr. Gladys writes in *Living Medicine* about the patience she learned when working on her biography. It took years longer than she expected. In retrospect, she admits that her impatience with the process was only a waste of energy. The end product was well worth the wait. If she'd skipped steps, to use her obstetrics metaphor, it would have been like delivering a premature baby.

As Dr. Gladys puts it, impatience probably causes more strain and stress on our lives than anything else. Our blood pressure rises; anger builds and our adrenals get exhausted. We age faster. (I have learned that being more patient is cheaper for me than buying expensive anti-aging creams; although I still do that too!) Life is a process. Patience and joy go hand in hand. How can you be impatient when you are laughing?

YOUR ACHING HEART AND BACK

What about the organ that pumps your lifeblood? When you have a heart attack, your heart doesn't attack you; it's telling you that you are forgetting to appreciate the little joys of life and it falls over in pain, describes Louise Hay in *You Can Heal Your Life*. It may not surprise you that my husband, Jeff, lowers his risk of a heart attack by taking high blood pressure medication. His recurring body message is from his heart.

To put his heart's message in perspective, on October 26, 2010 at 10:32 p.m., Jeff was one of twenty-seven invited witnesses to observe the lethal injection execution of the sociopathic murderer Jeffrey Landrigan in the Florence, Arizona prison. Jeff was the prosecuting attorney in 1990 who secured the death penalty for the cruel murder of Landrigan's second victim. The sound factual and legal record Jeff presented in the case withstood twenty years of appeals. While work such as this has been extremely gratifying and a public service, it has weighed heavily on his heart. My career major felony prosecutor husband has experienced decades of daily doses of witnessing the pain people inflict on one another. It's no wonder it has "pained" his heart.

A common pain that many people suffer is upper or lower back pain. What function does your back provide? Support. Certainly, some backaches are caused by sitting in front of computers in chairs that don't support you, but dig deeper. What emotional connection might there be? Other areas of your body could bother you, but instead it's your back. When your back hurts, might it represent your belief that you lack support from your boss, or from those on your work team, or from your family or spouse?

DIGESTION AND BELOW

What does your stomach do? Digests things, you say. When you reach for the antacids, what can you not stomach or assimilate? Are you digesting new experiences or are you afraid?

I can attest to what your digestive system does to you when you are afraid to make a change to live your scream. In the extreme, if you cannot stomach who you are, you may develop ulcers. Your stomach may hurt due to a fear-based belief that you are not good enough. Your endless attempts to please others exhaust your digestion.

Affirm what you want and then know that it will actualize. This kind of knowing is based on trust, which is a state of mind where intuition reigns supreme. I didn't have this trust. Instead, I covered up my body's backtalk by gobbling down a half-gallon of TUMS every couple of months.

While the next part of your body may seem rather private, if your "privates" are calling for attention, your energy in that area very well could be blocked. As Muvo, the Zulu Sangoma intuitive healer suggested, I needed to examine my feelings about issues of male and female power, or lack of it, in my life.

The sexual organs create pleasure as well as life. In retrospect, my lifelong struggle with difficult menstrual cycles and my ultimate hysterectomy make perfect sense. While I'm slightly embarrassed to share this with you, I'm doing so because I think it could be instructive for you. The best example I can give is what I personally experienced: I dutifully followed society's path of success and denied my pent-up creativity. My uterus fell. While

I preferred a natural remedy, it wasn't an option for a completely fallen uterus.

When discussing whether I should have an operation with medical intuitive, Laura Alden Kamm, she explained to me that an unhealthy uterus relates to frozen creativity. The loss of my uterus was symbolic. I had pushed for money and success all my life. The strain of problem solving—mine, my family's, and everyone else's when I was president of GreenEnergyCo—caused me to "use all my juice." Laura observed that if my uterus was spent, remove it. It was metaphoric: my uterus could not hold its form or position anymore. Nor would my life hold the same form. And I'd never again hold the president position that previously existed. On November 11, 2009, I had a successful hysterectomy. Now I wonder why I didn't do it sooner. Letting go of my uterus helped me let go of the loss I felt. And I haven't had the pain and mess associated with more than forty years of cramps. Wooowee!

Often, an unhealthy bladder is a common problem that accompanies the removal of the uterus. (But in my case, my bladder was healthy.) Bladder problems may arise from being annoyed—"p.o.'d," (as a metaphor) at a partner. Prostate issues can signify to a man as he ages that somehow, in his mind, he's less of a man. A common issue I've seen with my fifty-plus male friends is the hourly trip to the bathroom to pee. I still see them as real men—I wish they could.

YOUR LOWER CONNECTION WITH MOTHER EARTH

Your knees, like the neck, according to Dr. Gladys, have to do with flexibility. Explore whether your pride, ego or stubbornness restrict their movement. Do you want to move forward, but are fearful of bending or changing your ways? Remember, life is flow and movement.

Feet are fascinating. Feet can literally and metaphorically move you forward. My four-year-old godchild moves on happy, dancing feet. A friend, who is an older retired executive, shuffles her inflexible feet, as if she no longer has anywhere to go. Since retirement she has lost a sense of purpose and you can see it in how she moves.

How grounded are you? Another part of your feet, your "soles" are your interface with Mother Earth and the rest of Creation. "When maintained in full and balanced contact with the Earth, they [our feet] tangibly keep us connected or nonseparate. Lift a big toe, roll a heel inward and the connection is broken. We've forgotten who we are and become disconnected," states Matthew Taylor, PT, Ph.D., RYT.

I first met Matt Taylor when I was training for my second one-half marathon, and my right knee kept hurting. My friend, an orthopedic surgeon, recommended a surgical procedure called a patella release. Matt observed how I ran. He noticed that my right foot rolled inward when it struck the ground. That collapsed the right ankle, which, in turn, put pressure on my right knee. By strengthening my left hip and adjusting how my foot hit the ground, I ran the event without knee pain! I didn't have knee surgery. It was also fascinating what he discerned about my personality just by how I cantered. He observed that I leaned forward and approached the world head-on.

A close friend developed plantar fasciitis. This occurs when the plantar fascia on the bottom of the foot becomes inflamed. It's not a disease. It's soft tissue injury from abnormal forces in activities. According to Matt, your sore foot can relate to a tight pelvis from not breathing, "settling" for less, or overtraining. Planter fasciitis can also be linked to not speaking your own truth. Your throat and foot are connected in this manner. The bottom part of your foot is pulling away from the Earth and losing its interconnectedness with your basic foundation, in effect.

My friend's connection with our Earth "groans" literally in real pain—the separation of the fascia with the rest of the foot as he puts weight on it when walking on this Earth. He is off-balance at this time in his life and disconnected with those close to him.

Think about it: when your feet hurt, your freedom of motion is restricted. The pain decreases your ability to be active (unless you swim a lot). Foot pain can cause you to become socially isolated, which leads to more suffering and disconnection. What foot pain symbolizes for my friend with plantar fascia is that he likes his alone time, and yet his greatest fear is of being alone. Some of his quiet behaviors, and now foot problems, tend to isolate him during social functions and from participating with people. This seems to support the theory that the very thing you fear is what you create! After all, you are directing a lot of energy toward what you fear.

Bunions can be a sign that you are pushing against life. You want to change things in your world but are not succeeding. Aren't the interconnections between how you walk on the Earth and what causes you to suffer worth considering? Where are your feet as you read this? Foot alignment and contact is yet another metaphor, a mirror of sorts, of whether you are in touch with your scream. When you are afraid, anxious or withdrawn, in what position are your feet? How does the position of your grounding affect your overall posture? Does it create discomfort? Do you stand tall or hunch over as if life is beating you down?

When you are out of alignment, many things become more difficult—not just walking and hiking to socialize and be with people, but balancing, lifting and sitting. Matt challenges us to think of how the ego puts us into tortuous footwear and training regimens!

I now see so many connections, or metaphors, between what hurt in my body and what was going on in my life. As I looked back through my journal, I noticed that when I was contemplating firing my incongruent, deceptive leader, my right foot swelled on a daily basis. The right side of the body relates to our masculine side. I realize now that it represented my not being sure of how to move forward as our top leader. I had been "bitten" by this rattlesnake—this leader's dishonest accounting of project costs—and I didn't want to get bitten again, so I was treading, both lightly and literally, at the time. Within days after the leader was terminated, my foot felt fine.

OFF BALANCE AND SEEKING UNHEALTHY RESPITE

How else can anger and fear manifest in physical events in your life? A sudden wakeup call is a serious ailment or an accident. I remember several times when I almost longed to be in an accident.

I was working more than fifty hours a week (even when I took weekends off), plus I was the mother of two small children, a wife and had many social obligations. If I were laid up, I could heal and rest. Fortunately, I must not have thought about it that seriously or long enough, because it didn't happen. Have you ever had these thoughts?

I was in and out of the hospital quickly when my kids were born. I hadn't had any hospital stays or serious surgery before my hysterectomy in November of 2009. I was flabbergasted at the outpouring of calls, gifts, visits and sentiment following my operation. While flattered and feeling loved by my network of dear friends and family, I saw the irony of it. I was being consoled for not nurturing myself all these years, for building up resentment and frozen creativity in my uterus, and for resorting to an expensive operation to remedy it! Neither my friends nor our health care system has rewarded me equally for the preventive measures I've taken to care for my health and myself. Something is very wrong with this picture...more to come on that later.

Think about the circumstances that surround a serious illness or accident in your life. Could there have been mental thought patterns that attracted the event to you? If you have anger and frustration pent up from not feeling the freedom to speak up for yourself, do you become accident-prone? Could it be that you got so angry that you wanted to hit people, and instead you got hit?

When you are angry with yourself and feel the need for punishment, an accident would be just the cure, wouldn't it? Even if it's not your fault, it allows you to turn to others for sympathy and attention. You get your wounds bathed and you have bed rest, but you also get the pain. It's as if our society says it's OK to blame something else for what happens in our life. When you are this out of balance, you are not living your scream. Again, examine what your body is telling you.

CONGESTED OR FLOWING ENERGY THROUGHOUT THE BODY

My acupuncturist, Dr. Kelly Hsu, an M.D. who also trained in

Chinese medicine, referred me to an excellent book, *Between Heaven and Earth: A Guide to Chinese Medicine,* by Harriet Beinfield, L.Ac. and Efrem Korngold, L.Ac., O.M.D. The authors were among the first Americans to be trained at the College of Traditional Acupuncture in England and to be licensed in California. If your fears are blocking the release of the old, you will have "congestion," according to the authors. Energy can flow healthily or be blocked within your body. The basic bodily function of elimination offers a clue to which of these conditions is occurring. While not a subject you might associate with a leadership book, healthy elimination is essential to living and leading with a balanced body, mind and spirit.

The colon represents your ability to let go and run healthy energy through you. It signifies the ability to release that which you no longer need. While I hate to admit it, I've not been so fortunate to have a daily morning ritual. I used to hold out for several days in the past. But when I changed my diet, released my old survival pattern—the fear of not having enough—and left being an attorney, my constitution literally changed.

Look for patterns. If energy is not flowing, it may be associated with a pattern of staying in an unfulfilling job, hoarding possessions, staying in painful relationships, not loving or forgiving yourself or trying to always be in control of your environment. I think back to my twenties when a ski instructor told me to "go with the flow" rather than concentrate so hard on how to execute the technique. I was too much in my head trying to be in control. As you believe and trust life, energy will begin to flow and relieve the congestion. Things will unfold in the best manner for you. The synchronicities that come your way will be uncanny.

Dr. Gladys makes an interesting observation in *Living Medicine.* Forgiveness breaks the bonds that hold the blocked energy that causes illness. She points out that the Bible calls Jesus the Great Physician who did not treat dis-eases, but healed people by forgiving their sins. She also refers to Chinese medicine wisdom that says pain comes from blocks in the life-force energy, our *chi.* Acupuncture is one way to increase the flow of chi. Fear and anger block energy. Laughter, music and beauty shift that block and also allow energy to move again.

MEDICAL VIEWS OF THE CONNECTEDNESS OF YOUR BODY'S DISEASE AND YOUR UNDERLYING EMOTIONAL CENTERS

In *Living Medicine*, Dr. Gladys explains the science and art of medicine through the example of your endocrine system. The endocrine system influences almost every cell, organ, and function in your body. It's instrumental in regulating mood, growth and development, tissue function, metabolism, sexual function and reproductive processes. Studies show that biofeedback can help people have some control over their endocrine glands, such as the adrenals. By taking control of their thoughts and emotions, people can learn to lower blood pressure and heart rate. (You may be familiar with the example of the Hindu Fakir who can slow his physiological functions down to a level where he could be pronounced dead.)

What Dr. Gladys is saying is that how you feel about yourself and what you think affect your physical well-being. By examining your underlying emotional centers, you will gain information about where your thoughts are not serving you well and creating imbalances.

Different systems and traditions identify our life-force energy as our *chi*, spirit, *prahna* or *kundalini*. It's the rising energy that activates our spiritual centers, that activates our hormonal glands, known as energy centers in the Hindu tradition. The New Testament calls the life-force the "seven churches."

What follows is a simplified introduction to your energy centers. Energy centers are the centers of the vital energy in the body that are responsible for balance at all levels of being—physical, psychological and spiritual.

You can learn about yourself and when you are not acting in alignment with who you are by examining to which energy center in the body your pain relates. Clues are conveyed through your energy centers. You can access this information by identifying which area has congested or flowing energy within it. The energy centers overlap the parts of the body that I discussed in the previous section.

In the audiobook, *Igniting Intuition: Unearthing Body Genius*, Christiane Northrup, M.D., and Mona Lisa Schulz, M.D., Ph.D., describe how to recognize unhealthy patterns in your own life. You can change the unhealthy patterns and your cells' health by changing your thoughts, relationships and beliefs. We will delve into how to do that next. For now, let's focus on identifying what's going on within the energy centers.

Before you dismiss a discussion of energy centers and changing your cells as "out there," know that Doctors Northrup and Schulz base their advice on scientific data. So do many others. For example, psychiatrist and physician, David R. Hawkins, M.D., Ph.D., conducts research on human kinetics and how the body responds when people speak truth or falsehoods. All the body's organs are linked to meridians of energy that are also linked to acupuncture points that are linked with specific attitudes. In *Power vs. Force*, Dr. Hawkins wrote, "There's nothing mysterious about these vital internal communications, and they can be demonstrated in seconds ... if one holds a particular negative thought in mind, a very specific muscle will go weak; if one then replaces the thought with a positive idea, the same muscle will instantly go strong. The connection between mind and body is immediate."

Medical expert opinion now surges with the belief that unresolved emotions held for a long time contribute to illness. The body says something needs to change, and there's power in this knowledge. From the works I mention here and others like them, you may gain even more clues of where you store your fear in the form of pain or dis-ease. Your role is to first identify it so you can release it. Instead of asking, "What's the matter with you?" you may be better served by asking "Who's the matter with you?"

We'll start from the lower part of the body and work our way up through the energy centers, as they are described in *Igniting Intuition*. Notice that the emotional energy centers are organized according to the colors of the rainbow, ROYGBIV.

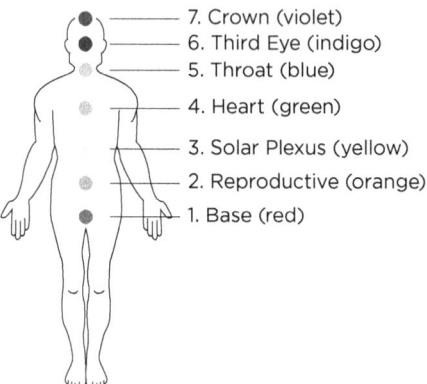

THE FIRST ENERGY CENTER

The first energy center is located at the bottom of your torso, between your legs. It represents your basic emotional needs for survival. It's your foundation, your home, Earth, family—all that which helps you form your sense of belonging, safety, security and roots. This energy center is associated with the eliminatory system, legs and feet. This center is cross-referenced in Chinese medicine with the element of Earth, and its color is red. When you don't feel your basic needs are safe and secure, your "foundation" shows ailing signs. Your belief system, judgments and any feelings of lack or relations to money emanate from here. (As I later describe, my friend from early childhood feels that the world is collapsing in on her. She is in financial shambles. She's lost her home. She's had hip replacements. Her external world is literally mirroring her internal "world." Her favorite color is red!)

THE SECOND ENERGY CENTER

The second energy center is located two inches below the navel. It represents your relationships, intimacy and emotions. The Chinese element is water and color is orange. This energy center is associated with the reproductive and pelvic area. Problems in these areas may indicate frozen creativity. (Yes, as you know, I'm familiar with this problem.) In Drs. Northrup and Schulz's experience, women who lost their fathers early are prone to looking for relationships to replace them. This emotional issue can appear physically as reproductive organ or cervix issues. These doctors find that when these women learn to say NO, and don't view their relationship with men as "serving the one above her," their emotional and physical issues improve.

THE THIRD ENERGY CENTER

The third energy center is located in your gut, your solar plexus, adrenals, and represents self-esteem and social roles. The Chinese element is fire and color is yellow. Health problems associated with an imbalance in this center include digestion issues in the stomach, liver and small intestines.

Obesity and inactivity are related to the third energy center. Imbalances in this center go both ways—not enough healthy eating and too much exercise or visa versa. You can restore balance by eating healthy and through exercise. Exercise increases beta endorphins. You can use them as a pick-me-up. However, the overstimulation of beta endorphins can become addictive. It's like the Lay's® potato chips syndrome—you can't eat just one. If you need to run marathons, you may be addicted to the production of these endorphins, and need as much help as one who does not exercise. The subject of weight and healthy eating is discussed in more detail below because it's such a prevalent issue in our American society.

THE FOURTH ENERGY CENTER

The fourth energy center represents the heart and healthy love. That is, a balance of giving and receiving. The Chinese element is also fire and the color is green. If you have difficulty with emotional expression or problems with partnerships, it can contribute to heart disease. In Drs. Northrup and Schulz's view, heart disease in the U.S. is related in part to Americans' problem with showing anger. We think there's something wrong with it. And if you have high levels of hostility, you may be prone to a heart attack. By learning to express hostility you can lower your likelihood of heart disease.

Heart disease may also signify that you are not living your passion. Maybe your passion used to be your kids. Now what? "I have the dwindles," declared one of Drs. Northrup and Schulz's clients. She had a heart tumor and was advised that she needed to discover her new passion. It was travel.

Men who retire can have similar or worse issues. Statistics for policemen who retire at age fifty-two show a 70 percent chance of dying, typically from heart disease, within the following three years. Retirement becomes the death of their passion.

To change, to renew an old passion or take up a new one, takes a leap of faith. Faith is located in the heart center. Recall that the heart has an electromagnetic field that's stronger than the brain. When you are in touch with your heart, it regulates the other parts of your body. Balance and alignment, (in other words, healing), occur when you practice appreciation from your heart, and balance giving and receiving. To change this imbalance, the doctors advise you to forgive yourself and others.

These doctors observe that if you have an "unhealthy love," you may experience breast cancer. They see a higher incidence of cancer in patients who have a history of being stoic and who bury their anger—all of which are associated with the fourth energy center. Dr. Schulz tells of a woman who had breast cancer and stayed in her relationship with her cheating husband. The breast cyst created the "relationshipectomy" and catalyzed her divorce. (Fortunately, she listened to her body and changed her life. My mother did not choose that path.)

Cancer can also be triggered by unhealthy passion: hate, often in the form of self-hatred, and anger and rage from believing you are less than you are. These doctors, like Dr. Bernie Siegel, see cancer as a dis-ease caused by a deep resentment that you've held for a long time until it literally eats away at your body.

THE FIFTH ENERGY CENTER

The fifth energy center is located in your throat. The Chinese element is air and the color is blue. It includes your throat and mouth, essentially your voice, and represents who you are in the world. It also includes the thyroid glands, which are associated with your will. Issues that reveal themselves in the fifth energy center can relate to intuition and communication. Health problems that manifest may involve your speech or thyroid. Physical problems with your feet can also be linked to this area. You can get stuck not living your truth. (Recall the planter fasciitis example earlier in this chapter.)

THE SIXTH ENERGY CENTER

The sixth energy center represents your third eye, insight. It's located in your forehead. It also includes the pineal gland. The energy here resonates with clear thinking and clear vision. The Chinese element is space and the color is indigo (some sources say violet). If you experience health issues with your senses, you may be off balance with your spiritual path. Nurturing the sixth energy center allows you to integrate your intelligence with your intuition. Distress in this energy center can be manifested by ringing in the ears, for example. Here the ego can trap you into limited, narrow, right and wrong views of your life. All I know is that I have not had to take decongestants after decades of recurring sinus congestion since I began journaling for this book. Maybe it's coincidence; maybe the process of writing down these ideas began the integration of mind and heart that balanced this energy center?

THE SEVENTH ENERGY CENTER

The seventh energy center is located in the top of the head and controls the cerebral cortex, head and upper spine. It includes the master of all the glands, the pituitary, because it produces hormones that stimulate and control the functions of the other endocrine glands such as adrenals, thyroid, ovaries and testes. The Chinese element is space and its color is purple or violet (some sources say crystal light). It's called the crown energy center because of its highly spiritual nature. It represents your relationship with Heaven, just as the first energy center, also known as the root energy center, represents your connection with Mother Earth. If you feel separated from a spiritual path, you may experience brain and nervous system disorders.

You'll know you have found your scream when your mind, body and spirit are connected and in balance.

While different traditions have variations on the energy center explanations above, there's a common theme. Your mind, body and spirit are connected. When balanced, the more likely it's that you have found and are living your scream!

To live in alignment with your scream you will want to identify and release thoughts, beliefs and patterns that limit you. They may be showing up as dis-ease. The dis-ease signifies that you are not balanced in mind, body and spirit. Drs. Northrop and Schultz suggest that you look for the energy center closest to the area of your body that's giving you feedback in the form of dis-ease. This may be the energy center that's affecting the malfunction. Look for the lesson in the ailment, seek the positive purpose for the message that your ailment's sending to you and be honest with yourself. Offer thanks to your body for the input.

Drs. Northrup and Schulz correlate past traumas, such as abuse, abandonment or heartache, with current physical ailments. Past traumas do not CAUSE the physical ailment, in their opinion, but tell you what patterns are unhealthy for you and create your petri dish for dis-ease. In other words, dis-ease is a significant voice of your inner leader that tells you intuitively what needs to change.

CELLULAR MEMORY

To completely be in balance and rid of an ailment, you may need to rid yourself of stored past negative emotions. The physical ailment is just a symptom. Cellular memory is real. It is a powerful driver for our healing and wellness. Working as a medical intuitive, Laura Alden Kamm has noted that the cellular memory of our body and its organs often hold the key to healing. In an email dated December 14, 2010 Laura noted, "Our cells hold an intelligence that goes beyond functionality and chemical levels of intelligence." In her trainings with integrative health-care providers, she teaches them how to incorporate their natural intuitive ability to access cellular intelligence. Weaving concepts from traditional Chinese Medicine and "Energy Medicine," Kamm's work helps re-establish cohesion within the body's systems. For example, this work can address the emotional intelligence between a donor organ and the recipient's body. Laura explains, "As it has been with the Integrative Medical Team at Columbia Presbyterian Hospital, the team has experienced how they have changed as practitioners and healers, and have witnessed exciting and intriguing results in their patients as they incorporate the integrative approach in Energy Medicine."

Recently, I gained an interesting perspective about cellular memory firsthand in a session with a self-described Quantum-Pathic® energy healer, Sherry Anshara, in Scottsdale, Arizona.

Sherry's QuantumPathic® perspective suggests that our cells retain "memories" of our past experiences. Whether we experience joy or trauma, our cells remember the context and the emotions we felt. Our cells retain the experience unless we release it. If we're unhealthy, it means we have negative experiences that we haven't released. We have to bring the memories that we've stored in our cells to the conscious level so we can let them go and reclaim our health.

I learned that this type of energy medicine combines physical and mental healing with the energy approach to heal the whole being. It's founded on the knowledge that all living beings and living systems are composed of energy: that thought and intention definitely influence energy; and that ultimately all things co-exist within one unified field of energy. This appealed to my energy background. But I approached this session with healthy skepticism, too.

I had my hysterectomy surgery just two months prior to my session with Sherry. I assumed that I put the lack of nurturing issue behind me. I felt extremely healthy. I did have a nagging issue with the groin area of my left leg, however. There was an intermittent dull pain. She observed that while I surgically removed my female organs, my body hadn't completely let the past experience go. My recent nurturing of myself hadn't yet made up for at that time, fifty-three years of ignoring it. I now was to nurture myself at a cellular level and come into my power as a female, according to Sherry. Wow. This was not an explanation that my left (analytical) brain understood.

I lay on her very comfortable, cushioned table where she performed some massage-like manipulations. Within one minute, she noticed my left hip was protruding higher than the right as I laid flat on my back. There was a total body twist from my left side to my right. She physically pushed on my left side while I performed and she talked me through some release and breathing exercises so that I would become less stiff in the shoulders and head.

She had me visualize the left groin spot and asked me to describe what I saw as inhibiting movement. I was not to think about it. What picture first popped up? While it seemed odd, I responded that there was a walnut locked in a titanium one-and-a-half inch box. I am not sure where that came from! Well, this was certainly an experience to "get out of the box." She then had me see the area not as a closed box, but as a room of windows and skylights, and to see myself standing in it.

"How old are you?" Sherry asked. Age sixteen popped into my mind. Why that age, I don't know, but she said to let the body answer. I felt like Alice in Wonderland. She had me reflect what was happening at this time of my life. My mother had married my evil stepfather a little over a year earlier. My mother had always been my biggest cheerleader. She had supported my siblings and me by attending our important school and sports events. Now we had to share her. Perhaps after that event the separation between my mother and me had become stronger? Perhaps I need to forgive my stepfather so that the lingering pain would be released? Sherry also offered from her perspective, that my birth parents made mistakes and that I should let them go. They didn't know me at all. My precociousness terrified my parents. The past is gone. I am to give unconditional love to myself and forgive.

I shed a few tears that came up from somewhere. I hadn't thought about being sixteen at all in my adult life. I have had all kinds of dreams about fairy tales since leaving GreenEnergyCo. At my birth, my mom was twenty-four and my dad almost twenty-nine. She said my mom was actually the equivalent of age sixteen and my dad was the equivalent of age fourteen in maturity when I was born. They were trying to live the fairy tales, but when they crossed the drawbridge they found that the castle was a dungeon. That's why they divorced when I was ten.

To put this in perspective for you, I don't routinely go to psychiatrists or spend time on the past. I don't believe in blaming external circumstances for my life circumstances. However, I do see an intriguing metaphor here for how the cells might hold old beliefs and patterns that can creep up as unresolved physical pain later. Whether it's cells holding old beliefs and patterns, or negative emotions such as anger and hostility or feelings of unworthiness being held within you, the mind-body connection seems irrefutable to me.

Examining your current beliefs about past events is worthwhile to create balance in your mind, body and spirit. While not always aware of it, I see it as dragging around a huge bag of trash that I've never dumped! My left leg has felt looser ever since my session with Sherry, so the session certainly didn't hurt me.

This one session intrigued me, so I looked into it. Striking examples of cellular memory are reported cases of transplant recipients suddenly assuming brand new behaviors, attitudes, habits and tastes that the donor possessed. One such example is reported in a Montgomery college paper. On May 29, 1988, a woman named Claire Sylvia received the heart of an eighteen-year-old male who had been killed in a motorcycle accident. Soon after the operation, Sylvia acted more masculine and strutted down the street. She was a dancer who previously walked much more gracefully. She began craving foods she disliked, such as green peppers and beer. She had a dream about her donor and eventually met the "family of her heart." The donor's family verified that her new attitudes, tastes, and habits closely mirrored their son's.

My experience with cellular memory certainly opens my imagination to the expansive possibilities of our emotional connections to our physical reality.

THE CONNECTION BETWEEN LIVING YOUR SCREAM AND YOU AND YOUR ORGANIZATION'S HEALTH CARE COSTS

So, how does finding and living your scream apply to your daily personal and work life? Obviously, you and your employees bring your personal selves to work—balanced or imbalanced, congruent or incongruent with who you are and what you value. When you are not living in your heart's joy and suffering from the physical cries of the consequences, are you optimally productive? How about your team members? You may be 'getting the job done' but how much more could you accomplish—more joyfully and more meaningfully—if each person were living in congruence with his or her scream? It would be one big celebration!

As you all know, good health is indispensable to fully enjoying most experiences in life. As you age, this becomes a top priority. If you have maintained your health, of course, it's easier to continue. However, it's rarely ever too late. The medical information in the remainder of this chapter is like the Cliffs Notes version on different therapies, treatments and interventions, so take from it what works for you. Hopefully, it will provide an overview on how to simply and cost-effectively maintain balanced health.

Dr. Andrew Weil, a thirty-year leader in integrative medicine, challenges corporations to adopt simple ways to contain health care spending in *Why Our Health Matters*. He suggests that organizations partner with government agencies and academic centers to evaluate innovative solutions for managing common health problems, especially integrative treatment.

Integrative treatment, with some use of alternative natural treatments, has been my preferred method of medicine for many years, although it wasn't called that in 1979 when I dove into understanding it. Dr. Gladys adds the strength of using your physician within to describe living medicine. I have found effective results using the "best of" all of these methods. Instead of first resorting to synthetic drugs and surgery to treat health conditions such as those employed in clinics and hospitals by conventional Western medicine, integrative medicine cherry picks the very best, scientifically validated therapies from both systems. In his *New York Times* review of Dr. Weil's book, *"Healthy Aging: A Lifelong Guide to Your Physical and Spiritual Well-Being,"* Abraham Verghese, M.D., commented that Dr. Weil "doesn't seem wedded to a particular dogma, Western or Eastern, only to the get-the-patient-better philosophy."

As Dr. Weil explains, conventional Western medicine is often both expensive and invasive, yet, for handling emergency conditions such as massive injury or a life-threatening stroke, one would certainly resort to it. Alternative therapies are different from integrative medicine, I have learned. They are closer to nature, cheaper and less invasive. Some are scientifically validated; others are not. "Complementary" medicine is used to describe blending an alternative with a conventional treatment, such as using ginger syrup to prevent nausea during chemotherapy.

Dr. Weil's work is guided by this definition: Integrative medicine is healing-oriented medicine that takes account of the whole person. It gives consideration to all factors that influence health, wellness and disease, including mind, spirit and community as well as body. It emphasizes the therapeutic relationship and makes use of all appropriate therapies, both conventional and alternative.

You have seen evidence of what the 50 to 100 Best Companies do. Predictably, Dr. Weil expounds in *Why Our Health Matters* that by offering workers discounted gym memberships, smoking cessation programs and more nutritious cafeteria food, companies and organizations will see an increase in productivity and reduced employee absenteeism. They'll also enjoy lower health care expenditures.

And while Dr. Weil describes the increased role that companies can play, ultimately it's your choice as an individual to take care of yourself. "At the root of good healthcare is an acceptance of each individual's responsibility for his or her own health," he tells *AZ Generation Health Magazine* in February 2010. Alcoholics Anonymous's success is based on this principle. You need to be responsible for your own care, for you to heal and be physically balanced. The system is not going to do it for you.

In today's Western society, due to the complexity of knowledge that a Western doctor must learn, one doctor alone cannot always interpret the data to administer medicine, so the primary doctors can send patients to specialists. In effect, general practitioners take power from the patient and give it to the specialist. Your family may be experiencing what our family is experiencing now—employers' rising heath care costs and lower employer contributions. Or maybe you pay for your own health care insurance. You see a generalist, have tests done, then see a specialist and there are co-pays for tests done of which you weren't even aware. It almost seems patients are no longer real people. This practice teaches us to feel that science knows more about us than we know about ourselves (not so!). As patients, we've given away the responsibility to care for our own health, haven't we? Think about the phrase, "health-care delivery system." It suggests that the doctor is like a mail carrier who can deliver health to your doorstep! Your language, the very words you—and society and the media—use, have power.

In *The Physician Within You*, Dr. Gladys encourages patients to be partners in their own healing. Those who follow the rules may be inclined to accept their doctor's diagnosis rather than believe they have power over the cure of many conditions. Their physical body may be treated and relieved temporarily, but is there a true, lasting healing?

When doctors cannot perform the heroic work of fixing the broken machine, they sometimes blame the victim. And patients get frustrated by their powerlessness. Suing for malpractice is an act of revenge in an attempt to regain power over the doctor, but it doesn't reclaim our true self-power.

A validation of this idea is conveyed in *Blink*. Malcolm Gladwell reported on independent reviewers who listened to recorded patient-physician interactions. (The names in the recording were obscured to protect privacy.) The reviewers accurately predicted who was accused of malpractice, based solely on the tone of voice they heard. If the surgeon sounded dominant, he or she was likely in the sued group. If the doctors merely sounded less dominant and more concerned, they were typically in the non-sued category. The observed difference in the doctors' interactions was entirely in how they talked to their patients, not in the complexity of medical training or explanation. It's just a matter of simple respect.

I can relate to this observation. During one of my company-paid-for executive physical examinations, the lead physician complimented me for how long I could run on the treadmill (longer than some of the firemen) at my age and on how many push-ups I could do as a woman. I matter-of-factly described how I had explored "holistic" health (for lack of a better term) and wellness since age twenty-two. The doctor launched into a tirade about medical malpractice, our legal system, the FDA, American Medical Association, and why he cannot suggest herbal or alternatives due to the threat of litigation. I was taken aback, but let it go. Surprisingly, a few days later I received an unsolicited apology letter from him.

So, own your health; partner with your physicians; ask plenty of questions, including those about alternative treatments as a starting point before resorting to invasive treatments (assuming your situation is not life-threatening, certainly). Encourage your employer to offer insurance coverage for preventative wellness or set up a medical flexible spending account to cover the cost of your pursuing it. Over the thirty years, many of the physicians who have helped me enjoy a vibrant, energized life did not accept traditional insurance. It has been worth the modest investment.

HOW TAKING RESPONSIBILITY FOR YOUR OWN HEALTH CARE BENEFITS YOU AND YOUR ORGANIZATION

As I took responsibility for my own health, I learned more and more over time about the many forms of alternative and integrative methods of healing and how they affected me personally, as I have mentioned. I visited traditional Western-trained medical doctors who also studied other forms of healing. I followed up on materials to which they referred me so that I could gain greater understanding and learn how to listen to my physician within. The contrast and comparison of the "best of" Western and Eastern medicine is detailed in *Between Heaven and Earth*. The perspectives helped me gain awareness (from both the left brain analytical side and right brain intuitive side) to more effectively discuss diagnoses or treatments with doctors the few times I visited them, so I'll share some of its basic concepts with you.

The authors explain that Western philosophy is dominated by "causal thinking." Events occur in a series, like a line of falling dominoes, with each falling domino being the cause of the next domino's fall, including the effect of the preceding domino's fall on the domino that just caused the next one to fall. The presumed pattern of events is a linear sequence that cannot be re-arranged.

In contrast, acupuncture and other forms of Chinese medicine presume that you can reorganize an existing pattern, for example, a pattern of disharmony, into a harmonic pattern of relationships. Once you do so, the original cause will disappear because the conditions in which the disharmony was rooted cease to exist. Chinese medicine views health as an organism's ability to respond appropriately to a wide variety of challenges in a way that insures maintaining equilibrium. It considers the source of dis-ease as any challenge to the body with which the body cannot cope, whether the challenge is a harmful substance or a bad feeling. The adage, "The man is not sick because he has an illness, but has an illness because he is sick," aptly expresses this view. Recall that this idea is akin to the question I raised in my discussion of the energy centers: "*Who* is wrong with you?" instead of "*What*."

Flowers growing in a garden need adequate light, water, air and soil. Similarly, humans need a climate with an adequate amount of energy—an excess or deficiency of emotions and life activities destroys the pattern of energetic flow. Chinese medicine follows the philosophy of *yin* and *yang*. This philosophy proposes there must be a balance between the internal process of nurturing yourself (yin/female energy, or white female energy, according to the South African Sangoma Zulus), and being engaged in the external work of the world (yang/male energy, or red male energy, according to the Zulus). To continue the analogy, if there's an infestation of pests, the gardener has to apply strong measures, like poison, but has to be careful not to irreparably damage the garden. A Chinese doctor is careful to help restore the resilience and strength of the body while prescribing treatments to help fight a disease.

Between Heaven and Earth explains that in theory and practice, traditional Chinese medicine is completely different from Western medicine, both in terms of considering how the human body works and how illness occurs and should be treated. As a part of a continuing system that has been in use for thousands of years, it's still employed to treat more than one quarter of the world's population. Since the earliest Chinese physicians were also philosophers, their ways of viewing the world and human beings' role in it affected the way they view medicine.

Perhaps Western doctors are like mechanics compared to the Chinese gardeners. Since the days of Descartes, the Western worldview has been that Nature and humans are machines governed by mechanical laws. Unfortunately, the mechanics don't keep up the required routine maintenance—that is the owner's responsibility! But then the doctors have to intervene to execute emergency repairs and replace non-functioning elements. Doctors, then, are the mechanics who fix broken body-machines. Instead of looking at the body as an integrated system, Western conventional medicine sees it as a bunch of parts, and they remove faulty parts in isolation from the other organs.

Interestingly, prior to the Middle Ages, the people of Western Europe were more like indigenous people. That is, the Europeans had a unified view of their Universe: they viewed themselves as an integral part of everything that was both seen and unseen. They were connected with Heaven through God and with Earth through Nature. The break with this organic sensibility came with the decline of the feudal society, as cities grew and as the Protestant Reformation undermined the Roman Catholic Church. Europeans believed they could attain mastery in the world through their own willful efforts. Heaven existed outside of Nature, barely within human reach. A schism occurred between the sacred and the secular, Heaven and Earth, life and death. The new "religion" was that of Science, as explained in *Between Heaven and Earth*.

Much later, with the advent of the Industrial Revolution of the late 1700s, an even greater dislocation occurred when factories caused people to leave the countryside to seek urban jobs. Insanity and poor health became more common as people lost their connection to Nature. And in the next chapter, you will see today's continuation of problems associated with the lack of connection in the rise of lack of self-esteem and resulting increasing suicide rates. It was during the late 1700s when science became the new religion that Western medicine took a foothold. That's why it's more oriented toward intervention than prevention!

The purpose now in conventional Western medicine appears to be to keep the machine running rather than to enrich life. Western culture's center is commerce, industry and information. We produce the world in which we live by exerting power over Nature. We don't co-create! In an effort to achieve mastery over the world, has Western medicine and, moreover, society lost connectedness with Nature and humanity? And how does this relate to the increased unhealthiness and obesity in our communities? We will explore this more before this book ends.

When you find your scream and live it, you become balanced in mind, body and spirit. As you increase your own self-awareness in this process, you'll naturally connect more with the world around you. You most likely won't become one of those obesity or heart disease statistics.

BALANCE IN ALL THINGS FOR THE HEALTHIEST YOU

Balance has been and still is a learning process for me. Laura Kamm challenged me in our second session in 2002 to take notice when there's an equal amount of light and dark as the sun sets, when all is peaceful. Try it. It's quite the experience in discernment. Well, if you have read this far, you have deduced by now that subtlety has not been a strength of mine.

Some of the Western way of thinking is, if some is good, more is better. No pain, no gain, as my aerobics teachers say. (I probably said it too right after Jane Fonda was my instructor on VHS tapes). This may not be so with the body, as I learned from Matt Taylor, who helped me run without the knee support.

Dr. Taylor was trained in physical therapy at Baylor University. He worked with soldiers and athletes prior to completing his doctorate in yoga therapies. He observed that I bent forward when I walked and did not stand up straight. I approached the world so head-on that I put a strain on my lower back. Due to teaching step aerobics for twenty years, physiologically I'd over-developed my quadriceps, and my hamstrings became imbalanced. Because my left hip was weaker, my right ankle was pulled and placed pressure on my knee. These imbalances created a vulnerability that resulted in my injury. To heal, I had to strengthen my hamstrings and left hip, thereby bringing them back into natural balance.

What I was challenged to explore emotionally, however, is what inflexibility—what was I resisting—that contributed to the knee being so sore? As I reflect, during that time, a shift in me was accelerating. I knew "inside" that GreenEnergyCo would have significant changes ahead and I wanted to prevent that. I did not want to "move forward." I wasn't ready yet. There were more beneficial projects that GreenEnergyCo could undertake and still more growth for our people ahead. The time to dismantle was not then.

In addition to stressing the need for balance in all things, traditional Chinese medicine advocates moderation in all things, philosophically and medically, and living in harmony with Nature. Prevention is a key goal, and much emphasis is placed on educating the patient to live responsibly. Traditionally, the Chinese physician is more of an advisor than an authority; he or she believes in treating every patient differently, based on the notion that one doesn't treat the disease or condition, but rather the individual. Dr. Gladys uses these principles in her practice of Living Medicine, too. Two people with the same complaint may be treated entirely differently if their constitutions and life situations are dissimilar.

Disease is also considered by Chinese practitioners to be evidence of the failure of preventive health care and a falling out of balance or harmony. This reminds me of the Peruvian guide, Don Americo Yabar's story of the Master who ate the sun directly, instead of consuming the apple to get a balanced amount of sunlight.

There's some confusion in the West about the fundamental philosophical principles upon which traditional Chinese medicine is based—such as the concept of yin and yang, the concept of chi energy discussed earlier, and the notion of five elements (wood, fire, earth, metal and water)—yet each can be explained in a way that's understandable to Westerners.

Let's look at the five elements, for example. The five elements and their relation to the complementary energy centers are grounded in the notion of harmony and balance. They offer another low-tech tool to aid in the observation of what is otherwise too hidden. As reading glasses bring into focus what is in front of my face (but if I hold the item out further, I can see!), the five elements show us our patterns of how we interact with the world. They aid "us in the divination of our certain place between heaven and earth," as the authors explain in *Between Heaven and Earth*. They also help the medical practitioner relate your imbalance to you as an individual.

There's a self-test in *Between Heaven and Earth* that you can use to determine to which of the elements you relate. I learned from the test, confirmed by my acupuncturist, that I am mainly wood and some fire. Wood is associated with a person leading her life as a *Pioneer*. This personification is of one striking into the wilderness with a bold, adventurous spirit to break new ground, face challenges, overcome difficulties and conquer the unknown. (This sounds a lot like the Calling Cards I drew years before I visited the acupuncturist. I have had many clues along the way.)

The *Pioneer* is action-oriented, whereas the *Philosopher*, who characterizes water, is preoccupied with seeking the truth. (Now this sounds like the CVI Innovator assessment characterization!) The *Philosopher* explores hidden mysteries through the medium of his own imaginative mind. The *Peacemaker* is stable, centered, relaxed and personifies earth. She is drawn toward being a mediator in the service of harmony and unity. The *Wizard* embodies fire and is magnetic and exciting, inspires faith that dreams can be realized and desires fulfilled. The *Alchemist* personifies metal and observes, studies, and analyzes phenomena to extract fundamental laws and principles in the service of a universal order.

The five elements theory for self-understanding describes the context within which we evolve. Knowing to which one you relate sheds light on the goals you set, the risks you take, the competence you manifest, your expectations, what threatens you and satisfies you. You are a combination of these elements but one predominates you as an organizing force. Your patterns of disease and health correspond to the element that typifies you also. This explains why some manifest stress as sinus congestion, and others as irritability with neck tension. For example, in *Between Heaven and Earth*, the authors explain that *Wood* does well under intense competitive pressure that upsets *Earth* and paralyzes *Water*. *Water* prefers to have time to think things through and *Earth* feels most comfortable when people work together cheerfully. You can see the similarity in the Chinese five elements theory to the theories utilized in the data-driven assessments that we reviewed earlier. The difference is that Western medical practitioners do not typically incorporate an understanding of who you are when prescribing your treatment.

Yin and yang describe the interdependent relationship of opposing but complementary forces believed to be necessary for a healthy life. Basically, the goal is to maintain a balance of yin and yang in all things.

Our contemporary culture encourages constant, often frenetic, activity. Being consumed with productivity, we don't replenish the self—we neglect it. To overwork, over-exercise, over-party and over-engage is to overindulge in yang, which leads to burnout of yin. (This harkens back to Muvo telling me my red energy, or yang, was out of balance, right after leaving GreenEnergyCo.) Consequences of this imbalance may be muscle, joint, bone, heart or kidney problems, perhaps as serious and sudden as a heart attack.

The key is to achieve balance, which means being flexible, diverse, moderate and in harmony with your own rhythms and needs. Chinese medicine uses acupuncture, herbs, diet, physical exercise, massage, mental discipline, and the modification of lifestyle habits as forms of therapies that re-establish the rhythmic swing of the yin-yang pendulum. I'm growing to understand the beauty of this ancient way of approaching the world. As we have seen, Dr. Weil, Dr. Gladys and other physicians are incorporating many more of these ways—clearly ones that are scientifically validated—into their practice of medicine.

During a consultation with a traditional Chinese medicine practitioner, the patient receives a considerable amount of time and attention. During the important first visit, the practitioner conducts four types of examinations, all extremely observational and all quite different from what patients usually experience with Western-trained doctors. First, the practitioner asks many questions that go beyond the typical patient history to inquire about particulars such as eating, bowel habits or sleep patterns. Next, the physician looks at the patient, observes his or her complexion and eyes. Chinese medicine practitioners also examine the tongue very closely, believing that it's a barometer of the body's health and that different areas of the tongue can reflect the functioning of different body organs. In the next chapter, I relate my visit to such a doctor and how different the examination was.

After observing, they listen to the patient's voice or cough and then smell his or her breath, body odor, urine and even bowel movements. Finally, the practitioner touches the patient, palpating his or her abdomen and feeling the wrist to take up to six different pulses. It's through these different pulses that the well-trained practitioner can diagnose any problem with the flow of the all-important chi. Altogether, this essentially observational examination leads the physician to diagnose or decide the patient's problem.

This type of diagnosis is very different from the procedures used in contemporary Western medicine, which includes laboratory tests of blood and urine samples. These tests are certainly useful. Much like the power in integrating intuitive understanding with the information from personality and values data-driven assessments, I encourage you to integrate the information from the best of Western and Eastern medical principles as it pertains to balancing your body.

FUEL FOR A BALANCED YOU

Your health and the food you eat are tightly interrelated. You have probably heard, "You are what you eat." The Eastern and Western approaches to food and health vary. In Chinese medicine, who we are determines what is most beneficial to eat. People who tend to be congested need decongesting food. People who are hot need cooling foods. Raw fruits and vegetables cool the digestion system (yin) because they promote the loss of body heat and secretion of fluid, according to the authors of *Between Heaven and Earth*. The Chinese believe Westerners overreact when we swing to radical purification and elimination through fasting and juice diets to counteract feeling out of balance.

An Eastern treatment for a person with hypertension goes beyond the Western advice of eliminating salt and saturated fats. That's because someone with high blood pressure can be strong or weak, congested or depleted, hot or cold; and Chinese practitioners consider all of these possibilities in the diagnosis. Chinese culture looks at food value as embodying sun, rain, heat, cold, dryness and wetness. Climate, the season and the illness at hand also determine what foods are best for you. People who are cold and dry need warm, moisturizing food; those who are hot and damp need cool, drying food. Raw fruits and vegetables cool (yin) you because they promote the loss of body heat and the secretion of fluid. If you are cold, damp and depleted, this diet would exaggerate the internal climate and add puffiness. Spicy warm foods (yang) absorb the heat of cooking and generate body heat and stimulate circulation. If you are hot, dry and congested, yang-type foods exacerbate your issues. Salad may be therapeutic food for one who is hot and dry.

Often in Western medicine, we mask signs of poor digestion. With gas, we chew antacids—ahh, the TUMS. Or we gulp Pepto-Bismol® to stop up our system. We'd rather take medications than change our diet.

FOOD AND YOUR CONSTITUTION

It took me some time to understand the importance of food. There's so much conflicting media and social information—and then there's what you grew up with that has emotional attachments. When I was young, we fended for ourselves when it came to meals. My mom worked and went to college. My sister, brother and I had our sports, school activities and learned how to microwave (once they were invented). I had two waitressing jobs when I was sixteen and usually grabbed something at the restaurants where I worked. Occasionally, at home, we had a cooked casserole.

Needless to say, I didn't learn much about healthy eating. (Media and marketing information still doesn't help clear the confusion. What is no "trans-fat" anyway?) On top of that, to emulate the magazine cover images of young women, I dieted to stay thin. I tried every diet. Remember Richard Simmons, Fit or Fat, the Zone Diet, the Scarsdale Diet, the Atkins™ low-carb diet, to name a few? I eventually learned that diets don't work!

You will discover why diets don't work in the next chapter on how to release your fear of change. You will learn how to change your eating behavior, if you need. In this chapter, I want you to focus on when your body is identifying for you that you are not balanced and are out of alignment. You are not living your scream when your body talks back.

There was a literal backfire to my low-calorie diet choices that consisted of many raw vegetables. At one point, my hands turned orange because I ate so many carrots! Later in life, my family demanded I find a "cure" for the backfire. They threatened to sign me up to compete on television's the "Man-Show," for the all-time smelliest flatulence! (This is truly embarrassing for me to admit to you readers who know me!) Flatulence is a fairly common human state and "remediable."

As the saying goes, the teacher comes when the student is ready. I learned about the best diet for me unexpectedly in my late forties. A health-conscious friend gave me a book about the ayurvedic way of viewing diet, *The Complete Book of Ayurvedic Home Remedies*, by Vasant Lad, B.A.M.S., M.A.Sc. Ayurveda is an Indian Sanskrit word that means "the science of life and longevity," according to Vasant. It's based on the timeless wisdom of India's 5,000-year-old medical system.

Ayurvedic medicine emphasizes that we come from Nature, and to be healthy we must live in balance with Nature. Nutrition is viewed as a fundamental way of balancing the body. Our innate constitution is imprinted at birth. It consists of the five universal energies of space, air, fire, water, and earth (that I mentioned above in the energy center section), which are combined into three fundamental energies, or *doshas*, according to Vasant. Air and space constitute the dosha of *vata*. Vata is the energy of movement. Fire and water constitute the dosha of *pitta*, which is the principle of digestion or metabolism. Water and earth make up *kapha*, the energy of structure and lubrication.

Here are some very generalized characteristics of each dosha. Every person is made up of some aspect of each. However, you typically have a dominant one or combination of two.

Vatas tend to be light in structure and form and are usually taller and thinner than average. Vata, when in balance, is creative, light, subtle and filled with new ideas. When out of balance, the movement of air in vata creates instability and fear. Vatas' tendency toward movement and instability can result in poor digestion, insomnia and psychological problems.

Pittas are mostly fire, with some water. They tend to be medium build and muscular. Warm, friendly, outgoing, expressive, rational, strong, courageous and heroic describe them. When out of balance, anger, hostility and resentment, along with stress, can result in high blood pressure and heart disease. Pitta is related to *agni*, the digestive fire, and when agni is too high, strong indigestion or ulcers can result.

Kaphas are a combination of earth and water. They tend to have a heavier build with large bones. They move more slowly, cautiously, have sweet, gentle natures, stable minds and good long-term memory. Kaphas, in balance, are meditative, deliberate and focused. When out of balance they tend to be lethargic and sluggish. Kapha digestion tends to be slow and they tend toward congestion and respiratory problems.

Deepok Chopra's website has a survey with more in-depth questions so you can better determine the constitution that you favor, and what foods will help keep you in balance. The reference is in the back of this book.

Let's compare my ayurvedic constitution to what you've learned about me in this book. I'm a pitta-vata. My digestive constitution is mainly pitta, which is a hot dosha. I learned that ayurvedic, worry-free teas, such as cinnamon or peppermint, could help with my digestion issues. For example, instead of TUMS, a fennel tea works wonders for gas relief. I should eat cool, not cold foods. Hot spicy food causes gas. To become "uncongested" (not constipated) I needed more leafy greens.

When I was introduced to ayurvedic nutrition, I had no idea what dosha or pitta meant (other than pita bread—ha!). Eventually, I consulted with Laura Alden Kamm to corroborate what I was experiencing.

Until I met with Laura I thought I was eating very healthy foods—yogurt and a banana for breakfast and power bar for lunch after my workout. Laura grimaced, and had me visualize yeast fermenting in a beer vat. The yogurt sat in my craw with the banana, and fermented. Boil and bubble, double trouble. She calmly explained that yogurt is too sour and aggravating for pitta. Heavy, oily power bars have too many carbohydrates for me. I need protein more than carbs. I complained that ever since my son was born, I could no longer eat raw veggies. She agreed.

Slightly cooked vegetables are better for me because the raw ones are too harsh to digest. The digestive capabilities of my liver were off because my acid, the fire—angi—was too high. Absorption was not occurring. Laura suggested I lay off salsa for a while, too.

I was amazed at what Laura could detect. Forget Oprah's personal cook—this information is as personalized as it gets! Laura said I was not eating enough food overall. By eating so little in a day, my digestion was sluggish. Choose chicken and shrimp, not red meat, because it's too hot, too sweet, and takes too much energy to break down to digest. My adrenals need protein. I also need to run glycogen through my brain and body. Grazing rather than eating big meals is better—three small meals, two snacks—because my stomach cannot handle a heavy load. I should lean toward foods that are slightly sweet, not sour. (Naturally, my favorite tastes are spicy and sour.)

I should choose cooling granola, apple juice, cinnamon and egg or some other kind of protein in the morning. Blueberries are good; bagels are not. A little bread and butter is good for one who is more pitta than vata. The fire would calm fastest by drinking cooked milk with cinnamon or nutmeg.

Food is my medicine, and Laura's prescription went further. Because I need fuel from glycogen from my liver to my brain during the day, lunch is important, not dinner. I put way too much pressure on my system by exercising at lunch time. I need real, whole foods. A pitta is strongest from 10 a.m. to 2 p.m. For me to not lose vitality, I needed something more like peanut butter and jelly or uncooked honey at lunch. I certainly hadn't learned this by reading the Zone Diet book.

She examined my constipation issue. My constipation problems related to my emotions that were tied into to my stressful survival experiences when I was twenty-two. Because my life was so out of control, a natural reaction was for me to protect myself from that again by attempting to control my environment. The unintended consequence of my experience was that I blocked things from going through me, emotionally and physically. But how can you perform optimally, if things aren't flowing, so to speak?

For some people, it's simply a poor diet of overcooked and processed foods, lack of water, and sedentary lifestyle that exacerbate their digestion problems. When emotional blockages manifest physically, food can become impacted in the colon. Your emotions also affect how well you assimilate food. If you eat when angry, it hampers digestion. The simple guideline for digestion is: eat what you can digest effectively. Feel better after eating than before—not stuffed, but that pang of hunger that caused you to eat is quieted.

Laura concluded our nutrition session by explaining that when I was back in balance, bitter and astringent leafy greens would continue to calm my digestive fire. Now, on many mornings I have a green shake of fresh berries, organic spinach and kale, banana, and almond milk with dehydrated greens. Be prepared, it looks like algae, but is not unpleasant tasting. This creates a comfortable balance of alkalinity in my body. I feel totally energized, and I'm "regular" and smell-free! She taught me that I'm the only one who can monitor my natural resources.

While this information is highly personalized to me, I offer it in hopes that you are intrigued to explore the best nutritional balance for you and that you achieve the relief and vibrancy that I feel!

My husband decided to take a different route to feeling better, however. He's a pitta-kapha. His personal preference is to eat high-carb foods. His ayurvedic constitution, however, would be better balanced if he ate many more vegetables. One of the consequences of his diet is that he has the kapha tendency toward acute nasal congestion. Jeff recently had sinus surgery due to a fungal infection that contributed to his congestion. The results have been fantastic. Sometimes, Western intervention is the way to go, but I encourage you to consider the benefits of food choices that honor your individual makeup before turning to invasive procedures. That will save you time and all of us money in the form of reduced heath care costs.

Have you noticed the return to buying local organic foods at farmers' markets? Can this be called "retro" since our ancestors grew crops organically, as well as respected and understood the land? (The ancient celebration and tradition of "knowing the land" will once again have our respect.) While not always readily available in your area, when you can buy locally, there are many nutritional benefits to doing so.

PREVENTING OBESITY AND DIABETES

As you have read, I have been committed to a healthy lifestyle for decades, instigated in part by my mother's short life. I'm very concerned about our workforce, and our society's epidemic of obesity and diabetes. Did you know that one in four American adults—that's 57 million people—have pre-diabetes? Did you know that one in three Americans born after 2000 are expected to develop diabetes in their lifetime, if we continue on our current trajectory? These two issues are the source of a majority of our health care ailments and costs. Yet 50 to 70 percent of all diseases are associated with modifiable health risks and are preventable. Diabetes is just one of them. Diabetes is a leading cause of heart disease, stroke, blindness, kidney disease and nerve disease. You have the power to prevent or delay diseases such as diabetes, right now. (See www.valleyymca.org in the References and Resources section.)

If you are challenged by obesity or diabetes, you are less likely to fully live your scream or a life of your dreams. There may be individual exceptions, certainly, where people have learned to live in joy despite the burden of carrying too much weight or not being able to produce insulin properly, but for those of us who don't fit this description, there are ways to prevent or turn around these trends. Type 2 diabetes is linked to blood sugar levels, not just weight. If you are thirty to forty pounds overweight, you would want to test for pre-diabetes. You can successfully live with type 2 or type 1 diabetes. However, if you can prevent it, your life will be easier. Pre-diabetics are likely to turn into type 2 diabetes individuals within ten years if they do nothing about it. Once you have diabetes, there's no reversal. Preventing the likelihood of becoming a diabetic has a three to one payback for the insurer; and of course there are the many benefits that accrue to individuals who avoid getting the disease.

As the public policy chair for the Valley of the Sun YMCA, I have been active in advocating preventative health and wellness in our communities. I see the encouraging results of the Y's 2010 Diabetes Prevention Program (Y-DPP). With simple lifestyle changes such as eating healthier and incorporating physical activity up to 150 minutes per week, or achieving a modest 7 percent weight reduction, a person with pre-diabetes can prevent or delay the onset of the disease by almost 60 percent.

The Y-DPP is based on the landmark program funded by the National Institutes of Health and the Centers for Disease Control and Prevention. The research proved that the YMCA could effectively deliver a group-based lifestyle intervention for about one-sixth the cost of supplying the diabetes medication Metformin for a year. Y-DPP works for all age, gender and race subgroups. Insurers like UnitedHealth Group are getting on board. Your company or organization can choose providers who cover more preventative services.

Think what preventive programs like this could do to contain health care costs in organizations. How much do you, as an employee, spend on your portion of health care costs? How much does your company spend on its contributions? The entire way our society looks at health must change. Progress is slowly being made. Health care companies and insurers are beginning to pay for more wellness and prevention programs. But each of us and our co-workers should demand more!

In the next chapter, you will learn how to make changes you desire. This program is one of several that are available to you once you decide to move in alignment with your scream.

BALANCE THROUGH YOGA

While we wait for a cure for what I believe to be a broken American health care system, there are simple preventative health measures and ways we can stay in balance, such as yoga. Think of the cost to repair the enormous number of sick people that the American lifestyle generates! We have heard from many doctors who agree that our society is constantly looking for high-tech solutions—a new magic pill, a new surgical procedure. "But what if we went low tech instead, giving people yoga strategies? It would be the biggest bang for the buck in terms of making an impact on the world," proclaims Sat Bir Khalsa, a Ph.D. in neurophysiology and professor at an affiliate of Harvard Medical School. He has dedicated his life to proving his belief.

In May, 2010, he told an interviewer with *Yoga Journal* that his legacy is to prove to an evidence-based American health care system that yoga should become the preferred "medicine" of America, prescribed by doctors and paid for by health insurance. Khalsa compares yoga to a toothbrush for the body and mind, stating, "... but what about mind-body hygiene? We have nothing for that. If we'd use yoga as regularly as our toothbrushes ... and if schools taught it, doctors recommended it, and parents reinforced it, people would have a tool that reduces their stress, or at the very least manages it, while building self-awareness."

There's a common perception in the minds of conventional scientists: Yoga is either trivialized as something for cosmetic purposes to slim your butt, or it's perceived as a "goofy, New Agey, 'out there' kind of practice," Khalsa says. I agree with Khalsa, who also says that while it's not sexy stuff, what makes the most sense and works most effectively is lifestyle change. Yoga is really all about changing your lifestyle.

Khalsa conducted a study with teens and found at the end of a twelve-week program, those who had taken yoga versus taking a physical education class reported less anger, fatigue and more resilience than the control group, reported *Yoga Journal*. The teens were thankful to have gained tools to combat stress and reported how they used breathing patterns to go to sleep, in athletics and before tests. Khalsa believes that if forty- and fifty-year-olds who grapple with insomnia had started practicing yoga and meditation as children, they wouldn't be facing sleepless nights.

Also, if adults with type 2 diabetes and obesity had learned yoga techniques in high school, their health outcomes would be better. The increased body awareness learned through yoga in a recent study showed it had a greater effect on the participants' weight than did the exercise aspect. They became aware of why they ate and stopped eating when full. Khalsa foresees that, while a lot of older veteran scientists will resist yoga, it's just the nature of bias and belief. He recalls the "cigarettes don't cause cancer" diehards. "Often it's the next generation that can finally enact a shift."

That generation is all of us, right now.

WHAT NEXT?

Dr. David Hawkins, in *Power vs. Force*, exposes what he calls the bogged-down bureaucracy we have for a health care system as the only one in the world where people have declared bankruptcy because of their inability to pay. He observes that systems become ineffective and wasteful when they're overburdened with fear and regulation. No kidding. Fear burdens both human and organizational systems!

You and your company can lower your health care costs by making a "wellness investment" in finding your scream and living in alignment with it. When people are out of alignment they get ailments, as we have seen. You can't ignore the relationship between what type of illness you have and your emotional imbalance. When my employees had foot problems, it was an immediate sign that they were not grounded in some fundamental way with who they were compared to the life they were living. Either they fundamentally were not in the right job, or they dreaded going into work each day and their balance was thrown off kilter. So we created a safe environment to explore the root cause of their imbalance.

Everyone wants to succeed. Once you are aware of your strengths, you can. Sometimes you discover that you are reaching too far outside of your natural and trained abilities. This is the premise behind the "Peter Principle." You've seen it, perhaps in others. Recognize it. You'll be happier doing something where you can succeed rather than faking it and being fearful. Putting this kind of pressure on yourself undoubtedly results in illness.

All people want to be connected, to belong. Finding the best-fit for you and for your employees provides this satisfaction. When you work out of joy and do what you love, your physical health will reflect it. As within, so without.

Many intuitive health experts opine that at the root of dis-ease is the seed of not forgiving yourself. The most important relationship is the one you have with yourself. You can be a best friend or your harshest critic. This is a very common issue. Your view of your self-worth = your net worth. Look in the mirror, sit on a chair and talk to yourself. Tell yourself that you are worthy of creatively expressing yourself in work that matters to you! Guess what blocks intuition and access to all the answers you possess within? Fear and low self-worth. Suffering is a residue of pent-up energies that accumulated from your past. Forgiveness releases these energies. When you confront your ghosts of the past, you can move beyond them.

We can learn from all of the sources of medicine—the indigenous people, Chinese practitioners and Western doctors. You can blend the best of all worlds in addressing your health—once you choose to take charge of your own health!

EXERCISES

1. Where does your body consistently hurt? What does the function of the hurting part of your body tell you about where you may not be in alignment with what you value? What fear might be stored within you?
2. What energy center relates to the part of your body you identified above? What might that tell you about where your energy is blocked?
3. Take the free on-line test to discern which dosha describes your digestive constitution. http://doshaquiz.chopra.com.
4. List what you can do to take more responsibility for your own health.

SEVEN

RELEASE YOUR FEAR

Things do not change; we change.
— Henry David Thoreau

You have used your intuition to find your answers within. You have explored your core using your intuition and data-driven assessments to become very self-aware of who you are and what you value. You have applied the first two principles to yourself as a person, a leader and as an organization. You have questioned whether your findings are true, and by listening to your body, you realize that you have pain where you are out of alignment. Now what? You will learn to apply the third principle to release your fear of change and re-align with your scream to live your dream.

Think of fear as F.E.A.R., an acronym for "False Expectations Appearing Real." Fear is the anticipation of something that has not and is not likely to happen. The emotion of fear is the root cause of blocked energy. Your personal power then is limited, and ends where your fear begins. Fear blocks you from seeing new opportunities. Fear can paralyze you. You believe you cannot move forward to change, become aligned with your scream, and live your dream. Fear can show up in your life as anger or frustration, impatience, feelings of unworthiness, lack of trust, resistance or separation.

To release your fear, you must first identify what it is that makes you afraid. Are you afraid you will never fill those big shoes? You may think you have no fear. Or perhaps you think that you have things you want to change, but they are not based in fear. I believe, as do many other authors and experts, that your feelings and emotions emanate either from survival, which is fear based, or creation, which is love based. It's more likely than not that what prevents you from living a life of your dreams is the very fear of change itself. If you are acting in ways that don't serve your highest and best self, you can bet there's an underlying fear that needs to be confronted.

The process of change requires not only that you become acutely aware of your fears, but that you own and acknowledge them and the valid purpose they once served. After you have identified your fears, you have to unlearn your fear-based feeling or response, release it, and replace it with your desired way of being. Dr. Joe Dispenza explains this process in greater detail in *The Art of Change*.

Dr. Dispenza knows firsthand the process of change. At age twenty-three, Joe was looking at the possibility of permanent paralysis after a spine-crushing bicycle accident. Joe was faced with a life-changing decision. His doctors believed that his only hope of walking again was a surgical procedure that even if successful could leave him permanently disabled and in constant pain. Joe refused the procedure, opting instead to recreate his own physical body by literally "changing his mind." He laid on a board for weeks, having friends and family change the angle of the board to promote blood flow to heal. Ten weeks later, without surgery, he was back at work, completely healed and pain free.

We all have a bushel basketful of beliefs that we don't question, and many are fear based. Your beliefs create your reality.

It's not what happens to you in your life, but how you interpret what happens to you that makes the difference in a fulfilled or unfulfilled life. If you interpret the events from a fear-based belief system, you will not be living your dreams!

I encouraged my younger son Shane, to confront his fear-based beliefs early in life. One such instance was when Shane would make excuses about riding the bus to grade school. He would purposely be late so I would have to drive him to school. This did not fit with my busy schedule. More importantly, I was concerned that Shane was a glass half-empty pessimist. My personal philosophy is "There's no such thing as can't," so I vowed to show Shane another way. We dug deeper. Shane revealed that he did not want to ride the bus for fear he would be beaten up by the much older bully, a neighborhood boy. I understood the valid purpose his fear served. Certainly, not riding the bus may have protected him from a potential pummeling, but Shane's fears seemed to be exaggerated.

I was describing Shane's pessimistic outlook to a fellow soccer mom during one of Shane's games. She was a psychiatrist and referred me to the book, *The Optimistic Child*, written by experimental psychologist, Martin E. P. Seligman, Ph.D. Dr. Seligman's work guided me in helping Shane to "de-catastrophize." He explained that planning for the worst case is a big drain on energy, ruins your mood and is a waste of time, because the feared event is unlikely to occur.

Have you ever noticed that when things are okay for fear-based thinkers, their respite from fear is only temporary, because if they don't have fear, they add it? Well, I was determined to help Shane help himself.

I posed the worst/best/likely case scenarios to Shane: "If you ride the bus, what is the worst that could happen? You get beat up so badly you have to go to the hospital. What is the best that could happen? You get on the bus and the ride is uneventful. What is likely to happen? You may get called a name when you walk by the bully, but otherwise the bus driver is watching and won't let anything serious happen." Shane became much calmer. He had a tool he could use to put his fears in perspective. He decided to ride the bus—most days.

YOUR BELIEFS CREATE YOUR REALITY

Let's look at the nature of beliefs. A simple one about opportunity is based upon the saying, "The sky's the limit." Here's a photo of my son Shane, when a senior at Arizona State University and President of ASU's Skydiving Club. He is hurtling toward the ground at 180mph before opening his parachute. Shane's belief and reality in this moment is that "The sky is not the limit, the ground is!"

Once you begin identifying when your beliefs, perceptions or judgments are filtering situations—situations that can be perceived in more than one way—you can move forward and change your lens. The first step, as we have discussed, is self-awareness. Awareness is the ability to observe, take note of, integrate, and make use of the information presented for the purpose of expanding your perceptions of reality. Changing your beliefs is also about expansion.

I caught myself imposing my beliefs erroneously in a simple situation. I was hiking with my daughter and our gentle, twelve-year-old, fifty-five-pound tricolored Australian shepherd dog, Samba. We were on a narrow dirt path in the tall pines along a stream in Northern Arizona. Samba loves to romp off path, into the stream for a dip and back. Samba was fifteen feet in front of us on our way back to the trailhead parking lot. We saw people walking four big dogs on leashes about one hundred feet ahead. I yelled at my daughter to run and get Samba back on leash. Too late. The people with the four dogs all quickly turned around upon seeing our loose dog.

I believed we frightened them off the trail due to our lack of courtesy to leash our pet. I dreaded potentially running into them in the parking lot. Sure enough, we met the group that we had chased away there. I apologized profusely (it's a small town and we might run into them again). They were not upset with us at all. Their perspective was to keep our dog safe. You see, across the street from the trailhead parking lot was the pound. They were volunteers who took unknown dogs for walks. They were not familiar with these dogs' dispositions. I had completely misread the situation. My daughter became upset with me for yelling at her when we were having such a lovely time.

This understanding became helpful to me as a leader. As I began to change my beliefs and look at situations more neutrally, I realized that members of our work teams could enhance their perspectives and performance by doing the same. On one of our training days, we were told the story of a successful diamond cutter in New York, Geshe Michael Roach. Each day, Michael would gaze up at his Wall Street skyscraper building before entering. He would be in awe at the beauty of the river running beside it, reflecting off the beautiful granite walls, and the facets of light bouncing off the thousands of windows, much like a well-cut diamond. He was grateful.

One day, he noticed a young man who was also looking up. "Beautiful, isn't it?" he said. This man grimaced and bemoaned the fact that on this day he was at this building. You see, it was that time of the month when he had to wash its many, many windows. The moral to the story is that this building is a neutral object, a building—no more, no less. It's the perceptions and beliefs that you bring to the situation that make the difference.

As I mentioned earlier, the misconceptions that my Asian leader and I had about one another got in the way of communicating effectively. When a facilitator guided us to understand that we approached problems from different perspectives, we left our emotions on the sidelines and heard one another in a more neutral fashion.

Here's another example. While over time I ultimately gained the respect of a different male executive, early in my career he described me as a "bull in a China shop." This was how he perceived me because he had a different approach to leadership. I had not broken anything, and only had a track record of continued success. But my action-oriented, impatient, persevering approach did not fit his style or environment. Later, he acknowledged that my strengths were essential for leading during GreenEnergyCo's lean startup phase. When there's no road map, you need a machete to find your way through the jungle. He changed his perception and eventually complimented me for my skilled leadership.

Malcom Gladwell in *Blink* offers an interesting illustration of how perceptions (and stereotypes) used to rule music auditions. Fifty years ago there were no women tuba players in professional orchestras. Everyone auditioned live in front of the decision makers. Guess what happened when the auditions were conducted with the musicians playing behind screens? We now have many women tuba players. Malcolm describes how to prevent making negative snap decisions. He reveals the many biases we all have. Try testing the level of your own neutrality (or biased beliefs) at www.implicit.harvard.edu.

I encourage an exuberant expansion of your beliefs and perceptions as a person and as a leader! To know more, notice more! The greater your awareness, the more it will drive you to feel, heal and deal with life's situations and possibilities.

LISTEN TO WHAT THE "RIGHT AND WRONG" WORDS YOU USE SAY ABOUT YOUR BELIEFS

The words you choose to use are telling clues about what unquestioned beliefs you hold within you. Your words exemplify your thoughts and beliefs. You come into the world knowing who you are. The way your family and others respond to you in specific circumstances creates belief systems that come into play in the same circumstances in the future. These beliefs kick in whether or not they are healthy, pure beliefs, according to scientist and healer, Barbara Ann Brennan in *Light Emerging, the Journey of Personal Healing*.

Lewis Carroll explores the importance of understanding our identity, language and the role of ego that develops as we grow up in *Alice's Adventures in Wonderland* and *Through the Looking-Glass*. I acted as Alice in the musical in junior high, so Alice became very personal to me. While there are many interpretations, you can see her search for her identity. After she falls down a rabbit hole, she meets creatures that constantly demand she identify herself. She becomes unsure of herself.

The white rabbit challenges her perceptions of class when he mistakes her for his maid, Mary Ann. He challenges her perceptions of good manners by assaulting her with dismissive rudeness. Her fundamental beliefs face challenge at every turn and she suffers an identity crisis. Will she choose to retain her notions of order or grow up and assimilate into Wonderland's nonsensical rules? Alice has to overcome the open-mindedness that is characteristic for children. Apparently, adults need rules in their lives—rules they blindly follow without asking "Why?" When the Mad Hatter longingly asked Alice to stay in the wacky fantasy Wonderland world, she said, "I can't because there are questions I have to answer."

In *Through the Looking Glass* after Alice has grown up, she still wrestles with her identity and she discovers language has the capacity to anticipate and even cause events to happen. Alice, for example, recites the nursery rhyme of Humpty Dumpty sitting on a wall and having a great fall. Humpty Dumpty inevitably actually falls. Words give rise to actions simply by being spoken in Wonderland. She learns that your perceptions and beliefs create your reality, but it may not be the reality that everyone shares.

My father was an engineer who turned into the best-deal-getting-purchasing agent at General Electric for forty years. He was adamant about what was right and wrong, good and bad. For example, when the gas tank gets to one quarter full, it's right to fill it to best protect the car; it's right to conserve and only use two sheets of toilet tissue; it's right to only have one pair of shoes, saddle oxfords, because they are black and white and should go with everything; and you duct tape one of two light switches so that you conserve on your energy bill. (Dad, in Heaven now, GreenEnergyCo actually has much more sophisticated conservation measures!) You should adhere to these rules and if you don't you are bad. You are not worthy. That's what I was trained to think. I have since learned that thoughts of being less than worthy are not healthy and need to be changed for a fulfilled life.

My father, I later learned, thought he was loving and protecting us and keeping us safe as children. His father harshly and routinely criticized him. (He would scream and was very scary, I remember as a young grandchild.) My father thought that if he taught us the "right" ways, we would be saved from such worldly criticism—the many voices that would all sound like our grandfather.

We all strive to have others accept us and to do the "right" thing according to our parental voices. However, as we mature, while we may know in our gut that we no longer agree, we repeat our learned pattern. Barbara Ann Brennan says, "We present our mask-self to the world according to our beliefs of what we think the world says is right, so that we can be accepted and feel safe."

I learned at an early age to be very self-critical and to always do the 'right' thing. Now, I am not so hard on myself and it allows me to walk MY path, not the one my parents wanted for me. I understand there are many "right" ways of living, not just my father's way. So the lesson here is to examine your words that reflect your "beliefs"—the truths you have created—and determine from where they are emanating. By identifying and changing the underlying fear-based belief the situation may instead provide opportunities.

For example, have you ever had the need to be right? At least among the many engineers who grew up with me and worked with me, it seemed to be a genetic trait, practically! Their words clearly indicated when I was right versus wrong.

Here's a lesson I learned about the "right way of doing things." When you are doing a home improvement project, do you make a list of what you need so you efficiently go to Home Depot one time? As a busy professional woman, mother and wife who craved more energy, that was the ONLY, and surely, the right way to get things done. This was until my husband taught me that just because he goes to Home Depot four times throughout the day, and I don't, my way does not make me right and him wrong. I changed my belief, but it hasn't changed the reality of how many trips he makes.

My changing my perception has been one of the keys to staying married for over 28 years, though! All experiences offer learning and acceptance when you don't let judgments of "right versus wrong" and "good versus bad" be descriptors of a situation—when you decide to change how you look at things. You get to choose—do you want to be happy or do you want to be right?

Just as many of us are not taught how to listen to our intuition in school, we are not taught how to listen to our self-talk either. Word choice is important. If you say, "Oh, stupid me," where does that lead? The more you pay attention to your words and make them match how you want to think and believe, the more success you will have in creating the life of your dreams. Our Peru trip leader, Carla Woody, studied neurolinguistics. Neuro-Linguistic Programming™ (NPL) is a way of changing the relationship between someone's mind and language in order to affect their behavior. She played back for me the way I described my debate about having a hysterectomy. I said, "I guess I could suck back in my uterus and not need the surgery, but removing it just might heal the old wounds." These words became my reality.

WHAT ARE YOU AFRAID OF?

In retrospect, can you see what beliefs that have created your reality now hold you back from becoming what you aspired to be when you grew up? What are you afraid of? Is it the fear of not being a superstar? Of failure? Of disapproval? Of a loved one leaving you (separation)? Of being fired? Of settling for a job that pays the bills? Do you fear you are not worthy enough, and are suffering from low self-esteem? Or that the world is not safe, so you cannot trust what may happen? Do you fear an early death, of heart attack or of getting cancer, like one of your parents did? Take a minute, breathe, and just let it come to you. Jot it down and begin journaling. I am sure you can identify fear-based barriers and limitations that you repeatedly encounter. You can either shine the light on them or live in their shadow.

I like to think that I have no fear. I am generally fearless. However, in peeling back my own onion of a self, I have found fear-based beliefs lurking in the layers. Like most everyone, I discovered some limiting beliefs that these fears have created in my life. They are a fear of not being nurtured in loving relationships and a fear of having financial freedom. I learned that the cure for the first one was to completely love myself and the rest would follow. I now have faith that the financial security that I need will come in unexpected ways if I live in alignment with my scream.

I identified the first fear-based beliefs that I would not be nurtured a few years ago, when elephants kept dominating my dreams. Maybe you recall the movie *Dumbo*, about the baby elephant with big ears who is ridiculed for being different. When the kids at the circus tease Dumbo, his mother defends Dumbo and is posted as a mad elephant, put in a cage and chained. Dumbo visits his mom, who reaches her trunk out of the cage and picks him up. She sheds a few tears as she rocks Dumbo in her trunk, while the gentle, touching lullaby, *Baby of Mine* plays in the background. During the song you see all the other animals in the zoo snuggling with their parents.

I had a special affinity for the Disneyland Dumbo ride, even as an adult. When visiting the Smithsonian Museum, I saw one of the original Dumbo Disneyland ride cars on display and my eyes immediately welled up with tears. I didn't get it. I now realize that Dumbo's situation has such special sentimentality to me because I had internalized a feeling of abandonment after my mother died. I saw most of my other friends with loving parents and as one big happy family. "I am all alone now," was my belief. Because I was so responsible and stalwart in 1979, I looked at my situation as survival. I never looked back. I didn't think anything about a lack of nurturing. I am just glad I identified a fear-based belief that I could change to allow me to feel more love for others and myself.

Are there clues about fears you may possess in your dreams? Do fear-based associations reveal themselves to you through books you read as a kid? Messages may be waiting for you to decode—messages that will help you identify your fear-based beliefs.

After you identify your fears, or fear-based beliefs, you will need to own them and validate them. My fear of money took some deeper understanding. In March, 2005, I visited an acupuncturist for the first time. Dr. Tom Ritchie was a Western medical certified anesthesiologist who left his practice to become an Eastern trained acupuncturist.

Dr. Ritchie explained that by eliminating congestion and activating the circulation of chi, acupuncture interrupts and disorganizes patterns of illness. In the first exam, he asked many questions about how I approached life and he analyzed my tongue, especially its color—whether it was white-coated or healthy and pink without red on the tips or sides. Mine was white-coated. Look at your tongue: it provides clues to your overall health right now! He took my pulse in various places on my wrist. He observed that my breathing was very shallow. He assessed which of the five elements I leaned toward—wood. "Wood reflects strength but can also be rigid," he said.

His initial comment was that while I looked extremely fit and healthy on the outside, my pulse was weak and indicated that I did not nourish myself on the inside. I had never had a doctor say anything like this to me before, although I very rarely visited one. I related that I had cut back my work week hours significantly from the early GreenEnergyCo startup days. Dr. Ritchie offered that a few days of arriving to work later "did not a lifetime shift make." He also taught me to understand how much we bind up our own energy with our own thoughts and tensions.

Dr. Ritchie taught me to ask myself about things I wanted to change but hadn't. "What is it about the behavior I want to change that is benefiting me so that I don't change it? Why am I creating this?" I realized that my concern about not having enough money embodied an underlying fear. I tensed my shoulders as if someone were always looking over them.

For thirty years I had been terribly tight in my raised left shoulder. Dr. Ritchie asked me to what I thought it may be related. Was it my relationship with money? He asked if my concern was motivated by love or fear? My first reaction is that it was in the best interest of my family to be secure. Dr. Ritchie gave me this insight. If you want to change a behavior or belief and you haven't, then you must perceive some greater benefit by maintaining it. What is it about how I look at money that benefits me?

Hmmmm. For example, did I squirrel away money for my kids' education to protect them from having to work? Or was it because I was afraid I would not have the money otherwise? There's a difference. Later, I sorted out these variances with a friend who is a developmental psychologist. She illustrated how money fears differ. Her parents had provided all the resources to cover college and basic living necessities. Anything extra had to be paid by her. Finally, at age sixty, she overcame her fear-based belief about making unnecessary expenditures and she got a pedicure.

After more introspection, I realized my money anxieties actually are not related to not having money or not being able to make it again. I know how to do that. It's a signature strength of mine, after all. My angst is about never wanting to repeat the exhaustive effort my past route took to accomplish it! I developed an underlying belief that making money was the result of intense effort. This is a fear-based survival belief. I could replace it with a love-based creative belief in abundance.

I choose to release that fear. When I catch myself acting from scarcity, I stop and spend the money to buy an extra pair of shoes—that aren't black and white oxfords. (Please note that I am not encouraging you to spend more money than you have.) I trust and have faith that the money needed for our family and the charitable causes we support will be provided at the right time and in the right manner. I go with the flow (more often than I did in the past, at least). I look for synchronicities and opportunities in every situation.

If you are worried about something, ask if it is motivated by love or fear. What might be at the root of a money fear you may have? What is it about not changing your self-limiting behavior that you perceive is beneficial to retain?

This doesn't mean each of us doesn't lapse in the changes we set for ourselves. But the fewer times we repeat old patterns, the more we grow toward what we want to be. I visited Dr. Ritchie two years later when I was painfully in the midst of shutting down the commodity portion of GreenEnergyCo. He diagnosed that "the general was working overtime," referring to my liver. He sensed there was "much wind in my liver" and it was not stable. My right ovary had extreme nervousness. (In hindsight, there were many early signs of the impending hysterectomy, but I thought I was as healthy as a horse.) He prescribed some herbs to help balance the liver, and they seemed to help. The herbs effect was subtle, as compared to a quick "cover up" (TUMS) or other pain medication. Eventually I saw improvement and didn't take the herbs anymore.

One more observation about the connection between fear and money is from a study of self-made, true millionaires, conducted by researcher, author and expert on the affluent, Thomas J. Stanley, Ph.D., in The *Millionaire Mind*. All the millionaires ranked the ability to overcome fear in decision making among the top five common traits. So if you want to be a millionaire, release your money fears, among other things. Dr. Stanley found that the common strengths among all self-made millionaires were integrity, tenacity, willingness to take risks commensurate with returns, choice of a profession that fully utilized their known strengths, making no fear-based decisions, a supportive spouse and discipline.

Many of these self-made successful people overcame obstacles by "bucking the system." This is akin to steel not being hardened unless hammered. They also were blessed with constructive parents who did not teach them to build negative self-talk barriers. These millionaires were indeed millionaires, not just "balance-sheet" rich. Their opulent homes and cars were not financed to the hilt. If you review Dr. Stanley's case studies in greater depth, you will note that many of the principles to finding your scream are also those exhibited by these millionaires.

A FEAR-BASED BELIEF SYSTEM IS NOT HEALTHY

A fear-based belief system will not likely be the path to becoming a millionaire or to being healthy! According to Dr. Gladys, fear itself is a major cause of hypertension, for example. We have discussed the mind-body connection between deeply-held, fear-based resentment that eats away at your body and may appear as cancer. I suspect that many of you or people close to you have experienced cancer or have a genetic predisposition to a life-threatening disease. I have a clear genetic predisposition to breast cancer like my mother, according to many Western physicians. Yet, I have no fear that I will get cancer like my mom did. I don't eat like she did; I am not as inactive as she was; I don't think like she did; and I don't harbor the deep disappointment of two failed marriages in my heart and body. I celebrated the year I turned forty-seven—the age when she died—with a huge party, and I am still kickin'!

You are not your genetics! However, if you repeat the same behaviors that your parents did, be on the lookout for clues of history repeating itself. Your DNA carries many potential patterns, not just those of your family, and you can choose to break those patterns or follow them. You can outgrow a legacy of family confusion if you learn to understand the purpose of your fears. Once you see into the heart of the matter, through awareness, you can release the patterns of recurring pain. Understand that at one time, these family legacy fears may have served a valid purpose, but now they don't serve you.

Many times you can overwrite your genetic code by changing the way you believe and perceive! I understand that there are children who are born with serious conditions and that under some circumstances the ability to think and believe differently may not change their genetic course in life. It may be that they are here to help family members grow through dealing with the illness or disability. I reconcile the inherited disease situations by believing that there are powerful growth and development opportunities for those living with such conditions.

There are possibilities and stories of incredible healings in all settings nonetheless. There are many stories of sick people who overcame their fears and healed. Their bodies talked back with a powerful, instructive message, until they stopped denying their scream. In *The Physician Within You*, Dr. Gladys tells of a close family friend, Jeff, who was young, just thirty-three, single, successful, and was diagnosed with a brain tumor. He was told he would lose coordination on his right side and his eyesight. Doctors cut into his skull to relieve pressure on his brain. He decided against chemo and radiation. He then went to Dr. Gladys, who he had looked up to with admiration since his youth.

Jeff began meditating and visualizing. He had just come off a relationship with a woman he loved and he was depressed. He knew fun and money were not enough in his life. He dropped to one hundred thirty-five emaciated pounds. Dr. Gladys put him on a diet of fish, fowl, many green vegetables, fresh fruits, sunshine and fresh air, but he had no one to love, not even a dog, and pondered his reason to live. Then he shifted to thoughts of wellness, not sickness. One day he looked in the mirror and realized he would live in the world and look at the tumor as a friend that awakened him to life. He visualized his tumor breaking up with a white light healing it. He continued to visualize for a year and the tumor stayed benign. The tumor became a blessing to help him solve his own search for meaning in life as he regained his spirituality.

WHO CAN YOU CHANGE?

Try this: Place your hands on top of your head, and push your head down. Now with your eyes, look up and ahead. What can you see? Barely in front of you? What perspectives are you missing when you lock yourself into unhealthy, fear-based, past ways of being, believing and perceiving? Take your hands off your head. Look up and around. Can you see a lot more of the landscape now? Who created the ability to see differently? You did!

For who can you change? YOU CAN ONLY CHANGE YOU! To distinguish what is yours to change and what is not, consider this. If you can change the issue without anyone else's help, it's yours. If others, by necessity, have to be involved to create the change, it's not yours alone. If your opinion or help is not requested, it's not your role to try to change someone else.

You are only the master of yourself, not others. I can change the choices about food that I put into my body, but I cannot change my husband's choices, for example. I can set an example by eating healthily and by being active and exemplifying vibrancy, but I cannot make him exercise—or nag him into it. (I have tried unsuccessfully and it just made him want to eat more to get back at me. Jeff's comment when reading this manuscript was; "This is because husbands are stubborn!").

It's difficult, at first, to have no one else to blame for your lack of health, wealth and happiness. However, if you continue to repeat negative behaviors and don't face and then release your fear of change, are you being loving to yourself? Who can choose to nourish you other than yourself?

You can also choose to examine your limitations, frustrations and blockages from a meaningful perspective. When you accept your part in creating your life situation, without blaming yourself or anyone else, and approach your life with the attitude that everything you encounter has a significant purpose, you will unblock the victim conditioning that saturates you and our society. This will enable you to work smarter, not harder, like that CFL versus the old Edison light bulb, and to be in your full personal power. Beliefs can also be viewed like magic in some respects. Magic is the ability to conjure something into form, and beliefs do just that.

Patterns that seem to repeat themselves since childhood, whether you define them as "good or bad," will not change until you take actions to break them! In the words of Carl Jung, "That which we do not confront in ourselves we will meet as fate." If you wake up and do the same thing each day, will you change? When you recycle thoughts or beliefs from the day before, you create more of the same reality.

If you believe you are not to blame, the failure cannot be your fault, for example, you will be locked in your present way of being. Our society has practically institutionalized the idea that "We won't let you fail." From your early days in school, if you are a baby boomer, a Gen Xer or Millennial, you were taught you would advance to the next grade. Heaven forbid if you failed. It's not your responsibility to deal with your failure. No wonder many of us fear failure.

Dr. Seligman, the experimental psychologist I mentioned earlier, illuminated this for me in his work. He associates the fear of failure and prevalent low self-esteem over the past 40 years with the advent of the No Child Left Behind era. He characterizes our present day society as "the feel-good society," compared to the depression era (those of the silent generation) before, which he calls the "doing-well society." This era's efforts to increase kids' self-esteem and happiness have resulted in increased individual freedoms and satisfaction that have turned into consumerism, recreational drugs, grade inflation, statistically higher depression, and suicides.

There has been a simultaneous slide away from self-responsibility for our actions. Individual investment in endeavors larger than self—those of God, Nation, Family, and Duty—have not been stressed as important. Because there's so much emphasis on the individual, the effect of failure is over-exaggerated. Dr. Seligman's observations in *The Optimistic Child* and more recently in *Authentic Happiness* are that when you find purpose and meaning in life by contributing to causes larger than yourself, the more meaning you will feel your life has. You can take his free online tests at www.authentichappiness.sas.upenn.edu.

A feeling of failure can lead to outright depression. Dr. Seligman notes a significant rise in depression in our society, a disorder of individual helplessness. When you are self-important and fail, blows are astronomical. People guided by the feel-good approach intervene when the child fails so that the child feels better. The former doing-well society endorsed mastery and optimism. The focus was on being a part of something greater and changing helplessness into mastery. Dr. Seligman believes that sometimes children need to fail and feel sad, anxious and angry. We make it harder for them to achieve mastery when we step in and save them from the fall. By cushioning them from feeling bad, we actually make it more difficult for our children to feel good and to experience flow and mastery. Many of us were raised in the "no child left behind" era. This contributed to our blaming someone other than ourselves for our present-day situation. If we want it to be different, we need to accept our own responsibility for making the change within us.

    I learned this in my twenties when caring for my brother. I tried positive reinforcement and negative reinforcement to get him to help clean and care for our trailer and his used car. I coaxed him out of his room where bowls of half-eaten food remained for more than a week. I could understand some despondency but I wanted to help. I finally sought an ASU counselor's guidance. Counseling was a free service to law students. She told me to "stop placing the pillow under him to break his fall." I couldn't do it for him. He had to address his own issues.

AWARENESS IS HALF OF THE SOLUTION

When will the pain of where you are be greater than your fear of change? Leave your trauma drama behind. To transform, which is to go beyond change and see a whole new set of opportunities, you must create a new path. It's like a path in your lawn or the mountainside that is worn from many feet. The grass does not grow. When you walk on new ground, the old path starts growing new grass and becomes covered When you choose to transform, you will create new energy. This is how quantum leaps occur scientifically. The atom begins to vibrate due to an increase in energy and the atom takes a "leap." Once you become aware of how often fear enters your decision making, you are halfway to the solution. You will take that leap to the new you when you catch yourself repeating the behavior you have decided to change.

    When you become aware of the role of fear in your decision making, you can begin to free yourself from it. Be wary of trading safety and security for creative freedom; once you do, it's hard to reclaim freedom. It has been said that security is for those without freedom. Personal freedom is the prerequisite to pioneering new parameters of possibility. (Say that three times fast!)

    You must find a safe and creative way to own and express

your stress and negative emotions. Take a breath before letting your anger explode. It's not *what* happens to you but how you *react* to it. You know a fear-based limiting belief is there as soon as it shows up—you feel frustrated. Wherever you feel challenged in life—whether it's about money, sex, health, a job, relationships or spirituality—it all comes down to how you manage your energy. You are signaling negative beliefs about yourself when you explode in anger. Your thinking is not working in your best interests. Ask yourself, if it were a matter of life or death, could you let it go? Just give yourself permission to let it go, IF you had to, for starters. This is how you begin to unlearn old behaviors and change.

What happens when you first change? It's likely you will encounter resistance from your loved ones, friends and your own ego. However, when you change and no longer react in the same way, it opens a new set of choices to others. Eventually, when you change, others' responses to you will change, too. It may seem like they changed, when actually, it was YOU!

BE YOUR OWN WITNESS AND CATCH YOUR EGO "SHOULDING" ON YOU

When confronted with the initial difficulty of change, I reached out for help. It's said that when the student is ready, the teacher will appear. As mentioned, I was referred to the work of Dr. Stanley Block, who is a physician, psychiatrist and psychoanalyst with more than forty years of experience. I learned that unaware egos and personalities focus on limited personal aims, social status and all fears through his book, *Come to Your Senses, Demystifying the Mind-Body Connection*. Higher consciousness will threaten an ego that is based in lower consciousness. The lower-consciousness ego will fight using fear against the changes you desire. Your ego is limited by judgments, perceptions, beliefs and assumptions that don't allow you to arrive at a place of fulfillment. By recognizing when your ego is creating your negative self-talk, you learn to come to your senses, thereby improving your quality of life and your performance.

Certainly in the corporate world, I took actions and saw leaders exemplify the ego in action. I observed and was taught to let the ego rule. I had to unlearn this behavior.

We learn how to care for our bodies and brush our teeth, but what are we taught to do about negative thoughts and emotions? How do you know if it's your intuition or your ego talking? When you listen to your intuition, it will come in the form of a fact, as data, according to Laura Kamm. It will not be emotion-ridden. The intuitive call or clue can evoke an emotion, but the message should be neutral. This is one way to tell if it's true inner wisdom speaking to you instead of your emotion-filled ego that does not want you to change.

As I understand ego-based thoughts and feelings, they are those dictating how you "should" be and how the world "should" be at each moment. Whenever you feel that these ego-defined requirements are unfulfilled, you experience tension, fear and physical distress, according to Dr. Block. Your ego takes daily life trials and creates a world of opposites: right/wrong, good/bad, success/failure.

Dr. Block relates a case study of a sales clerk who would go home irritated and resentful after listening to gossip all day from her co-workers. She would think to herself, gossip is bad—they should not be doing that—why are they? After understanding her ego was making a judgment, she noticed she viewed her work differently. When co-workers gossiped, she would smile to herself. After that, she stopped allowing their actions to dictate her reactions. If she caught herself judging them for gossiping again, she let it go and focused on doing her best at work. She became less tense. Tension will build as you try to change something you cannot control, such as happened with the co-workers' behavior in the case study. The clerk decided she could control her reaction, though, and did.

On occasion at work, you may be thinking, "I'm not doing this right." Before that negativity starts a chain reaction of blame, tension and anxiety, step outside of yourself—be your own witness—and see what you are doing to yourself by letting the ego rule. In that moment, catch yourself and LABEL it: "I'm thinking that I'm not doing this right," suggests Dr. Block in *Come to Your Senses*. Labeling your thoughts is a performance enhancer. You acknowledge the behavior and move past it.

Also begin to step outside yourself when you are in a situation that you are trying to change. See yourself as if you are a witness looking at you. The more often you catch yourself in the act of repeating a fearful or undesirable behavior, the quicker you will retrain your body. The repetition required is akin to teaching a pet a new trick. Detach from those impulsive feelings and assess the situation neutrally. What are you supposed to learn from it? As you catch yourself in an act of repeating the same patterns of self-sabotage, you can learn to stop the behavior midstream. You will chuckle about your new revelation.

If you are impatient, this everyday example will apply to you. That driver in front of you is so slow and you have places to go! You weave and pass him on the side and jump back in front of him. Recently, I caught myself starting to turn the wheel and speed up to pass. I stopped and said, wouldn't it be funny if I did this and we ended up at the same place. Sure enough, I was giving a speech and the person I resisted cutting off was there to watch me. Had I acted in my prior usual manner, I would have been very embarrassed and had at least one person in the audience thinking I was a jerk before I ever began my presentation.

Do you look to the opinions of others to define you and what you should do? Don't let the ego "should" on you and prevent you from moving forward.

A close friend of mine, who I will call Nina, is the poster child for the world "shoulding" on her. She is a lovely, sweet woman, and a dedicated schoolteacher who makes daily, meaningful differences in our children's lives. She lost her father six months after my mother died in 1979 but our lives have taken different paths. Nina believes she got a raw deal with her father's early death and that life is hard. She suffers from many health maladies and tends to blame her conditions on overdoing sports when she was young (which certainly has some validity) and to genetics.

She has arthritis in her joints, and has had two hip replacements before the age of fifty.

In all the years I have known her, Nina has allowed the world to "should on her." She overextends herself based on what others will think of her. She will have a party, buy everything, decorate and cook, even though she is way behind in preparing for teaching, or laundry, or bills or tending to basic finances. Because she never lets anything go, her hips are frozen with anger and frustration. As we have seen, pain is a strong signal from deep inside the body's intelligence, indicating that your emotional health is out of balance. Stored and stuffed emotions take a great toll and eventually old, built-up energy will be released in the form of painful physical manifestations. When you carry pain and don't release and let go of the past, your body will faithfully show you the results of your repressed feelings. Guaranteed.

The metaphor of Nina's internal life breaking down is exactly what you can objectively observe externally. Until recently (she is on a new path of hopefulness!) she held onto many of her father's things that she's had since 1979. The fear of throwing something away dominates her decision making rather than living in the clarity of having no clutter.

 At one point there was a path just big enough to walk around her bed to the bathroom. There were more than five empty white five-gallon detergent tubs sitting around the narrow space to get to the washing machine. There were dead plants scattered around. Every wall spot was consumed with a box or something. When opening all cabinet doors, items would spill onto the counters. Because she could rarely find anything, she would have to buy another bottle of ketchup, for example, and would end up having six, but she wouldn't know where they were. Bath toys were in the back of the bathroom shelf from over fourteen years prior when her children were young. I won't even describe the garage—not that you can see any of it beyond all the stuff piled up in it.

Nina took the weight of the world on her shoulders for the benefit of her family. Nina's husband tried to "compress" her so that he would feel more important. Her internal infrastructure was breaking down from all the pressure, tension and "shoulds" she allowed to be imposed upon her. Her external world looked the same with the clutter collapsing in all around her. She believed life was hard and overwhelming. It was true, this became her reality. Don't get me wrong, I have my own issues, as I have revealed throughout this book. I just find her story visually illuminating for the saying: "As within, so without."

Where do you begin to dig yourself out of the clutter when you have collected things for decades and have been afraid to let them go? You must gather up the courage to face the fear you have been sidestepping for years. You must come to your own personal realization that a new way will be better than sticking with the familiar. Nina has now made a vision board and understands that she can do what she most loves, which is to be sociable and help others—after she clears out the clutter, and attends to her finances. She is a Merchant/Lover under the CVI method and would be a high "I" (Influencer) under the DISC method. She naturally gravitates to being with people and playing. Business and finance are not her strengths or interests; however now knowing that, she is taking action to "plug the gaps" by getting more help in her weaker areas. She is visualizing a new life for herself once she cleans up her path. She is (literally) walking a new path. You can too.

Much like your ego that "shoulds" on you, assumptions and judgments create roadblocks. Assumptions are things you take for granted. Assumptions filter the way you see your reality. You know the saying to "assume" makes an "ass out of u and me." You can become aware of your assumptions. Is a fish aware of its surrounding water? Awareness causes you to observe and notice things. Many times you don't question the way you see things, just like the fish. By looking at a situation without old judgments and beliefs, but instead, with new eyes, you have new possibilities.

Judgments are roadblocks. They are mere products of our conditioning (like my assuming I need to be frugal because of the influence of my dad allowing me only one pair of saddle oxford shoes). When you break through the road block, you can reach the truth of your own heart and see life as it really is and can be.

You tend to see what you value. You see the figure, not the background in a picture. Without the "on," you cannot realize what the meaning of "off" is. The ego that causes you to identify yourself as one with your personality, your "I," brings protection to the way things are right now. The ego blinds you to other things that exist, like the background. Without the interval, you cannot hear the rhythm. Painters and weavers know you must have the background to see the pattern. Their awareness is different. They don't assume you focus on the figure. It's the space that allows you to see the image. Seeing things as they are without allowing the ego, assumptions and judgments to color them will open a world of love and compassion to you.

WALK THROUGH YOUR FEAR

You must identify when your ego, judgments, assumptions and beliefs are in your way, as I discussed. You must become aware of whether they are based in fear or love. Because until you open your eyes and confront your fear, it will chase you. You cannot walk around your fear or run from it. What you resist will persist. You must face your fears to release them. You must acknowledge and walk through them. Percolate or perturbate!—meaning think about it, let it come to the surface and deal with it, or let it agitate you.

There's a very simple example, told in 1925, of a woman who was afraid to walk under a ladder. She was advised to face her fear and walk under it. She wanted to open a safety-deposit box in the bank and when she walked into the building, a ladder was in her way. She quivered with fear and turned back. When she reached the street, she decided to return and walk under it because she would not be back in town to get to the bank for some time. It was a big moment for her. When she retraced her steps, she found the ladder had been moved and was no longer in her way. (I found this story in *The Game of Life* by Florence Scovel Shinn.) So often this is what happens when you face your fear and have faith.

As described, Nina repeatedly says life is too hard. I doubt she really believes that in her soul, but guess where her energy is directed and what is being created—hardship. She is exhausted and tired, as many of us are. Life certainly can be challenging for any in the human race. The difference is in how we face the challenges. Our growth and success in life can be measured by our ability to manage chaos, and walk through it. If we face no challenges, we will not grow and achieve—just like the kids who have pillows thrown down for them before every fall; just like our youth who are passed to the next grade when they have not truly faced the challenge. The key is to have faith, pull over to the shore, and walk along the bank instead of exhaustively swimming up river against the current.

HOW DO YOU RELEASE YOUR FEAR AND CHANGE?

To summarize the steps to release your fear and change, first you must identify and face your fear. Or at least recognize it and be guided, not paralyzed by it. You must own it and not blame anyone else for where you are in life. Validate that your underlying fear may have had a valid purpose—e.g., the fear of being hungry drives you to make money.

Next you learn how to release your fear-based belief, the one that emanates from survival. You will replace the old belief with the new way that you decide to be—one based in love that is from the deep creative forces within you. One that is congruent with your scream! Resist your ego trying to pull you back into old familiar patterns to preserve your former identity. Don't let the ego persuade you through fear and false perception that the effort to change is greater than the pain of staying as you are.

Previously, we focused on identifying what our fears are. Think back to where your body hurt. It was telling you not only where you were out of alignment with your scream, but also what fear resides in your body. If you resort to TUMS, for example, you may not be digesting new ideas and experiences. If your back consistently hurts, you may fear you are not supported in this world. These fears keep you from being balanced in mind, body and spirit and from being aligned.

If you want to change your fear-based beliefs, you must reinterpret your beliefs about what has happened to you in your life. My two siblings and I are in very different places in life, emotionally, physically, and socioeconomically. Genetically, we each have intelligence and similar life circumstances during our youth, but the outcome has not been the same at all. I understand now that they have internalized a very different reality of our past events than I have. I see that the dramatic differences in our lives are due primarily to how we think, believe and perceive the past events and the world. As a result, we made many different choices along life's path.

I am grateful for the strengths I developed as a result of having so much responsibility so young. I don't believe life is unfair. I take the events as opportunities to learn and it all ultimately fits! When you believe life is unkind, unfair, hard or cruel, that there's nothing you can do, there's never enough, or it's someone else's fault, an underlying seething resentment can build and can show itself as illness. I have learned that my outer world experiences all directly correspond to my inner world of thoughts, feelings and desires.

When you encounter any situation in day-to-day life, you actually project your perceptions on the event, coloring in whatever you want to see by way of belief. You are always interpreting reality. You are a pioneer preparing a path for a new interpretation of reality, and you are pushing against negative beliefs that have become indisputable (but erroneous) facts.

It helps to learn to ask why, what and how: Why are these people in my life? What is my contribution to this process? How can I change my actions to create a harmonious resolution? What is it about that person that annoys me—is he or she a reflection of a shadow trait of mine?

When you pose and answer these types of questions you will become self-empowered and much healthier. You will see your beliefs 'manufactured' certain perceptions about the past events that could be viewed in a very different and more affirming way— just like the Diamond Cutter and the window washer's view of the granite building with many, many windows.

To begin to release your fear and change requires you to perceive the world differently not just in your head, but also in your body. Let's focus more now on how to unlearn the old patterns that your body has memorized and overwrite them to create the new way you want to be.

UNLEARN WHAT YOUR BODY HAS MEMORIZED

As a layperson, I have found it easy to understand the way neuroscientist, Dr. Joe Dispenza explains the process of change in the CDs, *The Art of Change:* "To change is to think greater than we feel in the same circumstances." Your body memorizes ways of being, just like athletes such as Shaun White can throw the double McTwist snowboard trick without thinking about it. He has both physically and mentally rehearsed it with an enormous amount of repetition. Well, the body memorizes other emotional and negative thoughts and behaviors, too, such as suffering and low self-worth. When an emotion or behavior is repeated for ten, fifteen or twenty years, your body automatically, without thinking, acts. It's the master over your mind.

You have memorized the response so well that you don't know how to change it (assuming you are aware enough to identify it). Let's say you have had repeated instances of rejection in your life. How do you react when someone says "no" to you? Do you fall back into the repeated pattern of dejection? Does your face instantly go red? Or do you ask, what am I to learn from this situation? Can you step away and think of it as a new opportunity? When you let go of the old painful patterns, you gain clarity to enter through the gate to become what you most long to be.

To change requires you to change how you feel, not just what you think, according to Dr. Dispenza. The habit has to be overwritten. A habit is a *re-current*, often *unconscious* pattern of behavior that is acquired through frequent *repetition*. It can be changed with awareness and practice. Journalist and author Lynne McTaggart shares an incredible example of the power of the "repetitive" habit of a professional pianist who went to prison for seven years in *The Intention Experiment*. He mentally rehearsed his songs and finger movements while incarcerated. The night after he was released, he gave a flawless performance despite the fact that he hadn't actually touched a piano in seven years. The body has a mind of its own.

Many of the experts who I have studied describe this mind-body dynamic similarly. For example, Sandra Blakeslee, Ph.D. and Dr. Joe Dispenza state that your personality (which you can change) creates your personal reality. Emotions are energy in motion. Recall that Dispenza said in *The Art of Change* that thoughts are the language of the brain and feelings are the language of the body. The body is in essence, the subconscious mind. The unconscious does not know thoughts from real events. Our body does not know the difference between when a thought is real, i.e. happening in our environment, or when it's produced by a dream or worry, explains Dr. Dispenza. When survival emotions are activated, the chemicals that signify fright, flight or fight are released. People can turn on this chemical stress response all day simply through worrisome thinking. But we can't endure the chemical stress response for long periods of time, and it can create dis-ease. This is why it's so important to examine where your body consistently hurts and relate the function of that part of the body to the emotional centers associated with it.

Dr. Dispenza describes that when your mind and body work together, they produce the outcome, the change, the result. You can say you want to change and that, "Now I am happy," "I am not an angry person," but these declarations only engage the conscious mind. The test is what happens when you are in conflict mode? Does your body overpower your conscious state and react stressfully, as it has memorized to do in the past, despite your mind's contrary intent? You can begin to unlearn past behavior by catching yourself in the act and saying, "Stop!" when you are in the same circumstances and beginning to repeat the undesired behavior.

You can be your own witness, as I illustrated above. You have to unlearn the old behavior by repeatedly and consciously acting in your new, desired way of being. After a few weeks of catching yourself, you will be living as the new you—at least more often. We are only human and all have relapses in pressure situations. However, the more we practice, the better we get at living and acting congruent with our scream.

YOUR HEALTH AND YOUR SUBCONSCIOUS' MEMORY

When I talk with people about change, many say they desire to lose weight. Just by that word choice, the goal may be hard to attain. Why do I say that? If your desire is to be at a healthy weight for you, that is different than "losing weight." This difference matters consciously and subconsciously. While I have never struggled with obesity, my weight has readily fluctuated up by twenty pounds and down by ten. I have tried to "lose weight" many times—especially for special occasions, as I discussed. I was one of those, who, perhaps out of desperation, tried diet after diet, as if food were to blame for my failure to lose weight. Even though most of us understand that diets alone aren't the answer, why do we continue to attempt traditional diets to create permanent weight loss?

Close your eyes and think about your ideal weight. What comes into view? Is it a table full of all the things you can no longer eat? Or do you see yourself lighter, vital and feeling better about yourself? Those of you who see the first picture will have trouble eating in a manner that nourishes and honors your body. If you think in terms of deprivation, your subconscious may resist the change. When you feel within you that lighter feeling and the well-being produced by the feeling, you will likely have much more success in making choices that result in your being the healthiest weight for you. Diets and deprivation don't work. Visualize yourself as you want to be. You want to feel that same feeling that you will experience after you have succeeded. Some experts say 95 percent of people who attempt to lose weight using diet-based weight-loss programs eventually regain the weight and often gain more as their bodies try to compensate for the perceived deprivation.

The reason you don't see the change you want goes back to the first tenet—your answers are within—within your subconscious. Except your subconscious doesn't realize it's making you overeat.

According to the experts with whom I have worked, I have learned that emotions that don't serve you well are at the root of eating more than you need. I am not attempting to do a synopsis for you of all the medical eating disorder opinions out there, but instead to relate to you the advice of those who I looked to for guidance. Because these resources helped me, I am sharing who they are and how they can help you, too. I am the expert of my own experience, but I am not the diet expert. I refer you to some experts so you can pursue your own path of change.

Our relationship with food is complex. As human beings, our DNA is programmed to pack in food when there's abundance so we can survive during lean times. Additionally, Americans are culturally and subconsciously programmed to consume in large quantities. ("Want to super-size that?") From the size of our cars and houses to gigantic portions and all-you-can-eat buffets, we consume in abundance for a variety of reasons unrelated to our physical needs. If you have been to Europe, as an American, you cannot help but notice the smaller food portions served there.

From childhood, we have been programmed to clean our plates, to eat to be sociable and to use food for comfort and for many other reasons. How many times were you told that if you didn't clean your plate some child in some foreign country would starve? I was told it would be the children in Africa. While in the slum in Soweto, South Africa, I played with the kids, and I have seen that despite my years of cleaning my plate, sadly, they are still starving.

It seems as though we meet our demand for constant intense productivity with relentless overstimulation from caffeine and high-protein, high-fat, high-sugar foods. I know when I was training for the half-marathons that the power bars were considered the "way to go." However, as you read in Chapter 6, my digestion does not assimilate those high-protein/high carb power bars well. They may work for you—your body will let you know, in any event.

Some identify overeating with making a negative internal feeling go away. Briefly, you cover up that emotion with the experience of eating food, and then you regret eating so much. When you change your emotion, you will naturally feel better. As you do, you will make healthier food choices. The encouraging news is that habits of eating to cover up feelings within you can be broken with awareness and practice. Like political and religious beliefs, your belief about your body has built over time. When you lose weight, you can feel the difference in your clothes. However, if your subconscious body image is one of you as a heavier person, a slimmed-down body may not prevail until you retrain the subconscious and recreate a new body image.

According to neuroscience and medical experts, your subconscious fails to make the connection between the good it thinks it's doing (comforting you, giving you pleasure, etc. by eating to cover that negative emotion) and the weight you are gaining. The fact that your conscious mind is painfully aware of this connection has no bearing on the subconscious at all. At the same time, since the subconscious is the part of your mind outside your normal awareness, it's difficult for you to recognize that it's your subconscious that's inadvertently putting on the pounds. In fact, if you get distressed over your weight gain, the subconscious is likely to try to bring you comfort by making you eat even more! The key is to catch yourself when that emotion triggers you to eat, and to stop it! But first, you have to identify your triggers.

I had a dedicated employee who was about thirty pounds overweight. I learned that his wife, who was also very overweight, would cook southern fried chicken weekly for them. She knew it wasn't healthy, but it was tradition and had become a habit. The connection he eventually made is that during their poor Southern upbringing, the only memorable happy times in the trailer park were when they made fried chicken! Much of eating is behavioral and not conscious.

In our work staff meetings, we routinely incorporated health awareness sessions. We covered topics as simple as basic nutrition (in a fun guessing-game format), fun ways to be active and having pedometer measured walking competitions. I set the exercise example for my employees by working out at lunch (even though I later learned that wasn't the optimal time for my "constitution"). I encouraged them to be active on a schedule that worked best for them. Usually, any extra time needed to accommodate exercise could be made up without impacting our internal or external customers. We covered a portion of the fitness expense through the corporate benefits plans. The improved concentration and health of our employees more than made up for any scheduling or cost issues.

Often overeating and dieting go hand in hand in our culture. We get into the "eat, repent, repeat" cycle, as Michelle May, M.D., has coined in *Love What You Eat, Eat What You Love*. Some people eat in response to environmental triggers (time of day, presence of food, getting their money's worth, etc.) as she describes in Chapter 4. Others eat for pleasurable emotions like joy, celebration, reward, etc. Most have a combination of reasons. Emotions are simply information that we may experience as pleasurable or uncomfortable, describes Dr. May. I learned from her that until you deal with the emotion, your weight won't sustainably change. You eat to override that subconscious emotion.

Dr. May was our children's family physician. She calls herself a recovered yo-yo dieter for 20 years. She left her medical practice to pursue her passion of helping others discover a peaceful, joyful relationship with food, as she herself has succeeded in doing. Dr. May helps you rediscover when, what and how much to eat without restrictive rules. In her book there are many helpful, practical tips and strategies for developing a healthy, nourishing relationship with food.

If you are struggling with weight, your subconscious has likely mastered the feeling that eating comforts you. Or you may believe that once you start eating something you love, you cannot control yourself and will eat the whole bag of chocolates or gallon of ice cream. Many of you may be familiar with Oprah's struggle with weight. At one point, she chronicles that she weighed more than 230 pounds. Oprah's internal wounds from sexual abuse in childhood were soothed by comfort foods. She has tried many diets in the past and has lost and regained weight. Now she has a healthier relationship with food, much like Dr. May describes.

Recently, Oprah wrote: "My drug of choice is food. I use food for the same reasons an addict uses drugs: to comfort, to soothe, to ease stress. Next I tackled the food addiction, which is ongoing. As far as my daily food choices go, I'm not on any particular program. I've gone back to the common sense basics we all know: eating less sugar and fewer refined carbs and fresher, whole foods like fish, spinach, and fruit. But in order not to abuse food, I have to stay fully conscious and aware of every bite, of taking time and chewing slowly. I have to focus on being fully alive, awake, present, and engaged, connected in every area of my life. Right *now*."

Oprah describes that eating less or working out harder isn't the problem. She states, "It's about my life being out of balance, with too much work and not enough play, not enough time to calm down."

Oprah learned that she doesn't have a weight problem—"I have a self-care problem that manifests through weight." "When I stop and ask myself, 'What am I really hungry for?' the answer is always "I'm hungry for balance, I'm hungry to do something other than work.'" Oprah has reset her priorities and tries to do at least one hour of exercise five or six days a week. Her goal isn't to be thin, but strong, healthy and fit. She works out, eats healthfully, and is reordering her life "to do the spiritual and emotional work to conquer this battle once and for all."

Those of you who are conquering an unhealthy relationship with food must first understand what triggers you to eat more than for what your body is truly hungry. Journaling about what triggers you is very helpful to identify the root causes.

Second, learning about healthy food choices and having them available in your pantry helps.

Third, activity is fundamental. But it does not have to be in the form of hot, sweaty exercise in a gym! For example, Dr. Michelle May and I are fortunate to be able to hike in our saguaro laden desert mountains.

Dr. May has an exercise personality quiz in her book, *Eat What You Love, Love What You Eat*. You identify the time you like to be active, what rewards you like, where you like to be, with whom you like to be active—alone or in social settings—and what you like to do. A personal story Dr. May relates is that despite signing up for a half-marathon, and being capable of walking it, she realized she wouldn't be exercising on her terms if she had to train for it. She opts for being outdoors hiking or teaching yoga, now that she is a certified yoga trainer.

Dr. Gladys echoes the playing theme in *Living Medicine*. She encourages you to find the type of exercise that you truly enjoy. If it's too boring or hard, it becomes difficult and your natural tendency is to avoid what you dislike. It becomes work.

There are many things you can do to become more active, and it can be on your terms. It can match what you value. If you prefer being alone, start with a walk with your dog, if you have one. Take the stairs. Park your car further away from your destination. Or consider establishing a routine time with a friend. Because of the camaraderie, I rarely miss my regularly scheduled hiking and biking times with my friends. And by talking the entire time we get an extra cardio workout! We satisfy our emotional need for human connection and loving support while being active. We want to be with each other, so we prioritize our schedules to allow for our hikes. Anything that increases consistency, commitment and is active fun will work. When you become intent on the change, you will eventually establish an active lifestyle as your new habit.

You can adopt new eating habits, too. I used to unconsciously wolf down my food while standing or multi-tasking and walking around with the phone while munching. I have learned how to maintain a healthy weight for me. I regularly have some chocolate or dessert. I have wine periodically, too. Now I have retrained myself to make conscious choices about what I put in my mouth. I savor it, chew it more slowly and enjoy it more, all without a restrictive diet.

When you love and honor yourself, you will take practical

action to choose foods that nourish you. Consider how much time, energy and costs you will save feeling good compared to being sick and tired! Compare the co-pay or doctor visit cost and the time you spend on multiple doctors' visits and a multitude of tests. How much would you save and how much better might you feel by making a few healthier lifestyle choices? Good ol' Dr. Gladys will ask you as a patient, "What do you want to get well for? Is it to go right back to doing the things that made you sick in the first place or are you ready to make a change in your life and commit yourself to the healing process, which means an attunement with your total being?"

Might you fall back into a routine of guilty feelings that contribute to your eating? Are you someone who feels guilty about taking time for yourself? I believed it would be selfish for me to come home after a hard day at work and flop on the couch and watch TV or read a book. Instead, I changed my clothing and began dinner, homework with the kids, baths, and fell into bed later. My husband, instead would walk in the house, change clothes and sit down to relax. "How selfish," I would say to myself. "Men!"

It took many years, but I have come to understand that my husband's approach was healthier than mine and had more balance. After recharging, he would attend to the most important things that still needed to be done. His to-do list was shorter for good reason. Many things can wait and are not nearly as important as the priority of nurturing and taking care of you. For only you can do that. No one else can prioritize you taking care of yourself. When you do so, you remain healthy so you can be there to then care for others. It's like the flight attendant instructions to place the mask over your mouth first, then your child! Remember who you can change...

Do you own a car? If so, do you wash it? Do you fill it with fuel? When the low oil light goes on, do you cover it up and pretend there's no problem, or do you take the car in for servicing? If you ignore it, will the hassle of breaking down on the road later be worth it? Well, think of how many places your body takes you. Why don't you nourish it, service it and maintain it the way you do your car? Is it because you feel guilty or selfish when doing so? Let it go!

As I look back in my journal, I noted a huge breakthrough in 2001 when I signed up for a ceramics class on Monday nights at the local high school that my kids attended in Ahwatukee. I hadn't been to one since my early college days. As a busy executive, wife and Mother, at first I felt very guilty. After I adjusted my schedule to accommodate it, I began to beam when I brought home my first crude pots. My family got used to my being gone and began supporting me by attending to their own needs on Monday nights. However, they soon told me they didn't need any more "penny pots!"

To begin to unlearn that emotion of guilt, for example, and to prioritize yourself and your health, take out your first exercise. Review the time you wrote down that you spend on each of the eight areas of your life. Start with a baby step. Add ten minutes a day to an area that would nourish you and subtract it from another. In this manner, you will start to unlearn your old habit of thinking you are selfish if you take time for yourself. You will replace it with a new habit of nourishing and loving yourself.

So don't deprive yourself. Instead, eat mindfully. Override your subconscious. Find fun activities to get you moving. Learn how to establish a healthy relationship with food by acting on the practical advice you can discover in the material by Dr. May or Dr. Gladys or Dr. Dispenza, for example. (You can find references for these materials in the References and Resources section.) Make informed eating choices for lifelong health. You already learned how to identify foods that work best for your internal constitution. Once you decide to change the emotions underlying your subconscious reasons for overeating, you will eat only the amount of food that makes you feel better after eating and not continue to feel the hunger you experienced before. You will become mindful of feeling full, before you become stuffed.

VISUALIZE YOUR DAY "AS IF" IT UNFOLDED IN YOUR NEW WAY OF BEING

The secret to sustained change is that you must act ahead of the event. Your body must rehearse acting AS IF the new behavior already occurred. Martin Luther King thought, acted and lived as if blacks should be treated equally, even though he was jailed for his civil rights protest in December, 1961 in Birmingham, Alabama. In his famous speech, he said, "I have a dream that my four little children will one day live in a nation where they will *not* be *judged* by the *color* of their skin but by the content of their character." Great leaders have lived "ahead of their time." They understood how to activate their subconscious and intuition along with their mind to believe the external world was different.

Another great example is Jesus Christ. Jesus also gave thanks and lived as if his prayers were already answered before he saw the answer. When Jesus and his disciples were faced with how to feed 5,000 hungry people, a small boy produced five loaves of bread and two fish. According to the Bible, Jesus knew all would be fed and did not waiver in his belief. He could not actually see the reality prior to everyone being fed, but had faith nonetheless. We live by believing and not by seeing (II Cor. 5:7). Jesus blessed the five loaves of bread and two fish and used it to feed all 5,000 people with twelve baskets left over (John 6:1-14).

How do you visualize your day as if you acted in the manner you desire? How do you overcome that unconscious self that will be triggered when your hot buttons are pushed and you go into your old pattern of fear? You practice ahead of the moment. You see yourself in a triggering situation and become a witness who is seeing you respond in the desired manner, in your new way of being. You can also practice visualizing what you want to create in your life. You need to memorize that elevated feeling of getting what you want with all your senses before you get out of bed every morning. When you are in the flow you feel love, joy and inspiration. Energy goes to your heart and you feel lifted, which is the natural state of being.

Another technique to help you change when you find yourself sinking into an old pattern of unhappiness, for example, is to draw upon happy memories. These memories can reset your body. Recall that time when you were playing care-free. See it, taste it, smell it, feel it, hear it. Can you be happy and unhappy at the same time? No. A smile will come to your face and will bring you out of that old pattern of being.

Another example relates to a common issue that many people want to change—insomnia. If you consciously decide to sleep better but lay awake recapping your whole day, pull out a positive memory of your perfect night's sleep. Recall the thickness of your covers tucked around you. Be in that experience. Feel that pillow plumped perfectly. Re-create it and your body will come along. You will sleep soundly all through the night. This is a form of simple visualization.

As Joe Dispenza explains, by being thankful as if the experience you want has happened, you arrive at a state of "being," which is the state where the mind and body work together. Thoughts and feelings are aligned so your habitual behavior matches. In order to manifest what you want, you first have to create it within. So it's very important to visualize what you want.

In January 2011, I had a visualization performance enhancement session with coach Al Fuentes. I reinforced something I have been learning which is to "slow down to go fast." This is much like the concept of working smarter not harder. When you are clear, your focus is automatically on what is most important. Daily distractions don't take you off task. The results are achieved with less effort. As mentioned, to breathe is to run spirit through you. Choose to make time each day to get clear by mastering the flow of energy through you. You do this by breathing in deeply through your nose and out your mouth. Add visualization to your breath. If you could enhance your performance through the non-scary act of breathing and visualizing and were guaranteed results, would you?

Al Fuentes worked successfully with an ASU college wrestler who was born with one leg. He is now winning against wrestlers with two legs, using the breathing and visualization methods taught by Al. Al first showed me how to marshal my own energy. He had me raise my arm. He instructed me to resist him with all my might while he pushed down on my arm. I was strong. Then, through his breathing and pulling my energy up and away, he pushed again, and my arm went weak. (This is akin to the *Power vs. Force* theories proposed by Dr. David Hawkins to which I have referred). Al breathed deeply again and pulled energy up from the earth into my arm and pushed again. I was strong. He then taught me how to do this for myself.

As we were calibrating my breathing, it resulted in a deep, deep calm and peacefulness. I breathed in slowly, filling my abdomen then lungs for more than thirteen counts. I held my breath, and then released it for more than thirteen counts. As I continued this breathing, I visualized the intent I had for this book. I saw its message illuminate and leap off the pages, like a white light beaming into each reader. Many people had white lights flickering in their hearts like a candlelight service. I saw celebration as people found their scream and workplaces became places of joy and meaning. Despite this book's imperfections, the loving intent behind it radiated. The shoes each person dreamed of filling became their reality.

This practice can be applied to anything your heart desires. With practice and purpose, any time throughout the day, you can take a deep breath and have that end result visual picture pop into the forefront. This works much like the instant image that pops into your head that you associate with a sentimental song. For example, I see my sister singing the song at our wedding whenever I hear Dan Fogelberg's, "Longer than there've been stars up in the heavens, I've been in love with you." (Sappy, I know.) I am sure that when you hear certain songs, you can recall exactly what you were doing when it was first played for you. That is what I am reproducing with my breathing. I desire to visualize that thing I want in an instant—as a constant reminder. The ability to bring the visual of that performance goal that you set into your mind whenever you take a deep breath will produce the results you desire. No harm in trying, right? Just breathe.

REPLACE THE OLD WITH A CLEAR PICTURE OF THE NEW

It's important to create that visualization. Because when you decide to release the old and change, you need a picture of the "new." In other words, after you identify your fear, validate it and release it, you must be very clear with what you want to replace your old way of being.

To create the visualization of your new way of being, ask yourself, "What would I do in my life if I had no restrictions, of time, energy, money, health, family or other commitments?" Look at your answer. Did you say travel? If so, where's your next trip booked? Spend more time with your kids? Do you have kid time penciled on your calendar during the day as though it were equal in importance to any other appointment? Would you work harder? Ha. What actions have you taken to get to your desired reality?

You see, you move toward that which you think about often and a lot. You create mental pictures. Therefore, you must be very clear on what you want. The more specific you are, the better the visualization. Use all of your senses. Feel, see, hear, taste and smell what you want. If you don't know exactly what you want or where you are going, you may get somewhere else. Or as the saying goes, "If all roads lead home, there would be no need for country music."

Picture and feel your dream with all your senses. By listening within and exploring your core you become clear about your values and how to live more congruently with them every day. They will feed directly into this picture. You just need to release your fear and have faith that your desires will be delivered. Don't worry about how you will get there, just trust. Trust your heart's desires and amazingly and almost miraculously, the pieces will fall in place—in the perfect time and manner. The synchronicities of life have been increasing for me as I follow this truth.

TRUST—TAKE A LEAP OF FAITH AND SYNCHRONICITIES ABOUND

> TIMOTHY Q. MOUSE: Dumbo! Look! Have I got it! The magic feather! Now you can fly! *(Dumbo holds the feather in his trunk,*

then it slips away as Dumbo falls off the platform high above the circus ring, falling after the "magic" feather.) Dumbo! C'mon, fly! Open them ears! The magic feather was just a gag! You can fly! Honest, you can! Hurry, open them up! HURRY! *(At the last moment, Dumbo opens his ears and soars over the crowd.)*
— (Dumbo, 1941)

You don't need a magic feather. You just need to trust and have faith that your picture of what you want can come true. Let go of the "how" when finding your scream and living your dream. Trust, and take a leap of faith and soar.

Remember how I was in my element as a kid playing marbles outside on my knees? I have always loved Nature and wanted a cabin in the woods. I held it in my mind for thirty years, and when I left the corporate world my husband and I drove three hours from the desert in Phoenix to 7,000 feet in the mountains in Pinetop, Arizona. In that one weekend, we bought our full log cabin retreat. (Interesting that I am a "wood" according to Chinese medicine, and I am so drawn to that type of furniture and feel, instead of styles with clean, contemporary lines like metal and glass furniture). Our log home is complete with the antler chandelier, stone fireplace, wood stove, nestled in tall pines, juniper and oak. At night, it's under a panoply of stars. That was delivered to me in perfect timing, although I did not think so for many years prior, as I will explain!

The entire cabin experience is one of synchronicity. On our drive up north to our new retreat where much of this book was written, there was a juniper furniture maker whose shop I spotted. I pulled into his lot, reveled at his work and paid him to create our rustic, rough-sawn juniper tables and chairs. It was a one-man operation. He finished our fifteen-foot juniper dining room table and delivered it on Thanksgiving Day. On our next drive to Pinetop, we stopped by his former shop and he had vanished. It seemed that he was just there to create the joy in our home and then disappeared.

There's no such thing as coincidence. When you are in the flow, opportunities abound. The synchronicities of life are unlimited as your eyes become wide open. As you look through your new lens that is not filtered by beliefs, fears, judgments, assumptions and ego, you see the opportunity in each situation. My trips to Africa and Peru were not even inklings, four months prior to each trip. Getting shots, attending to home details, cancelling appointments and leaving the country for a month each time with so little notice may seem unusual. However, once you become available, these memorable opportunities happen.

In 2009, when my family was traveling across the United States during the hectic holidays, our plane landed very late in Atlanta. If we missed the last connection to South Carolina we would have to spend the night at the divey, dingy airport hotel. In an attempt to avoid this, I asked my family if anyone would move to a front open seat and dash to the next gate. No takers. I moved up the aisle and sat next to a middle-aged man with longer hair. I was in ready mode to bolt through the terminal. He talked continuously during our twenty-minute landing. He was a musician and it had taken him a long time to "find his scream"—the expression of the music deep within him and uniquely his. Now he was having success and helping younger musicians find their unique voices. That is how this book's title came about. I asked him if I could use his expression, "finding your scream." He said yes. I never saw him again. My family and I were not blessed to catch our connection, but I was blessed with this book's title.

Years before that, in 1982, when I was twenty-six, I was overworking myself in a law firm. I had borrowed a down payment, bought a little starter house and lived with my brother and a roommate. In April of that year I was standing on the balcony of the Snowbowl ski lodge in Flagstaff, Arizona, taking one last look before leaving. I loved skiing, and found it was a nonintimidating way to meet single men. The odds were more than fifteen men for every one woman who was a black-diamond-run, aggressive skier. At the end of that incredibly warm sunny day, I was admiring the men skiing in boxer shorts. The young women had on bikini tops and were being observed by a tall, red-headed man who was also leaning against the balcony railing about ten feet away from me. I remember it as clearly as if I were standing there now. He said, "Nice view from up here, isn't it?" My instant reaction was, "You have got to be kidding me. That is a horrible pickup line. I have to drive back to Phoenix now and work for twelve hours the next day; I don't have time for this."

He gently persisted and said he was on his way down from Oregon where he had been skiing on the B-level downhill racing tour. There were no legal jobs (1982 was a horrible recession for jobs) and he was going to stay with his parents in Arizona and look for work here. In the next half-second, Jeff said he has never seen a woman clear ten feet so quickly in all his life. I apparently leaped over next to him and struck up conversation. I do recall my mind computing—a skier, a handsome man and a lawyer-jackpot ...time is a-wasting! Twenty-one days later we were engaged; five months later we were married. I learned my husband, Jeff Sandler's nickname, "Sandman," on my wedding night! He is a 6:00 a.m. to 10:00 a.m. and 6:00 p.m. to 10:00 p.m. (lights out) optimal time person, and I am a 10:00 a.m. to 2:00 p.m. and 10:00 p.m. to 2:00 a.m. night owl. Oh well, too late. For better or worse and all that stuff. Literally, if I had been standing on the balcony at Snowbowl five minutes later Jeff wouldn't have been there and I would have been in my car heading home. Coincidence? Muvo's intuitive theory is that our ancestors destined it.

Why does it seem like we don't get what we long for? Sometimes it's not the right time. If you believe in a Divine order (Source, Universe, God, depending on your faith—I will just use Divine), then that explains the timing. For example, I realize now that had we bought our cabin any earlier than we did, it would not be the joyful mountain retreat that it has become for us and the many friends and family who join us. The added pressure of running and maintaining two households while being president of GreenEnergyCo, mother of two younger children with all their activities, and wife, may have led to a nervous breakdown. The responsibility of it most likely would have negated the joy of having and caring for visitors. When I step back and objectively ask, "What can I learn from this? Why am I not finding a cabin right now?" then I see that the timing is not right. I trust that it will come if it's meant to be, in the best way possible for me. Faith and trust are acquired skills.

Follow your heart. Trust that if you were supposed to be somewhere else, you would be, and that the Divine will move you and inspire you to move. I was stalled on this book and I meditated. I asked that a path to resolution be revealed in three days. I meditated the next day, placed my hands at the keyboard, and words just flowed. I did not second guess them; I just wrote what was coming through to me. I produced the poem that went to the heart of the main messages in this book in one hour. It is found after the Resources section at the end of this book.

Meditating and visualizing what I want and need has been working so well that I tried it on a simple matter. I asked for help in becoming one of the callers on Laura Kamm's talk radio show. I had tried for more than four weeks before meditating on it, without luck. Sure enough, the next morning, I was the second caller! Once you realize that the Divine wants to deliver what you clearly and comprehensively visualize, and you trust it will come in the way it's supposed to arrive, synchronicities abound!

Recently, synchronicity appeared in a charitable realm. I have been a thirty-two year volunteer for the YMCA, as I mentioned before. I started volunteering as a calisthenics aerobics teacher—the old jumping jacks, high-impact, hit the floor and do push-ups stuff—and grew to chair of a branch board and head of the Y Metro public policy committee. I choose to commit the time because the organization's values are aligned with what I value—the integration of mind, body and spirit, and it is committed to strong families, strong kids and strong communities. I was fundraising for their annual Strong Kids scholarship campaign and believed a neighbor had the inclination and means to contribute. He was a tri-athlete, believed in healthy lifestyles and in the Y's mind, body and spirit mission. He also happened to be the head of a regional health care industry company. I was disappointed when I sought a few thousand dollar contribution and it wasn't forthcoming. I just kept believing, meditating, praying and trusting that an answer would come. Two years later he was instrumental in ensuring our Y would deliver a revolutionary program that had been in testing to address diabetes prevention. As I described, the Diabetes Prevention Program is delivered in partnership with the Y and a health care insurer. Not only is it helping contribute significant program funding to the Phoenix YMCAs, more importantly, it's reversing the likelihood that pre-diabetic individuals will get full blown Type 2 diabetes by 60-plus percent. That sure beats a one-time few thousand dollar contribution!

You will find yourself in the right place at the right time if that is your belief. Your beliefs create your reality. To change, you must reinterpret what has happened to you in the past. Identify when perceptions, beliefs, judgments, assumptions and ego-based thinking color situations. Acknowledge and validate the purpose of your fear. Then, release your fear of change. Breathe and visualize the new way you want to be and fill the newly-created space with it. Trust and have faith that what you want will be delivered to you in the best time and manner. To practice releasing your fear, try the exercises below.

EXERCISES

1. What are you afraid of? What do you procrastinate doing (because there may be an underlying fear behind moving

forward)? What distracts you from accomplishing what you set your mind to do? Write them down because they are clues to your underlying fears.
2. Look at the list of the eight areas in your life that you ranked from one to ten in the first exercise. See how much time you gave each area. Add ten minutes to one of the areas that nourishes you and subtract it from another. Track yourself for three months, roughly the time to change a behavior, and examine if you have truly shifted your activities. Continue to practice until you live that change.
3. Write down what you would do in your life if you had no restrictions, no time, money, health, family or other commitments. Next, take one action toward that reality.
4. Identify when your "shoulds" become limitations for you or are based in fear. By journaling for more than nine years, it became apparent that there were themes that created limitations discovered by examining my own "shoulds." I should follow through, so I finished too many tasks. I should be a super Mom, so I became impatient if things didn't get done quickly because I had a lot to accomplish in limited time. Identify your "shoulds." When you catch yourself being caught up in the "shoulds" of life, try this: take your index finger and point it at your face and say, "My ego is shoulding on me!" Catch yourself when you say, "I should ... put on makeup before I go to grocery, or go to that social function to network despite the fact that I am exhausted, or volunteer for the PTA to show I am a good mom or dad, or work the weekend to show I am dedicated..."
5. To gain awareness of when the ego (fear) is holding you back, practice by asking yourself in the morning, if I were not afraid, in the next fifteen minutes, I would _____ (for example, read the newspaper longer, linger longer in the shower, make myself breakfast etc.). An affirmation that addresses fear, insecurity, or unworthiness is, "I deserve the best in the world that exists for me. I am safe and capable." Say that three times before your day begins.

6. Before you get out of bed give thanks for all that you have. See, hear, feel, taste and smell how you will act during your day as the "new you." Picture yourself in a situation where your hot button used to be pushed and see yourself acting in the new way you have decided to be. Visualize acting "as if" your new way of being occurred.
7. Write down what you want to create as if you were making a grocery list. Cut out pictures and make a vision board, or place it as the screensaver on your computer. Believe that where your thoughts, time and attention go, so goes your reality.
8. Go two weeks without criticizing someone close to you. Consciously catch yourself if you start. Write down any changes you see in your relationship after these two weeks.
9. Have you noticed recurring patterns in your life? Write a few down. For example, I am energetic, enthusiastic and a self-starter; but on the flip side, I can talk too quickly. This can be perceived that I am not a quality listener or that I am jumping to conclusions. Write the pros and cons of some of your dominant traits that may create limitations for you.
10. Explore your beliefs. Write down whatever first comes to mind without over-thinking your response. What beliefs do you have about health, wealth and happiness? Have you selected them consciously as you would choose the flowers you plant in a garden? What beliefs have you inherited as treasured family heirlooms? What do you define as your "good" traits? What issues do your family members have in common? What do you use your body for? What role does food play in your life? How do you feel about fun? Do you view the world as a dangerous, fear-ridden place, full of challenge and struggle, or is it a great adventure filled with bountiful opportunities? What do you think is possible for you to achieve in this lifetime? What do you believe you deserve from life?
11. From you responses in #10, write down the limiting beliefs you are discovering about yourself on small pieces of paper, one per page. Examine each belief very carefully to see how

you have designed your life around restrictive ideas. Words are symbols for how you have focused your energy. Take the papers outside, and much like my South African river cleansing, either throw them away into running water or bury them under a rock and let them go. (If you feel so moved, you can look for a healthy "muti" substitute and purge, but I don't think that is necessary.)

- Perhaps a visualization of the limiting belief rising into the air like a vanishing released balloon will work better for you. Remember, when you let it go, you make space for what you want, so be clear on what you desire to replace it with simultaneously!

- Then, affirm what you want: "I have vital health. I accept the responsibility for the changes in my life to accomplish this. I love and forgive myself." Even if this does not reflect your current experience, words set forth the direction for energy to follow, and when you hear them you will begin to change your beliefs.

CLOSING

LIVE YOUR DREAM

...girl don't let your dreams be dreams, you know this livin's not so hard as it seems, don't let your dreams be dreams.

— Jack Johnson, Dreams Be Dreams

The privilege of being President of GreenEnergyCo was a dream come true. There are innumerable tales of the people of GreenEnergyCo who found their scream. Some of the stories have already been told. Here are three more inspiring ones.

Our leader of a highly technical quantitative group, who I will call Lane, had much of our profitability in his hands. He oversaw the risk of commodity price movement going against or for us. He had been frustrated in the utility environment. He was underutilized and thus, a mis-fit. He was tethered from developing new products and services. We wooed him to our company where he could be creative and thrive. He became a best-fit. His contributions were endless. He developed new risk models that better preserved our profits. Lane brilliantly designed a dashboard of metrics that our customers could interactively use to assess their price risk with different types of procurement plans.

Lane took a leap of faith to join us. It worked wonderfully for all of us. When we closed the commodity division, he briefly re-joined the utility. He was nearing enough years of service to retire. Nonetheless, after having the full taste of freedom and fulfillment, he fearlessly changed jobs. Lane now has a dream job of directing the international energy procurement and green and traditional energy project development for one of the world's largest mining companies.

A lead in GreenEnergyCo's IT (Information Technology) area, Rachel, was lured away from our sister utility. When she started with us she opted to take the DISC. It revealed that she was naturally a high I (Influencer) and a high C (Compliant). You would expect the high C trait to fit in a utility's regulated environment. She rose to her very best-fit as a leader who, through influencing her people, created new computer interfaces with our customers and other utilities. Rachel explained to me that she joined us because she wanted to understand if moving into an IT management position was really the right path for her. She had excelled in the technical arena of "doing" things. By taking that leap, Rachel severed herself from all her prior expertise. Rachel had to confront not being an expert and learning everything anew. Rachel described the change as both a frightening and freeing experience.

Interestingly, three years later, Rachel retook the DISC. Her high Compliant style dropped in half and Dominant became her highest score after she became a leader within GreenEnergyCo. Eventually, when our commodity group wound down, she was readily re-employed by the parent company. But this time they saw her innovation and leadership capabilities. Rachel became the leader of testing the company's major systems, including cutting-edge smart-metering programs that had not been implemented on this scale anywhere else in the utility industry.

Rachel explained that her experience at GreenEnergyCo allowed her to return to the parent company with the certain knowledge that she could take on and learn anything. As Rachel revealed, "It also gave me the confidence and self-understanding to know that I could embrace a management career, since I could now see that my strengths were not just technical skills, but the ability to learn, map out business processes and technical requirements, and lead others in crafting new solutions."

And the third example is one of the wonderful synchronicity-of-life examples that happen when you have faith.

The leader, who I will call Greg, who now runs GreenEnergyCo's remaining energy efficiency services business line, found his scream in a most fortuitous and intuitive way. I received an unsolicited inquiry when word got out in the marketplace that I had terminated the former deceptive leader of this business line.

It's amazing how quickly such information spreads! Greg had just completed some business deals with his former company. He had taken a sabbatical of sorts. He had gone to the mountains on a several-day "alone time" trip. He told me he had searched within for what he wanted to create next in his life, which turned out to be the "Four P's"—people, passion, Phoenix, and pay, in that order."

Greg contacted me on a cold call, thinking he could help us "in some way." He knew he wanted to travel less and work in Arizona. He liked and was good at negotiating large commercial transactions and had more than twenty years of experience in the energy services industry.

Greg was familiar with transitions like the one at GreenEnergyCo, which happened in energy services companies from time to time. I was surprised and intrigued by his call, honesty and openness.

Nothing happened at first. Then, a few weeks later, I contacted Greg. We developed a loose scope of work and signed a consulting contract. We were both taking a chance. His role became clearer as he built rapport and credibility with us. Greg was following his gut that there was some future for him with us. After I left, Greg remained. Greg was made the president of the energy efficiency services group within three years of his initial exploratory call. The group that comprises GreenEnergyCo now is growing steadily and was recently recognized as one of the best places to work by a local business periodical. Greg's journey is a testament to the power of gaining clarity on what you want and having the faith to pursue your scream.

How can you turn your creativity, your scream, into your livelihood? There are many other examples of people who have found their scream and live their dreams. Look at how "the clues" in their life ultimately reveal their true calling. Below are a few from other professions that inspired me along the way. Many more are reported every day. Given the depressed economy of recent years, there's even more impetus for you to find your scream and draw upon that deep creative force within you. Lifetime jobs where you work securely for one big company in your life are vanishing. That is not necessarily a bad thing. However, you will need to create your future. My kids were advised as entering freshmen in college that 50 percent of them would land jobs four years after graduating that hadn't been created yet.

Take that leap of faith and trust how your heart's desire will come to you. Ask yourself, what is the worst that could happen? The best? The most likely—if you take a chance and pursue your dream? Maybe you can convert your existing job into one that better matches your scream. Or you may want to leave where you are and pursue another path.

My daughter, Shelby, is a constant reminder to me of how to keep the faith. Her whole life she has lived in the present moment and has not worried about anything. Lo and behold, it always works out for her. Shelby had not applied for any jobs prior to graduating from Arizona State University with a graphics art degree in May, 2010. As a planner, this was incomprehensible to me. I told myself, it always works for her. A neighbor gave her freelance projects just as Shelby's funds were running low. This kept her afloat.

After six weeks, I pressed her about to whom she had forwarded her résumé, and I sent emails to my business friends to make inquiries for her. She picked up another freelance project and was offered a job at that company. This position entailed tedious layout work. Shelby was capable of doing the company's projects but her heart desired a job that concentrated on the creative design aspects. Instead of succumbing to fear, as I might have when I was her age, she held out for a more appealing job. Within days, a friend from her same program in college called Shelby and told her to apply at her modern baby products employer, Boon, Inc., because she would be a perfect fit and they needed help immediately. It was that easy!

Leaving a prescribed career path might feel very unsettling, says Mike Marriner, "but the greater risk is staying in a job that isn't satisfying." (*Outside*, 2005.) In 2000, Mike was twenty-three and about to attend medical school and to play water polo at

Pepperdine University in California. He thought he had plotted out his life path. First, however, was a summer trip. Instead of getting a job or going to grad school immediately after he graduated, he and two buddies took a three-month, 17,000-mile road trip across America in a neon green RV. Little did Mike know when he stepped inside that RV for their first mile down the road that the trip would turn into a new career. His buddies and he interviewed more than eighty people from winery founder to lobsterman. The result was a hot new brand: ROADTRIP NATION. That serendipitous journey spawned books and documentaries.

Mike interviewed Boston Beer Company founder, Jim Koch, during his trip. Jim left a lucrative consulting job to make ale in his kitchen. Twenty years later, Samuel Adams is a much-loved brew. Marriner says, "People need to get away from all that noise and pressure at home, which cloud your vision of who you are… On the road, you learn truths firsthand—like the one about money not buying happiness." And when Mike pursued his destiny, cash eventually did come, too.

A friend of mine, Terri, found her scream twice in the last two decades. She was a highly capable, Stanford graduate with a master's degree in mechanical engineering, performing technical work in which she designed safety features for transportation vehicles. While well qualified—which can sometimes feel like a curse—she became increasingly miserable. After thirteen years of this employment, she bought a book about exploring what type of work is best for you. Through this, she discovered that she wasn't a "gear-head" engineer like the rest of the design guys with whom she was working at the time. Terri was relieved when she discovered that it was okay to be a mis-fit. She described to me how she took on her job with new fervor.

Terri started to accept herself and her unique contributions as an engineer. She saw for the first time that her best-fit would be in a more social environment where she could work more with people, not things. This opened her eyes to consider an opportunity she would have completely overlooked before. This position was a part-time director who would recruit and educate youth to the world of science and engineering. Her former employer offered to hire her back part-time as a consultant. She took deep breaths, a big leap of faith ... and jumped. Terri left her comfortable, secure corporate position and replaced it with the two consulting jobs. Her consulting business lasted for ten years until the economic downturn.

More recently, due to declining work as a result of the economic recession, Terri needed more work and income. Her intuition told her there was "something more," but she did not know what. I suggested that Terri consult with Dr. Sandy Kolberg, who had helped some of my leaders. Terri "explored her core" again through the use of the CVI and one-on-one sessions. The CVI revealed she is a Merchant (people person)/Innovator (creative problem solver) with top values of creative, cognitive and community. Sandy was a cheerleader for Terri, encouraging her to go for a new job in a startup organization to improve science and engineering education in Arizona. While Terri did not get that job, she had a great interview and was hired as the deputy director. She is still living her dream.

Another example of someone who lives her dream is Kelly Streeter, a thirty-year-old structural engineer graduate from Cornell who loves to go rock climbing. She uses her rock-climbing skills and roped rigging systems to scale and inspect architectural structures across the nation, from historic statehouse domes and churches to bridges. (*Outside*, 2005.)

Another scream-turn-to-dream story is the one about Debbie Allen. She acts, sings, writes and directs. Her career soared in the 1980s with the hit TV series, *Fame*. She choreographed the Academy Awards for years. At the ages of four and five she put on her shiny pink bathing suit, tied a pink towel around her neck, climbed a tree and danced on the roof of her house. Because she was black and challenged by segregation, she had to find her own path to dance. Eventually, she started her own dance academy to provide opportunities for dance for all. (Read more in *The Element* by Sir Ken Robinson, Ph.D.)

A dream life come true is that of a favorite celebrity of mine,

Jack Johnson. He is a multiplatinum folk singer-surfer and environmentalist. Jack records some of his hits in a small studio energized by solar power. (*Outside*, 2010.) Some top songs include one from the Curious George movie, *Reduce, Reuse, Recycle*, and most recently his CD and song, *To the Sea*. His song, *Dreams Be Dreams* is a perfect lead-in for this book's conclusion, as Jack advises us to listen to and act on our dreams or they won't materialize. His success is proof "that the seeds of luck can fall on fertile ground if you follow your destiny and don't lose your soul," according to an earlier interview with *Outside* in 2005.

Jack surfs frequently and doesn't forget his roots. He remains grounded through simple living and adventure. He started surfing at age five. A week after a premier pro event when he was 17, a wave tossed him onto a reef and left him with a coral-cut, torn-up face. While he healed quickly, he used the months he was in the hospital to improve his guitar skills. He could have been devastated and depressed by this event but instead, he turned it into gold: golden cords, golden records.

His recently-deceased father, a big-wave surfing pioneer, inspired Jack's newest CD. Jack reflected on this marked event in his life. "When your parents are gone it's a time to say to yourself, 'All right, now it's you. What are you gonna show us? What are you gonna do?'" Jack decided to finally sing about his love for the sea. (*Outside*, 2010.)

Everyone has talents, but do you have the courage to follow your talents where they lead? Are you sacrificing what you love to do for a job that pays more or that gains you approval from others? I initially did! When I overcame the fear of change and left being a lawyer at the utility, what happened to me? I got to *find my scream* and have the experience of a lifetime.

I took action to move toward a better fit. Remember, what you do right now is not who you are—it's just what you do, that is all. My hope is that the Scream to Dream Approach illuminates the way to find your life-affirming actions. I dream that you will be re-enchanted by your life's opportunities.

While perhaps not how you would define your list of 10s, I

define my life as totally meaningful because I constantly choose to do things that nurture me. This includes making a positive, meaningful difference for my family, friends, community and fellow workers. I am living in Nature part-time now and have abundant adventure. I am energized by inspirational speaking and writing, and by giving back to my community. I continue to influence energy policy to create a more sustainable environment. I make time before I get out of bed to be grateful for the day that I have created—as if it already happened. I am getting better at meditation and am growing spiritually. I am also "muti-free."

Yes, it takes effort to work within and to direct energy to change your thoughts and lifestyle patterns from counterproductive to productive. But it also takes effort to stay as you are. Which path better serves you? Which shoes fit best? While each of us is unique, we are all profoundly the same. The search for your own truth, love, compassion and equanimity are basic to all human needs.

My challenge for you is—how will you find your scream and live your dream? Consider this: to be more fully in alignment at home and at work, you will find your answers within. You will develop your intuition by listening while you are in a non-thinking state. You will explore your own core to discern your natural gifts and values. You will notice and become aware of when your body hurts, signifying that you are out of alignment. You will be inspired to change to become aligned. To do so, you will release your fears, first, by identifying them; then by acknowledging and validating the purpose of your fears; and finally by changing your beliefs through re-interpreting what has happened in your life. You will take more deep breaths and visualize what you want to create.

You will take a leap of faith and have trust that what you clearly want will be delivered in the best possible time and manner. When you accept complete responsibility for your life by identifying your scream, trusting and believing in yourself and your intuition, and overcoming your fear to live in alignment with your scream, you will live your dream.

It's time to activate your imagination, clarify your intentions, focus your energy, take action based in love, not fear, and expect results. As you do so, you will be fulfilled and in a healthy balance of mind, body and spirit. You will become the best person, and if it's your scream, the best leader. Your company or organization cannot help but be the best it can be when it's comprised of each of the best "you's." And as each one of us changes, the world will change. Mother Earth will smile on each and every one of us. It will be done one person at a time, one leader at a time. It's up to you.

Remember my revelation in the elevator at two a.m. when I declared that I would no longer be the rate case lawyer? I had a most amazing thing happen at that moment in time. I suddenly had a vision of a white dove flying out of a cage. And that has become a reality for me. I have been set free to be me. To find my scream, and live my dream. I am privileged to encourage each of you to do the same. I want you to be set free to be YOU and for you to find your scream and live your dream!

Makhosi, blessings from the highest spirit; hello and goodbye, from my heart to your heart.

REFERENCES AND RESOURCES

References are organized by their initial location in each Chapter. All websites are current as of January 2011. Additional helpful resources are mentioned in each relevant section.

ONE: HOW I FOUND MY SCREAM

Calling Cards™ 2000 'A Journey of Discovery'. The Inventure Group. www.inventuregroup.com.

ENERGIZE!

$E=Mc2$. http://www.worsleyschool.net/science/files/emc2/emc2.html.

TWO: TRANSFORMING TODAY'S LEADERSHIP

WHY WE NEED TO CHANGE HOW WE LEAD

Scharmer, C. Otto, Ph.D., *Theory U: Leading from the Future As It Emerges, The Social Technology of Presencing*, San Francisco, CA: Berrett-Koehler Publishers, Inc., 2009. http://www.ottoscharmer.com.

Self-awareness a top criterion for leaders. http://davidchao.typepad.com/webconferencingexpert/2010/06/bestbossesarethemostselfaware.html.

http://money.cnn.com/magazines/fortune/bestcompanies/2010: "100 Best Companies to Work For," *Fortune Magazine*, 2010.

http://outsideonline.com/culture/201005/best-places-to-work-intro.html: "The 50 Best Places to Work," *Outside Magazine*, May 2010.

http://www.greenbiz.com/news/2009/02/10/green-companies-do-better-during-downturn-study#ixzz1An9vXrcq: "Green Companies Do Better During Downturn: Study," February 10, 2009.

WHAT WOULD YOU LOVE TO CREATE?

Keim, Amanda, "Pomegranate Café," *Ahwatukee News,* October 20, 2010.

Miranda, Coty Dolores, "Mother takes children's product business to top," *Ahwatukee News,* December 3, 2010.

Intuition defined. http://www.merriam-webster.com/dictionary/intuition.

Inspire defined. http://www.merriam-webster.com/dictionary/inspire.

Spir defined. http://wordempire.blogspot.com/search?q=spir&updated-max=2009-01-17T13%3A31%3A00-08%3A00&max-results=20.

THREE: YOUR ANSWERS ARE WITHIN

Albert Einstein. Great-Quotes.com, Gledhill Enterprises, 2011. http://www.great-quotes.com/quote/8985.

Invictus quote. http://www.imdb.com/title/tt1057500/quotes.

HEAD VERSUS HEART

Dispenza, Joe, D. C., *Evolve Your Brain: The Science of Changing Your Mind,* Deerfield Beach, FL: Health Communications, Inc., 2007.

Institute of HeartMath®, www.heartmath.org.

Hawkins, David R. M.D., Ph.D., *Power vs. Force,* Carlsbad, California: Hay House, Inc., 2002.

Kamm, Laura Alden, *Intuitive Wellness,* NY, NY: First Atria Books/Beyond Words Publishing, 2006. http://www.energymedicine.org.

Laura Alden Kamm email 11/30/2010 defining psychic versus medical intuitive.

Resource: Evan Wise, management consultant, Managing Director of Management One®. http://www.management-one.com.

INDIGENOUS INTUITIVE WISDOM

Robert Ingersoll. Great-Quotes.com, Gledhill Enterprises, 2011. http://www.great-quotes.com/quote/229331.

http://www.intuitivemind.org, South Africa trip leaders, Nancy Rebecca and Yvonne Kilcup.

LEARNING FROM ZULU SANGOMA TRADITIONAL HEALERS

http://www.ancestorsspiritconsciousness.com, and http://www.youtube.com/user/spiritconsciousness, Sarah & Muvo, South

Africa Zulu Sangoma healers.

Arden, Nicky, *African Spirits Speak: A White Woman's Journey into the Healing Tradition of the Sangoma,* Rochester, VT: Destiny Books, 1999.

CONNECTING AND BRIDGING CULTURES

http://www.kenosis.net/carla.htm, Peru trip leader, Carla Woody, MA, CHT, founder of Kenosis, LLC.

http://www.kenosis.net/Retreats/PeruTrip.htm, Peruvian guide, Don Américo Yábar.

http://www.mayaexploration.org/staff_mendez.php, Alonso Mendez, Mayan translator, and http://en.wikipedia.org/wiki/Mayanism.

WAYS TO ENTER YOUR ANSWER ROOM

Grossman, Cathy Lynn, "When the Spirit Moves You," *USA Weekend,* interview with Rabbi Jamie Korngold, April 2-4, 2010.

McGarey, Gladys Taylor, M.D., M.D.(H), *The Physician Within You,* Scottsdale, Arizona: Inkwell Productions, 2000. This book is a dream analysis resource also.

Running the Rainbow is adapted and printed with permission from Laura Alden Kamm, *Intuitive Wellness,* NY, NY: First Atria Books/Beyond Words Publishing, 2006.

FOUR: EXPLORE YOUR CORE

Sides, Hampton, "Bear Grylls Has a Dirty Secret," *Outside Magazine,* May 2010.

Cannon, Janell, *Verdi,* Orlando, FL: Harcourt Brace & Company, 1997.

THE CORE VALUES INDEX™

Taylor, Lynn Ellsworth, *The Core Values Handbook: "How Can They Possibly Think Like That???"* Tukwila, WA: Taylor Protocols, 1992.

Core Values Index™ is created by Lynn E. Taylor and Taylor Protocols, Inc. The expert who administered and facilitated the use of this assessment is Sandy Kohlberg, Ph.D., founder of Strategems, LLC. http://www.strategems-llc.com.

TTI'S DISCPROFILE™ AND MOTIVATION INSIGHTS®

DISCProfile™ is created by William Moulton, Marston Ph.D; and Motivation Insights® is created by Eduard Spranger. http://www.ttiassessments.com/solutions/products-and-assessments/valuesmotivators. The expert who administered and facilitated the use of these assessments is Joy Schwertley, Ph.D. http://www.discoveryprofiling.com.

Yantis, John, "35 Entrepreneurs, 35 & Younger," *Arizona Republic,* October 24, 2010, quote by Bill Bonnstetter founder and chairman of TTI Performance Systems, Inc.

MYERS-BRIGGS TYPE INDICATOR®

Myers, Isabel Briggs, McCaulley, Mary H., Quenk, Naomi L., and Hammer, Allen L., *MBTI Manual (A guide to the development and use of the Myers- Briggs type indicator),* 1998.

Resource: While not scientifically validated, many friends and co-workers have found the information by former Olympic athlete, Dan Millman, about the life-purpose system helpful to improve their self-awareness. Millman, Dan, *The Life You Were Born to Live,* Tiburon: CA, New World Library, 1993. You can take a free test at: http://www.peacefulwarrior.com/index.php/life-purpose-calculator.

Resource: Rath, Tom, *Strength Finder 2.0,* NY, NY: Gallup Press, 2007. You can take free tests at: http://www.authentichappiness.sas.upenn.edu/Default.aspx.

FIVE: EXPLORING YOUR ORGANIZATION'S CORE

Copyright, 2000 American Management Association: The Management Course for Presidents: February 2001, Phoenix, Arizona, The Bradley Group.

Paraphrased in part from the "Lessons From Geese For The YMCA" from Jerold Panas, Linzy and Partners, March 2007. http://www.panaslinzy.com.

Lencioni, Patrick, *The Five Dysfunctions of a Team,* San Francisco, CA: Jossey-Bass, 2002.

Shinn, Florence Scovel, *The Game of Life: And How To Play It,* Rockville, MD: Arc Manor, 2008.

Piper, Watty, *The Little Engine That Could,* NY, NY: Platt & Munk Publishers, 2002.

SIX: HOW DO YOU KNOW IF YOU HAVE FOUND YOUR SCREAM?

YOUR BODY DOESN'T LIE TO YOU

Siegel, Bernie, M.D., *Love, Medicine and Miracles,* NY, NY: Harper & Row, Publishers, Inc., 1986.

McGarey, Gladys Taylor, M.D., M.D.(H), *Living Medicine, The Dwelling Place,* Scottsdale, Arizona: Inkwell Productions, 2009.

Hay, Louise L., *You Can Heal Your Life,* Carlsbad, California: Hay House, Inc., 1984.

Beinfield, Harriet, L.Ac., and Korngold, Efrem, L.Ac., O.M.D., *Between Heaven and Earth: A Guide to Chinese Medicine,* NY, NY: Ballantine Books, 1991.

Taylor, Matthew, PT, Ph.D., RYT, "Ask the Yoga Therapist," *Arizona Yoga,* Fall 2010.

Northrup, Christiane, M.D., and Schulz, Mona Lisa, M.D., Ph.D., *Igniting Intuition: Unearthing Body Genius,* Audio CD, 1999.

Hawkins, David R. M.D., Ph.D., *Power vs. Force,* Carlsbad, California: Hay House, Inc., 2002.

Resource: Sherry Anshara, on cellular memory. http://www.quantumpathic.com.

http://www.montgomerycollege.edu/Departments/StudentJournal/volume2/kate.pdf. Transplant story.

Weil, Andrew, M.D., *Why Our Health Matters,* NY, NY: Penguin Group, 2009. http://www.drweil.com/drw/u/ART02054/Andrew-Weil-Integrative-Medicine.html.

Weil, Andrew, M.D., *Healthy Aging: A Lifelong Guide to Your Physical and Spiritual Well-Being,* NY, NY: Random House, Inc., 2005.

Nolan, Kate, "Feeling Very Weil," *AZ Generation Health Magazine,* February 2010.

McGarey, Gladys Taylor, M.D., M.D.(H), *The Physician Within You,* Scottsdale, Arizona: Inkwell Productions, 2000.

Gladwell, Malcolm, *Blink: The Power of Thinking Without Thinking,* NY, NY: Time Warner Book Group, 2005.
The Dosha Quiz. http://doshaquiz.chopra.com, or you can take a free digestive constitution test at: http://www.ayurveda.com/online_resource/constitution.pdf.
Lad, Vasant, B.A.M.S., M.A.Sc., *The Complete Book of Ayurvedic Home Remedies,* NY, NY: Three Rivers Press, 1998.
Diabetes prevention. http://www.valleyymca.org/social/diabetesPrevention.cfm, and http://www.cdc.gov/diabetes/pubs/factsheet11.htm.
Barrett, Jennifer, "Healing Power of Yoga," *Yoga Journal,* May 2010, interview with Sat Bir Khalsa, Ph.D.

SEVEN: RELEASE YOUR FEAR

Dispenza, Joe, D.C., and Storr, Julie Ann, *The Art Of Change, Vol. 1: Q&A Series,* Audio CD, Reel to Reel Media, 2011.
Seligman, Martin E.P., Ph.D., *The Optimistic Child,* NY, NY: HarperCollins Publishers, Inc., 1995.
Roach, Geshe Michael, *The Diamond Cutter: The Buddha on Strategies for Managing Your Business and Your Life,* NY, NY: Doubleday, 2003.
Gladwell, Malcolm, *Blink: The Power of Thinking Without Thinking,* NY, NY: Time Warner Book Group, 2005. You can see how to prevent against a negative snap decision: http://www.implicit.harvard.edu.
Carroll, Lewis, *Alice's Adventures in Wonderland* and *Through the Looking-Glass,* NY, NY: Penguin Books, 2000.
Brennan, Barbara Ann, *Light Emerging, The Journey of Personal Healing,* NY, NY: Bantam Books, 1993.
Stanley, Thomas J., Ph.D., *The Millionaire Mind,* Kansas City, MO: Andrews McMeel Publishing, 2001.
Block, Stanley H., M.D., and Block, Carolyn Bryant, *Come to Your Senses,* NY, NY: First Atria Books/Beyond Words Publishing, 2007.
McGarey, Gladys Taylor, M.D., M.D.(H), *Living Medicine, The Dwelling Place,* Scottsdale, Arizona: Inkwell Productions, 2009.
Carl Jung quote. http://www.brainyquote.com/quotes/authors/c/

carl_jung_3.html.
Seligman, *The Optimistic Child,* NY, NY: HarperCollins Publishers, Inc., 1995.
Seligman, Martin E.P., Ph.D., *Authentic Happiness: Using the New Positive Psychology to Realize Your Potential for Lasting Fulfillment,* NY, NY: The Free Press, 2002. You can take free 'authentic happiness' tests at: http://www.authentichappiness.sas.upenn.edu/Default.aspx.
Block, Stanley H., M.D., and Block, Carolyn Bryant, *Come to Your Senses,* NY, NY: First Atria Books/Beyond Words Publishing, 2007.
Kamm, Laura Alden, *Intuitive Wellness,* NY, NY: First Atria Books/Beyond Words Publishing, 2006.
Shinn, Florence Scovel, *The Game of Life: And How To Play It,* Rockville, MD: Arc Manor, 2008.
Dispenza, Joe, D.C., and Storr, Julie Ann, *The Art Of Change, Vol. 1: Q&A Series,* Audio CD, Reel to Reel Media, 2011.
McTaggart, Lynne, *The Intention Experiment,* NY, NY: Free Press, 2008.
Resource: Kathleen Thoren, MA; http:// www.theamazingyousystem.com.
Blakeslee, Sandra and Mathew, *The Body Has A Mind of Its Own,* NY, NY: Random House Publishing Group, Tantor Media Inc., 2007.
May, Michelle, M.D., *Love What You Eat, Eat What You Love,* Austin, TX: Greenleaf Group Book Press, 2010. http://www.AmIHungry.com.
Oprah weight management quote. http://www.oprah.com/health/Oprahs-Weight-Loss-Confession/5.
Martin Luther King dream quote. http://www.mlkonline.net/dream.html.
Resource: Al Fuentes; www.alfuentes.com; www.mentalchamp.com.
Longer Than song. http://www.danfogelberg.com/lyricsphoenix.html.
Dumbo 1941. http://www.imdb.com/title/tt0033563/quotes.

CLOSING: LIVE YOUR DREAM

Auerback, Lisa Anne, "20 Dream Jobs: How to Make Work, Life & Play Your Greatest Adventure," *Outside Magazine*, September 2005.

Robinson, Sir Ken, Ph.D., *The Element*, NY, NY: Penguin Group, 2009.

Roberts, Michael, "Road-Tripping with Jack Johnson," *Outside Magazine,* June 2010.

MY SOUL SONG

Poem created in one hour by using intuition.

All that is shall be
pure as the driven snow.
Let it go, let it go.
I know, I know.
The way to go
is neither long nor hard.
It is a new backyard.

❧

The branch it waves so very slow
when laden with the heavy snow.
It is white,
to our delight.
And each limb will bounce back
with great might
to dump the snow out of sight.
But it is weak
when man comes to chop it down.
Frown, frown.
It falls with a sad sound.
Breathe.
The tree breathes and
gives us our breath.
And so we are one.
All connected
with planets and sun.
The world
is a ball of love
Just hidden under the snow.
Recognize the duality.
The reality.
The snow is heavy and
it creates pain.
How can we gain?
Gain insight to our tree's plight?
How do we stop the fight?
What goes up must come down,
CO_2 to the ground.
We must gain new sight
tonight, tonight.
We must hear differently
without the chaos
buzzing in our ears.
Hear the bee buzz
as it creates new life
with the pollen, it does.

❧

All is quiet now.
The possibilities await.
In this space
it is not full,
we don't have to pull.
We can refill
without a pill.
Just look for the light,
look for the light.
Insight, insight.
What is the might
of many nations
without a world to play in?
When our hearts are
light and full of joy
oh boy, oh boy.

MY SOUL SONG

Write a children's book I will
(Yoda says it will be a thrill).
Through delight of eyes
that see no uphill.
Make a snow cone
from fresh snow.
The warmth of the mouth
melts the snow away.
Rest and play.
Fill your day this way.
The yin and yang.
The dark, the light.
Balance is in sight.
Don't think.
Just be.

੨▲

Time to meditate,
a way to celebrate
the quietness, the calm.
Like new lip balm
for chapped lips,
it soothes like a psalm.
The dawn of a new light,
Insight. Insight.
Delight. Delight.
There is no fright
of what will be.
Acquiesce, naturally.

੨▲

Let it flow,
let all pain go.
In the noise stillness can be found.
Lay on the ground.
New nature sounds will abound.
The giving tree, let it be.

Let it be.
Tiptoe dancing with the feet,
you are in for a treat.
It is so sweet.
It is so sweet.
To be complete,
to be complete.
Find your scream
and live your dream.
It rhymes, why not?
If it will make you stop
doing what you are doing
that doesn't serve you well.
Oh hell.
Our hands are not replete
if not aligned with our feet.
Bang, bang.
We hit the ground.
Go round and round
until we turn and sway,
for clarity will come another day.

੨▲

Get out of your head.
Rid of thoughts of
what you dread.
Don't get out of bed
until you are a new you.
Until you are a new you.
Change may create fear
when it is near.
But it holds the hope
of who you are
When you are wishing on a star,
wishing on a star.
Your childhood dreams,

you hold dear,
you hold dear.
They are created with no fear.
Faith to create the step
under your feet.
Be upbeat.
Have a seat.
Listen with your inner ear.
Let the heart guide
the gleeful ride.
It is so easy you see.
Dr. Seuss' rhyming spree.
Live life in metaphor
and it won't be a chore,
or a bore.
Inspire,
by living your heart's desire.

Only a few are needed to show
the rest what to do.
Lead by example,
draw others near.
Show them to have no fear.
Love.
What are we supposed to do?
Love all.
Not just a few.
Forgive to live.
Let go
of every past blow.
Let go,
let go.
Why hold the past so near
when it is not your
friend, my dear.

Look with new eyes and
see the surprise.
What holds you back?
Avoiding a heart attack?
Or a pain in the back?
Or a stiff knee?
Stiff from inflexibility!
You are not who you are
until you live your wish
upon the star.
Until you sit with them afar.
Until you sit with them afar.
Breathe.

Feel the electromagnetic force
from the heart not the head.
If not, you may as well be dead.
Be alive.
Thrive.
Don't regress into survival.
It is so primitive you see,
believe me,
believe me.
Do not judge.
It is a lie.
Do not criticize.
See with affirming eyes.
Compassion feels
better than the rest.
Can you do it?
This is a test.
For if you believed,
you would be relieved.
You would "re-live."
You would give.

MY SOUL SONG

Time is on our side.
It will abide
by going slow
until we are in the know.
Time is not your enemy.
Befriend it with levity.
The words they come.
The words they go.
But criticism is a no-show.
It hurts so.
Be your own witness.
Observe the flow.
Step out of your skin
and watch the dream begin.
The world is dizzying.
The tears are drizzling.
From past pain.
Such an energy drain.
Such a drain.
What we have to gain
is to let go of the pain.
When life force flows through you
unblocked by the garbage,
the dust and rust,
it glides effortlessly
like clean rain run-
ning down your face
with grace,
with grace.
Disgrace, dis-ease, degradation,
be gone, if you please.
We bring that on ourselves
Like scavengers to a carcass.
Let's pass, let's pass.
Your gift, your ability,

It's as easy to see as
counting 1, 2, 3.
Find your scream
and live your dream.
Scream with joy,
oh boy, oh boy.
You are in your groove
and it is so smooth,
so smooth.
No force, only power.
Your natural power.
The one that flows.
The one that knows.
That comes up through your
toes and out your nose.
It is in you all the time.
It can even make you rhyme!

❧

Bliss, not a fist.
Cooperate, there is no debate.
Competition is for fools
who don't see the natural rules.
Laws of coherence.
Laws of abundance.
Laws of love.
What is within, is without.
There is no doubt,
there is no doubt.
So what is this all about?
Your calling--
All roads lead home.
To your home,
your heart.
Let's start.
Get smart.

Be a part.
The time is now.
The old way must die
and give way to new life inside.
Clear the garden
for the new seed.
Get rid of the weed.
For we can't fix it
from the outside.
It is within,
that is where there is our win.
Our win.
And when we win, the
world does too.
It gets created anew.
So the angels guide me to type.
They know what to write.
I am here to convey
The optimal way every day,
every day.
Is there more to say?
It will all be ok.
Ok.
When we are clear,
as to what we hold dear,
it will appear,
it will appear.
Set your intention every day.
Give gratitude
as if you already got your way.
No resistance is the key.
Discern differently.
Start from neutral,
the place to be.
Step back

and see differently,
see differently.
Emotions can't cloud your day,
no way,
no way.
Don't let the body rule.
Use intuition as a tool.
Feelings can be changed,
Reprogrammed for the gain.
Be aligned,
each and every time.
Catch yourself
when not
in the proper thought.

Feel what you want
with all your being.
See its color.
Hear its song.
All night long,
all night long.
Practice makes perfect,
that is the way.
Meditate to practice
every day.
10,000 hours of practice
make you a pro.
The Beatles know.
They know.
Happiness is yours to have.
Step out of the way.
Reprogram what you say.
Today.
Today.
What are you waiting for?

MY SOUL SONG

A better day?
Some help, you say.
It is here.
It is yours.
You possess it within.
You know the way.
Don't chagrin.
Don't take it on the chin.
Be what you want.
Pretend if you must.
It won't be a bust
For it all happens for a reason
in every season.
It happens for a reason.
It's not good or bad,
right or wrong.
It is just part of our soul song.
So get on your way
to creating the best
and brightest day.
Taste the chocolate.
Slurp the honey.
Watch the bunny
leave tracks in the snow.
Take it all in.

It is here for you—begin.
Just notice,
that's all ya gotta do.
All ya gotta do.
This soul song is not at an end
for it is a new beginning,
my friend.
Rest.
Sleep.
Dream.
Journey to your life's delight.
Your guide will hold you tight,
and help you gain the insight
needed for you
to help us all end this plight.
Live well,
each moment,
each moment.
None are a waste,
just a taste
of all there can be.
Create each moment
in Divine Glory.
Glory.

Photo Courtesy of Sean Richards

ABOUT THE AUTHOR

Vicki Sandler is a successful entrepreneur who navigated her own road to success, first as an economist studying behavior and markets, then as a lawyer and green energy company president. Through this journey she discovered her true inner leader. Vicki has a track record of inspiring transformation in businesses, her associates and her friends, and of transforming herself. She has honed her innate ability to see and illuminate what each of us can be through the process of clarifying what your scream is—that is, your unique voice of joy from your core. She believes each one of us has the ability to find our scream and live our dream. Vicki offers insights from her life and leadership experiences that show you how to align your and your employees' talents within your company or organization to best-fit. When you do, you will be your best, most fulfilled, healthy functioning self, as will be your company.

The Scream to Dream Approach is a multifaceted, multi-cultural approach to discovering your inner leader. When you lead from the inside out—inspiring and caring for the human beings who create, innovate and uphold the corporation—the people and your organization will flourish beyond expectations. It's what any CEO needs in order to be the most effective at this time in our lives. Vicki dedicates this book to sharing what she has learned so you can attain your highest, most fulfilled potential, too. Vicki inspires leaders, organization and association members to adopt the Scream to Dream Approach to living and leading. She is available for training, workshops and executive coaching to those who want to find their scream and live their dream! Learn more by visiting http://www.findyourscream.

www.ingramcontent.com/pod-product-compliance
Lightning Source LLC
Chambersburg PA
CBHW050856160426
43194CB00011B/2182